Transforming
Corporate
Performance

Transforming Corporate Performance

Measuring and Managing the Drivers of Business Success

Michael A. Milgate

Westport, Connecticut
London

Library of Congress Cataloging-in-Publication Data

Milgate, Michael, 1966–
 Transforming corporate performance : measuring and managing the drivers
 of business success / Michael A. Milgate
  p. cm.
 Includes bibliographical references and index.
 ISBN 1-56720-530-5 (alk. paper)
  1. Organizational effectiveness—Measurement. 2. Industrial
productivity—Measurement. 3. Total quality management—Measurement.
4. Performance—Measurement. 5. Industrial management—Evaluation.
6. Success in business. I. Title.
HD58.9.M553 2004
658.4'01—dc22 2003057994

British Library Cataloguing in Publication Data is available.

Library of Congress Catalog Card Number: 2003057994
ISBN: 1-56720-530-5

First published in 2004

Praeger Publishers, 88 Post Road West, Westport, CT 06881
An imprint of Greenwood Publishing Group, Inc.
www.praeger.com

Printed in the United States of America

The paper used in this book complies with the
Permanent Paper Standard issued by the National
Information Standards Organization (Z39.48-1984).

10 9 8 7 6 5 4 3 2 1

For CC, JAC, AE, DL, SN, MT and BW—for the friendship
and support when the times were tough.

MSR—thank you for the good times and
the good memories.

Many thanks to CC, RJL and SRN for their assistance in
proofreading and preparing the diagrams.

Contents

Preface

When I e-mailed Eric Valentine, my publisher, in early 2000 with a proposal for a second book for Praeger to publish, it seemed like a good idea. I was a full-time academic with the luxury of resources, especially time to research the book. Then, in mid-2001, I moved back to the private sector. In my previous work and current experience in the private sector, my performance has only been measured by the return on investment (ROI) calculated by accountants. Something that I could never fully understand as a nonaccountant was that growth, market share, public reputation, and shareholder value were all ignored as valid measurement tools in the organizations I was with.

As I write this Preface, having completed the manuscript, the world is a very different place. Not only has September 11, 2001, become one of those days in history on which people will remember where they were, just as they remember where they were when they heard of the assassination of John F. Kennedy, but there have also been a number of major corporate collapses that have affected the lives of employees, "mom and pop investors," and the returns being paid by investment, and superannuation funds, and so on.

Globally, there is major fallout over the demise of Enron and WorldCom and the role that their auditors and managers played, even reaching my home country of Australia, which was mentioned in congressional hearings into the role that Arthur Andersen, the Enron auditor, played in the largest corporate collapse in Australian corporate history, that of HIH Insurance. Australia also saw the collapse of One

Tel Ltd. (a telecommunications reseller) and Ansett Australia (an air-line). All these organizations had, on face value, healthy annual reports, which somehow, while still meeting the regulatory requirements, did not seem to accurately measure their performance.

Throughout this book, I have used the term *strategic* in the long-term sense, meaning to achieve an organization's long-term goals and objectives, as opposed to short-term operational measurement or annual measurement for regulatory purposes. In some ways I am departing from the conventional wisdom. The usual ways of measuring performance are inadequate; it is no longer enough to document the factors of finance, the HRM market, the shareholder, the health of the organization, and the organization's potential for future viability. New ways, even combinations (as with combination drug therapies for certain diseases), are now needed to ensure that the life of an organization for the new century has a chance of continuing.

Performance measurement appears to have become the critical business issue between the late 1990s and the first decade of the new century. As this book finds, it underpins or drives every element of organizational endeavor, it is a competitive differentiator in its own right and clearly not a vogue issue or passing trend. However, much of performance measurement is driven by "fads" being pushed by various consulting organizations or "guru" authors.

Each themed chapter examines the strategic dimensions of that form of measurement, the process itself, and best practice approaches through case studies, case reports, research trends, and advisor overviews. Guidelines and insights help rethink perspectives and practices concerning the overall approach. The book can be used as a "dip-in" resource, allowing the reader to either dip into a chapter that may be relevant or use the book from start to finish as a means of challenging the organizations approach to performance mearurement.

Chapter 1 examines the business and strategic contexts of performance measurement, along with shortcomings in contemporary practice. Chapter 2 has three sections, covering balanced business scorecards, the functional adaptation of these frameworks for human resources (HR) and supplier measurement, and other emerging business measurement disciplines, including corporate dashboards. Chapter 3 details the broader context of business excellence and performance measurement by considering their links to business strategy, the rationale and benefits of self-assessment, and the process in practice. Chapter 4 discusses the contribution of benchmarking to business strategy, improving performance capability in relation to competitive issues, and the emerging practice of transferring best practices. Chapter 5 has three sections that discuss process measurement in relation to organizational capability and business performance by detailing the links between processes, their measures and business strategy, process measurement in practice, and issues concerning implementation. Chapter 6 examines customer management in terms of strategic considerations, a review of processes and practice, approaches to multisource customer feedback, customer value and profitability, and systems/implementation. Chapter 7 considers strategic quality management, including leading corporate practices in terms of frameworks and approaches, guidelines on rethinking this form of measurement, and an overview of critical points for implementation. Chapter 8 discusses employee measurement, which is tied to business or HR issues and organizational capability. Three sections cover the business issues, how employee measurement relates to different dimensions of performance, and the emerging approach of multisource assessment. Chapter 9 discusses financial measurement in relation to value creation and adding value, widening and integrating measurement practice, the use of economic value-added methodologies, and cost measurement and management. Chapter 10 reviews critical trends in valuing knowledge, examines how knowledge management evolves, and discusses implementation and measurement issues, including emerging models and processes. Chapter 11 pulls together the overriding issues for strategic performance measurement by revealing its shortcomings, examining strategic reviews and audits, and providing guidelines on implementation.

At each level or theme, I recommend that you address both generic and specific questions with colleagues in other functions and disciplines. An agenda for change should ensue. And, despite the route map this book provides, there is no perceived point of arrival save that of saying that the broad intention of strategic performance measurement is to positively change behavior, which enhances business performance and the quest for superior results.

Context for Strategic Performance Measurement

CONTEXTUAL ISSUES

The word that most aptly describes the broad context for contemporary performance measurement is *uncertainty*. On the one hand, competitive corporate pressures and volatile business conditions often force a readjustment of priorities, resourcing, and response, while on the other hand, there is focusing and mobilizing of the organization, changing it and its complex interrelationships and activities, which is difficult at the best of times.

There are many other variables concerning business strategy and performance. These encourage uncertainty because the answers to key questions such as the following are unclear:

1. What kind of organizational capability is needed to shape sometimes myriad forms of responses from various stakeholders?
2. What are the drivers of better performance or greater stakeholder value?
3. How are these drivers tracked?
4. How is measurement effectively deployed?
5. Postanalysis, what action results?

Two other overriding questions are crucial: Can measurement drive internal change, improving performance and the delivery of capability against unpredictable external conditions? How might measurement positively influence or change behavior? Over a decade ago, the answers to these two questions would have been cut and dried, much like the practice of business management and measurement at the time. The former was control orientated against the annual strategic plan, while later, chiefly financials but also the classic metrics of cost, quality, and delivery, gave after-the-fact, input-related and non-predictive information.

In this context, line of sight between measurement, data, business decisions, action, and overall organizational performance was weak. Critical business changes were not captured until it was too late and, in some cases, measurement was an end in itself, great on effort and resourcing, but short in strategic return. The near failures in the 1980s of IBM, Rank Xerox, Sears Roebuck, Caterpillar, and Continental Airlines, among many others in top financial listings worldwide, bear witness to this statement.

MEASUREMENT SHORTCOMINGS

It could be argued that little appears to have changed,[1] despite a considerably widening performance measurement agenda in the last decade and a greater internal emphasis on nonfinancial indicators. This may create internal issues or debate, the aim of which is to reduce corporate dependence on purely financial measures of success in favor of more inclusive, stakeholder value–driven approaches. There is nothing intrinsically right or wrong about financial or nonfinancial measures, but the appropriate context is the issue. Barings, for example, had a culture highly oriented toward financial results, but there were no balancing mechanisms for measuring values and risk contexts. We now know the outcomes that resulted for Barings, which was sold for £1 to ING. If leadership prioritizes one form of measurement or another as good in itself, distortions can occur.

Measurement cannot be done in isolation. Instead, a framework needs to be developed that will ensure that the business delivers what is intended. The greatest danger is excessive financial measurement, the belief that adding measures means performance will improve. This is not to argue that the instinct to measure more is, of itself, dangerous, but people may immerse themselves in measurements rather than crucial interpretations. A shortcoming, therefore, is undue faith in what might turn out to be unbalanced measures.

On the other hand, there is a risk of being misled by too narrow measures, as at Barings. On the other hand, though a broad-based framework might have plenty of balance, it then requires much greater skills to interpret the results and data. This view is discussed in detail

in Chapter 8. Too many organizations waste time and money on measurement because they lack a clear focus of purpose and allow themselves to be deflected. Adopting the next management fad that comes
along as pressures of the moment change the destination or, put another
way, measurement can be taken too far as people become metrics
obsessed; as the saying goes, if you give a baby a hammer, everything
becomes a nail.

Considering these shortcomings, the following vignette from Chapter 6 on customer measurement is revealing. A large U.S. office services
organization made the correct strategic decision in committing to
"world-class . . . customer understanding." It deployed 105 separate
measures or research activities involving 200 employees, 17 departments, and costs of over US$1 million; however, customer retention fell
10 percent and satisfaction levels fell by 5 percent after one year.

By contrast, an example is provided from the area of employee
measurement. One manager proudly cited the fact that, after an
employee opinion survey, he compiled a document listing over ninety
actions for him to take, yet experts typically recommend adopting no
more than six actions at any given time. Three points are worth
highlighting:

1. There is a tendency toward overmeasurement.
2. Measures are often inappropriate.
3. The question of who should respond and act concerning data
   analysis or feedback is often overlooked.

In the case of the office services organization, there was too little
response or feedback; only 27 percent of findings were acted upon,
while the hapless manager overreacted and failed to focus.

As we shall see, balance is a crucial measurement issue. It is also
crucial to raise measurement to strategically significant levels, where it
has a direct impact on business performance and results.

STRATEGIC MYOPIA

Considering quality measurement (covered in Chapter 7), David
Lowe, a chief executive officer and Malcolm Baldrige Quality Award
senior examiner for a number of years, says he has witnessed much
activity carried out purely for quality's sake, with no regard for strategic objectives. The emphasis here is on the means and not the end.
Lowe's view is that there is no point in measuring quality or making
improvements if they do not impact on business performance and
profitability.

Nick Develin, managing director of U.K. consultants Develin & Partners, makes a similar point on process measurement in Chapter 5. He suggests that business performance measurement tends to be inward looking and, as such, cannot help to create capability that is more competitive. Develin regards this lack of perspective as the crucial strategic issue, along with delivering a superior market or customer position. He suggests that these capabilities cannot be achieved by applying existing measures to new processes. Success involves significant internal change in culture, structure, competencies, and behaviors. In effect, Develin suggests that organizations measure the wrong things in the wrong way and use measures too selectively, sometimes because they are the easiest to apply.

David Lascelles, of the U.K. consulting firm Paragon Consulting Associates, consults widely on self-assessment strategy, business excellence, and performance improvement. He suggests that "flavor of the month" packages are popular because organizations appear to have become "measurement crazy." This "craziness" has led to a scant appreciation of the keys to successfully managing a business and how tough it is to build a strategic performance measurement framework. This phenomenon is often crisis driven or, at least, driven by a fear of crisis, when the key is to allow strategic thinking to evolve.

These points on strategically focused measurement were substantially addressed by the 1995 Renaissance Solutions survey of over 200 organizations on defining and managing business strategies.[2] The project also included forty personal interviews with senior executives. This survey made a telling observation: "Overall, the majority of management systems are designed around short-term, control-orientated financial frameworks that are fundamentally tactical."[3] It then cited five common factors of performance measurement in participant organizations:

• Dominant financial or other backward-looking indicators
• Failure to measure all the factors that create value[4]
• Little account taken of asset creation and growth
• Poor measurement of innovation, learning, and change
• A concentration on immediate, rather than long-term goals

The report also revealed that, for business planning, targets were typically derived from departmental financial forecasts rather than from strategic performance drivers and the linkages between them. The report concluded: "Despite reasonably high level use, non-financial measures and targets are frequently treated in isolation from strategic objectives. They are not reviewed regularly, nor are they linked to short-term or action plans—they are largely ignored or 'for interest' only."[5]

SHORTCOMINGS TO BEST PRACTICE

The broad shortcoming of performance measurement in contemporary business practice can be summarized as follows:

- Measurement is an organizational preoccupation; the preceding references refer to excessive measurement, "flavor of the month" tactics, and metrics obsession hit the mark, with a tendency to overmeasure or measure for its own sake.
- Measures are inappropriate, of the wrong type, and measure the wrong issues; they lack focus and are unbalanced, inward looking, historical, and nonpredictive.
- Alignment with business strategy, performance, and profitability is scarcely evident, as is the linking of measures to strategic performance drivers; measures are, typically, tactical rather than strategic.
- Measures broadly fail to address competitive issues, competition, market or customer positioning, building capability, innovation, learning, and value creation.
- Data analysis and response to feedback are weak, which has implications for management practice, decision making, systems action, process improvement, and organizational response.

Much of what is covered here has its source in consulting, that is, from consulting organizations and even academics pushing their latest way of measuring performance and giving the results new and more meaningful use. As such, much of what is covered has only limited or nil exposure to academic critique or study, so the reader may feel this book supports the faddish nature of some of these approaches. However, the main objective was to bring together a variety of new approaches where they could be compared in one book so that businesses have a greater chance of success in the new millennium.

NOTES

1. Some of the case studies later in the book do suggest that much has changed, but the question that remains unanswered is if this will last and has become part of the long-term culture of these organizations or if it is just passing. Maybe if we wait another ten to fifteen years there will be a more definitive answer.

2. *Translating Strategy into Action* (London: Renaissance Solutions Ltd, 1996).

3. *Translating Strategy into Action* (London: Renaissance Solutions Ltd, 1996).

4. Though they do not identify the factors, which may mean that they do not know what they are or that the link among the factors being measured and how they create value may not be as clear as those involved would like.

5. *Corporate Performance Measurement Benchmarking Study Report* (Houston: American Productivity and Quality Center, 1996).

2

Performance Measurement Frameworks

THE CONTEXT FOR FRAMEWORKS

Three words recur throughout this book as desirable attributes for strategic performance measurement: *focus, balance,* and *integration.* Focus has both strategic and operational dimensions in defining direction, capability, and what the business or its activities are all about. Balance implies seeking an equilibrium for making sense of the business and strengthening focus. Integration is critical as it ensures the organizational effort fits into some form of sustainable response to strategic priorities and change.

It follows that the use of balanced frameworks for understanding and pulling together these three attributes is a first principle in attempting to rethink or introduce strategic performance measurement. Without the coherence of a framework, effort tends to dissipate and outcomes are diminished. This was the rationale for the emergence of performance measurement frameworks in the 1990s.

Performance measurement frameworks are systemic and relate to different purposes and contexts, from the predictive and descriptive to the prescriptive and within strategic,[1] process, and operations contexts. The value of these frameworks lies in:

- Encouraging a rigorous strategic review or analysis, which shapes the organization's destiny in the light of turbulent business conditions

- Setting a different perspective for reconsidering organizational capability
- Guiding users in determining critical success factors and performance indicators
- Providing a structure for more effective management and systems
- Establishing a more rigorous basis for rethinking key measurement issues as related to people, including performance management, communication, and compensation

Next we will review three balanced scorecards from different organizations, along with their applications, in effect, as strategic management systems. Functional scorecards for human resources (HR) and suppliers are covered later in this chapter, along with other performance measurement models that are attracting interest, for example, corporate dashboards and strategic deployment. The fact that other approaches or interpretations exist in different consultancies is worth emphasizing as those covered here represent, first, the lead model and, then, a scan of other variants and their offshoots.

THE BALANCED SCORECARD (BSC)

The classic scorecard was designed by Nolan Norton Consultants, KPMG Peat Marwick, and 12 Fortune 500 organizations.[2] It was then refined by Kaplan and Norton and modified by several organizations that use it.[3] The purpose of the balanced scorecard (BSC) is to attempt to understand the phenomena of business. It focused originally on defining the drivers of financial performance, understanding the shortcomings of its measures, and finding alternatives. Three dimensions evolved to shape the scorecard: nonfinancial performance measurement, an organizational systems framework, and an overarching management philosophy. It serves a corporate need for a strategic framework and a new measurement process. The BSC has four elements, as shown in Figure 2.1:

Financial—How do our shareholders see us?

Customer—How do our customers see us?

Internal—What processes should we excel at?

Learning—How must the organization learn and improve?

Driving each element is a small number of strategic objectives and measures, with weighting allocated dependent on organizational priorities. For example, the financial element might be worth 60 percent and customers 20 percent. Business unit and operational objectives and measures align with these objectives and measures,

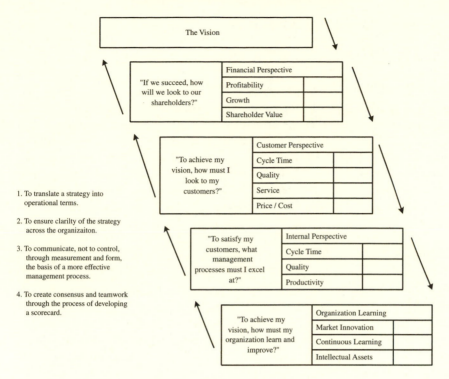

Figure 2.1 The Balanced Scorecard Provides a Framework

cascading right to the line and support units. Through the cascade, every measure selected can be ultimately related to financial results. As articulated in practice, the scorecard translates vision and strategy into understandable forms, which can trigger organization-wide actions. The BSC assists the organization to achieve consensus, focus, and clarity of direction through portraying its link with strategic objectives and measures. In this sense, performance measurement is interpreted as a dynamic chain of cause and effect relationships that disclose the key performance drivers.

The practical value of scorecards as a descriptive, but not prescriptive, tool should be emphasized as it enables users to clarify strategy and refine business structure in the context of continually changing business conditions. It is an integrating framework for managing change and implementing strategy, and clearly not another program, process, or initiative. A useful scorecard tells the story of an organization's strategy, as strategy, by its nature, is a set of hypotheses about cause and effect. The scorecard is a tool for better management by:

- aiding process management and improvement
- strengthening performance management by aligning employee goals and competencies to strategy
- acting as a strategic feedback system to ensure that strategy is on track and also to enable learning

As shown in Figure 2.2, the scorecard is, therefore, a balanced management system in which shared vision and strategy are reference points for the management process; achieving this balance enables synergy and a practical fit with other frameworks. The scorecard has a strong compatibility with the Baldrige and European Foundation for Quality Management (EFQM) models and helps embed any other change initiatives, such as Total Quality Management (TQM), into the system.

Applications of the BSC

The practices of specialist insurer, Cigna Property and Casualty (Cigna P&C) typify the context outlined here. Its business response to rapidly declining fortunes led to a strategic performance framework being introduced using a BSC approach. Extraordinary claims for catastrophes led to losses of US$1 billion between 1990 and 1993, which, along with poor quality underwriting and risk management, brought the organization close to failure.

Strategic redirection of Cigna began in 1993, resulting in a four-year transformation process through deployment of the BSC. The scorecard

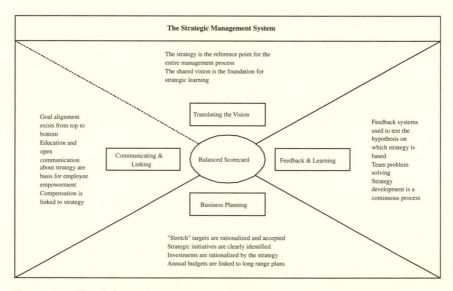

Figure 2.2 The Balanced Management System

was seen as a strategic framework for reengineering and improving business performance. In practice, it acts as a planning tool and management system that is tailored to the specific needs of each business unit. Over eighteen separate scorecards were in place by 1997, aligned to one master scorecard for the entire organization. Each has four quadrants common to the model in Figure 2.1, with some changes in element terminology, for example, those of Cigna are financial, external, internal, and learning/growth.

A critical point for Cigna was first to conduct a strategic review of the business and its risks and then make accurate assumptions about markets, customers, and four key variables:

- Business strategy
- Process/organization
- People/skills
- Information technology

These variables are intended to drive operational decisions. For each variable, executive missions were drawn up to guide future performance. The BSC has been the means for managing Cigna's transformation by integrating the four variables with an overall business vision that has achieved a seamless insurance service between field offices, agents, brokers, and customers. In this context, the scorecard is a tool for strategic direction and reviews, business planning, process design, and aligning management systems. Each unit thus has a clearer framework to run its own specialist business.

Underpinning this example is a feature common to most financial service organizations. Traditionally, they are focused on external financial reporting, with little regard for value in terms of service quality, speed, customer needs, or the needs of other stakeholders. As noted in Chapter 1, this approach to performance measurement tends to be historical and nonpredictive, which has strategic limitations.

As detailed in Chapter 1, NatWest UK recognized the issues of over-measurement and measurement limitations and in 1992 introduced a scorecard with four quadrants (financial, customer, processes, and organizational development). This has substantially evolved over five years.

A major development occurred with a 1995 restructuring that allowed six new business units to build and distribute their own scorecards in relation to an overarching corporate vision. The bank deploys a family of scorecards, all related to its core capability model, which is a strategic view of capabilities such as customer service and risk management. The result is a more meaningful, high-level business picture. One does not end up with just one overall scorecard, full of indexes that may be averages of averages and therefore relatively meaningless.

NatWest's scorecard has three attributes. It serves as:

- A practical framework for implementing strategy and performance management
- A management tool linking business, team, and individual objectives and rewards to strategic goals
- A mechanism for change management

Building the scorecard starts when one grasps these measures and drivers, which are at the heart of a solid performance management system.

By contrast, MichCon, a gas utility, has used the balanced scorecard to link strategic and business planning with strategic objectives and a matrix of critical process and subprocess measures. The four quadrants, with strategic objectives and lead indicators, are:

- Financial: improved returns, profitable growth, and reduced service costs; lead indicators are revenue-cost ratios and cost-per-unit measures.
- Customers: increase customer loyalty and improve corporate image as measured by price in relation ot that of competitors, service responsiveness and accuracy, and consumer satisfaction with community programs or adverse environmental issues.
- Internal: develop products and services, maximize system assets, and minimize operational problems; lead indicators are internal customer ratings and employee surveys.
- Learning: develop strategic skills, provide strategic information, and align personal goals (training hours per employee is an indicator).

However, critical elements of deploying the scorecard are its installation onto the corporate executive information system (EIS), communication, and compensation systems.[4] Organization-wide measurement data is entered into the EIS by every operational unit, with designated indicator owners being responsible for data quality and accuracy. In addition, strategic indicators, which track progress against goals, are maintained in another database by the business planning function. The system provides three views of data and information for analysis and action. First is an organization-wide summary for review at monthly goal meetings, followed by the strategic view for business planners, which displays goals and their indicators. Finally, we obtain an organizational view, which overlays processes within the organization.

More broadly, it is important to define a measurement communication process for reporting and discussing detailed measurement information in relation to the bigger picture of process improvement. Among the methods used are:

- Internal publications, including a weekly one-page update of performance against measures
- Work area postings of measurement information using charts and graphs
- Weekly or monthly unit and team discussions of results, targets, and improvement actions
- Electronic support: data and information are available to any employee with a computer
- Television: the MCTV (MichCon) video network, which broadcasts to most company locations, one program, *Monday Morning Measures,* describes the previous week's performance in relation to selected measures.

In terms of demonstrating the connection between the scorecard's strategic objectives and measures and those of individual effort, specific results are tied to employee objectives. Satisfactory performance in meeting these objectives leads to merit pay bonuses, and an additional teamwork incentive program is aligned with five key corporate measures:

- Customer satisfaction
- Safety
- Absenteeism
- Financial ratios
- Operational costs

An example of a teamwork incentive program is the so-called *enterprise agreement,* which rewards teams when they achieve operational savings, with team members sharing 50 percent of the gains. MichCon uses two forms of executive compensation linked to performance against the scorecard: a short-term pay plan based on financial and operating measures, and a longer-term, six-year performance cycle, which compensates based on peer-ranking positions.

In adopting balanced business scorecards or frameworks, key points are illustrated:

- Their use as tools for focusing mechanisms for strategic, business, and systems reviews
- Applying a strategic performance framework that links organizational capability with critical perspectives, that is, the four quadrants

- The deployment of families of scorecards, tailored to specific business unit needs and aligned with a corporate master
- Supporting deployment and decision making by integrating scorecards into executive information systems

Finally, a further point concerns addressing people issues in relation to a measurement framework by rethinking and designing special plans for individual performance management, compensation, and multisource communication.

The Dynamic Business Scorecard

One explanation for why performance measurement frameworks are attracting widespread interest (primarily in Europe and North America) is that business is experiencing a new age of measurement. Rather than being micro or metrics focused, this emphasizes the macro, big picture level, taking into account strategy, systems, and processes. Leaner structures are contributing to this interest, but, and more important, there is an increasing recognition that strategic measurement can drive the closing of significant performance gaps.[5] There is also a perception among executives with fewer resources at their disposal that a business has to be managed far more tightly and precisely than before. Among emerging scorecard models are quality award criteria frameworks (see Chapter 3) and others, variously focused around strategic thrusts, processes, core competencies, and stakeholder value.

In essence, the most effective frameworks are dynamic, adaptable to business change, and flexible enough to be tailored; they act as an organization's own large-scale business model. They introduce structure and discipline and should have customers right at their heart. The dynamic scorecard shown in Figure 2.3 represents the overview of how Forum Corporation's business scorecard actually works to its specific circumstances. Forum's message is that effective people and efficient processes offer value, which builds customer loyalty to deliver business results. In addition, customer loyalty triggers a feedback loop linking to the fundamental people and process elements.

Figure 2.4 outlines how performance measures align with the dynamic scorecard's boxes and how each measurement group is identified by an acronym such as CARES, TACTIC, SPECS, SCORE, and MAGIC (the latter, with a hint of double meaning, referring to business results). A critical point of the dynamic model is that links from one box to the other are explicit. Measures to the left predict those to the right, and the predictability of metrics is measurable in itself. Thus, the performance of the performance measures can be assessed, leading to the system's continuous improvement.

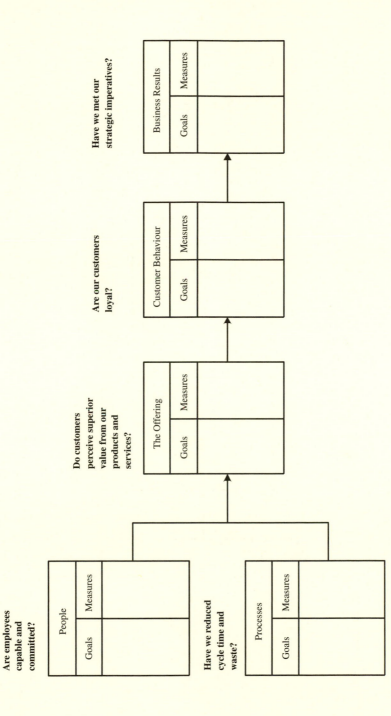

Figure 2.3 Dynamic Business Scorecard

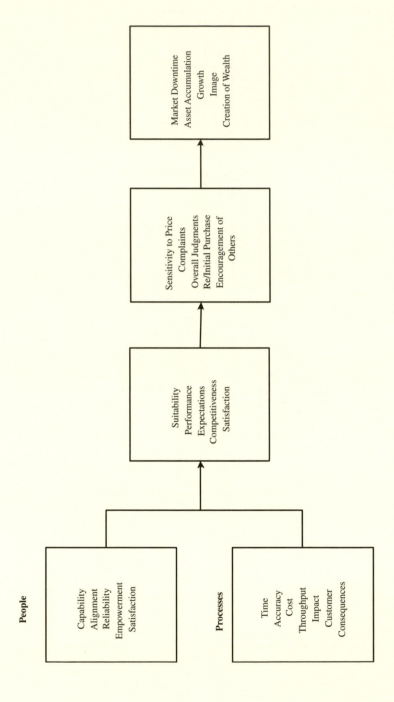

Figure 2.4 Dynamic Business Scorecard Measures

There are three phases for creating a dynamic scorecard: assess, invent, and mobilize. These, in turn, break into six steps:

1. Organizational assessment to establish the climate for measurement
2. Creating a representative and accountable core scorecard team
3. Defining business model, results, and measures
4. Conducting a measurement audit of current metrics, information systems capabilities, and gap analysis
5. Building the scorecard for EIS prototyping while planning implementation and communication
6. Implementing, including education and learning for support of procedures and processes

Apart from a master framework, the dynamic scorecard has other applications at executive and departmental levels connected to appropriate strategic and operational measures. For example, the goal of greater customer loyalty for the former will be measured by customer retention percentages, whereas day-to-day line activity will use a customer first-call effectiveness metric, among others.

Among the principal benefits of a dynamic scorecard is a powerful alignment between financial and nonfinancial measures, strategic direction, business goals, and critical success factors. Measures are thus linked up, down, and across the organization. It is possible for employees to recognize the scorecard's logic and how they fit into the big picture since they can measure their own performance, consistent with that of the organization. This line-of-sight employee involvement, plus the potential for learning, provide a significant motivator and builder of self-esteem, with potentially enormous payoffs.

The Value Performance Scorecard

By contrast, the payoff for the value performance scorecard is primarily in business results but also in stakeholder value. The model is shown at Figure 2.5 and is similar to the scorecards in Figure 2.1 in that it has four boxes with strategic goals and measures. However, there are significant differences in three of the four perspectives, as follows:

- Financial: business results—How do the stakeholders see us?
- Customers: customer satisfaction—How do customers see us?
- People: people satisfaction—How do employees see us?
- Societal: impact on society—How does society at large see us?

Any balanced scorecard should reflect the award evaluation criteria of the business excellence model chosen and do so by relating it to the established Baldrige, EFQM, or other chosen methodology. Customers,

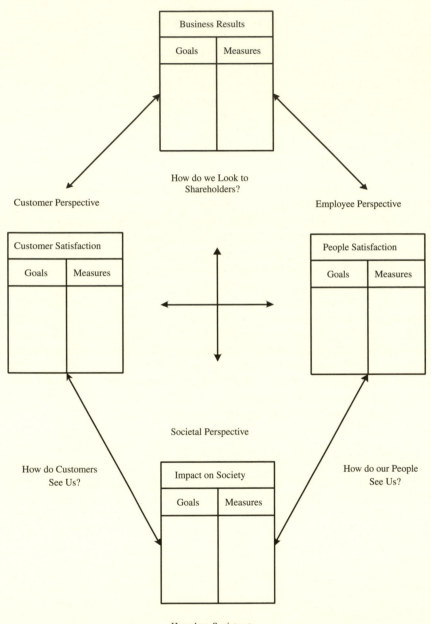

Financial Perspective

Business Results

Goals	Measures

How do we Look to
Shareholders?

Customer Perspective

Customer Satisfaction

Goals	Measures

How do Customers
See Us?

Employee Perspective

People Satisfaction

Goals	Measures

How do our People
See Us?

Societal Perspective

Impact on Society

Goals	Measures

How does Society at
Large See Us?

Figure 2.5 Balanced Scorecard

people, and societal measures ultimately drive financial measures, or business results. Scorecards should reflect all those organization's stakeholder groups that have needs to be satisfied. If they do so, they act as a predictive tool that helps make a critical connection: determing what is it that keeps you in business. Customer loyalty delivers better financial results, whereas satisfied employees give greater capability, productivity, and a capacity for learning or innovation.

The impact on society perspective is unique and links directly to one element of the outcome criteria in the EFQM model. This can be interpreted broadly, from impacts on suppliers and local communities, including employment markets, to environmental costs. Business and process measures do not traditionally relate to satisfiers for these constituencies of interest. Consider the effects, for instance, of a company that performs outstandingly against business excellence measures within, yet nonetheless issues a profit warning or reduces head count, as has happened in practice. A balanced and consistent measurement of these satisfiers is important for any organization with a substantial societal presence.

The performance scorecard also addresses emerging expectations of multiple constituencies in another sense. The trend toward corporate governance and sustainable business is resulting in new stock portfolios being launched, for example, with Paragon, as the market becomes more aware of the significance of more rounded business performance and nonfinancial measurement. The new portfolios emphasize business excellence principles, along with inclusive approaches to stakeholder involvement and value and their potentially beneficial impact on financial results. Chapter 9 covers this issue in more detail.

The markets are increasingly understanding that earnings per share (EPS) and price appreciation do not just happen, which is a recognition that was not evident several years ago (prior to the mid-1990s). Executives should focus on this issue and ensure that a balanced scorecard relates performance to stakeholder's satisfaction to value, or, what is keeping them in business.

Functional Applications of the Balanced Scorecard

Given its depth as a strategic management system, the balanced scorecard principle will continue to be widely adopted and further refined in user organizations as experiences in its implementation emerge. It is worth recalling that Cigna P&C regards this as a four-year process, after which tough cultural and behavioral issues begin to be tackled.

Hence, as this evolution continues, the alternative performance measurement frameworks cited previously will emerge, in addition to the design of dedicated process- or function-oriented scorecards. Hewitt Associates launched its scorecard concept for measuring the effectiveness of HR management in 1996, in line with wide North American and European trends for conceptualizing and rigorously evaluating what this function does. The scorecard attempts to strategically align and measure HR through four HR-related quadrants: financial, operational, customer, and strategic capability. Each relates to specific measures and questions, as follows:

- Financial: the financial impacts of people management and HR practices on business results, including HR costs and value added
- Operational: internal efficiency and effectiveness of HR processes, including productivity, quality, cost, and cycle time
- Customer: the perceptions internal stakeholders have about the effectiveness of HR practices and roles in relation to business goals
- Strategic capability: measuring how HR contributes to leadership, learning, and innovation, all of which, in turn, are contributors to competitive success

Fundamentally, the scorecard is a measurement process aligning HR strategies and programs with the business plan. HR measurements have traditionally focused on basic efficiencies, for example, length of time for processing claims, which in this case views employees as a cost. Measuring in this way provides little linkage with business strategy.

SUPPLIER SCORECARDS

By contrast, Sun Microsystems applied the scorecard principles, though not the specific concept, to the supply chain as a model for leveraging competitive advantage. Its vision for 2001, according to its annual report, was "to be recognised as the best at integrating suppliers, Sun and customers into a seamless value chain."

For suppliers, this has three implications: building alliances, promoting cost competitiveness through Sun's total cost of ownership program, and increasing customer responsiveness. To drive these supplier imperatives, the corporation has operated total cost of ownership and supplier scorecards for a number of years. The latter act as integrated, external measurement and recognition frameworks under Sun's supplier management process. This process is overseen by a five member Supplier Council and has evolved from a corporate renewal framework called Business Process Simplification. One element of this is the "Procure to Pay" guideline, which targets a reduction in the supply chain from 86 to 25 days and 20 percent cost reductions through increased efficiencies.

By outsourcing production, and focusing on fewer suppliers and the total cost of ownership program, Sun was able to grow from a start-up in 1982 to a US\$12.5 billion company in 2002. This may be attributed to Sun having core competencies, differentiated products, and involved suppliers. This involvement in the supply chain, which makes Sun's systems designs flexible enough to fit supplier processes rather than the reverse, produces higher yields and less costly parts, but one needs to understand that customers' needs are paramount and the hope is that they will see themselves as an extension of Sun.

The scorecard measures suppliers against the total cost of ownership criteria (delivery, quality, price, service, and technology), with targets stringent enough to drive continuous improvement. Although ratings are externally imposed and measured by Sun, suppliers are expected to assess their own performance. In practice, scorecard objectives expect all suppliers to achieve a minimum 85 percent satisfaction scores, with the top 40 producing a 25 percent overall improvement against the previous year. They are audited every quarter with strategic reviews. If suppliers reach these targets, they have guaranteed sales, knowing, for instance, the Sun business plan in advance, while the corporation is able to achieve its own strategic objectives of enhancing customer loyalty and driving down customer dissatisfiers.

The U.K. contract electronics manufacturer D2D has been a Sun supplier of printed circuit board components since 1990 and finds that adopting this supply scorecard has directly shaped business performance. In fact, the company has won an outstanding supplier award from Sun for a number of years in succession. To comply with Sun's requirements, D2D reorganized its manufacturing process, converting traditional production lines into more responsive customer focus teams. Each is dedicated to clients like Sun, acting as an "internal outpost" of the corporation's operations in D2D's own plant.

Introducing the scorecard has been all encompassing and has served to drive competitive difference. As a result, the firm obtains extra added value and gains distinct business benefits. Given the strategic importance of supplier scorecards, D2D has developed its own called the Vendor Accreditation Scheme, which 150 key suppliers have to use. It is guided and supported by teams from D2D and is essential for cost-effectiveness and business performance improvement.

BUSINESS FRAMEWORK VARIATIONS

Self-devised Frameworks

As indicated in the previous section, the balanced scorecard has led to the emergence of other frameworks and also to functionally oriented versions. Linking this point to the comment concerning a new age of measurement focused more on the macro business picture, other variations on the framework theme are developing and will continue to do so. Two such variations are detailed here: how scorecard use has helped organizations devise their own strategic performance measurement frameworks and the deployment of corporate dashboards. For example, stock transfer specialist, First Chicago Trust Co., systematically introduced the balanced scorecard but, in contrast to typical practice, does not, in itself, act as the organization's business framework.

Seeking to improve operating conditions, reduce service problems, strengthen customer performance, and accelerate growth, First Chicago Trust Co. developed its own framework for strategic performance measurement. It did so by identifying key nonfinancial measures that are ultimately predictive of financial performance:

- Customer satisfaction
- Employee satisfaction
- Productivity
- Quality
- Market growth
- Control effectiveness

By monitoring performance for each measure and taking appropriate remedial action, improved revenues, business growth, reduced expenses, and compliance with sector regulations have resulted.

Through this framework, measures are aligned to strategic objectives (leadership, operations, risk management, client relations, competitive standing, and so on), from which results follow. Of note is the fact that actual measures for the six categories are changed every year as the organization adjusts to marketplace influences.

A critical emphasis is placed on strategy. There must be consistent alignment between measures and strategy, which is not easy to attain or always obvious. Alignment will ensure that short-term efforts parallel long-term direction and will expedite some efforts; involving people at all levels is also important and involves giving them authority for setting measures and challenging processes. The organization needs to articulate its strategy in terms understood by management and staff and must have a basis for ensuring it is kept on track.

Many organizations are aware of the story of decline and renewal of the global machinery and engines firm, Caterpillar, which exemplifies executive complacency and weak strategic focus followed by transformation. From hitting record sales and profits in 1981, the next three years saw significant losses. Demand was down 50 percent as the group succumbed, due, primarily, to Japanese competition. In addition to these problems, Caterpillar had major cost disadvantages and structurally was in no position to respond. However, by reengineering over a twelve-year period (1983–1995), Caterpillar's management repositioned and transformed the business by focusing on nine strategic priorities:

- Customers
- Product introduction
- Manufacturing and logistics
- Decision making
- Eliminating functional "silos" and bureaucracy
- People
- Business processes
- Compensation
- Performance measurements

A case report to an international scorecard conference by Caterpillar revealed that the renewal effort was focused by the catchphrase, "the High-Velocity Company."[6] More significantly, performance measurement was a critical consideration in four areas: supporting strategy, driving behavioral change, focusing on the nine business priorities, and being based on the principle of key accountabilities.

As part of the reengineering initiative, Caterpillar devised its own balanced scorecard of eight top-tier performance measures:

- Quality
- Customer satisfaction
- Human resources
- Product growth
- Inventory
- Timeliness
- Productivity
- Financial

These top-tier measures were devised and launched in 1991, as driven by the two dimensions of people and process. For the former, a cross-functional performance measurement team of innovators and implementors designed a new process after assessing existing measures and developing the new measures through prototyping. All were integrated into a strategic system or framework. Key aspects of deployment, according to the case report, were education, training, and a tied-in reward plan which aimed to reinforce new behaviors among Caterpillar's 54,000 employees.

Business Dashboard

The founding principle of Caterpillar's self-devised scorecard was identifying its nine top-tier measures, which drive results. This requirement to track the strategic drivers of success has been a mission at the Conference Board in New York City, which has studied *best practice* strategic performance measures among global corporations for a number of years.[7]

As Figure 2.6 shows, an organization might be concerned with five key strategic performance measures: growth, client satisfaction, quality, business management, and environmental performance. The dashboard has the following elements:

- An actual index number representing the current situation for the elements

| Growth Measures | Target Index |
| | Actual Index |

| Business Management | Target Index |
| | Actual Index |

| Client Satisfaction | Target Index |
| | Actual Index |

| Environmental Performance | Target Index |
| | Actual Index |

| Quality | Target Index |
| | Actual Index |

| Other | Target Index |
| | Actual Index |

Figure 2.6 Sample Generic "Dashboard" to Track Strategic Measures

- A target index for the goal
- Each index is calculated from a series of weighted indicators, which *drill down* into the organization and underlie the key dashboard indicator, as shown in Figure 2.7.
- Executives determine, and change as necessary, the underlying measures and their assigned weights.
- Weighting may be done on an indexed scale of 1 to 100, an alphabetical scale of A to E, or through any other tracking system useful to the organization.
- The framework accommodates a situation in which underlying measures may apply to more than one strategic dashboard measure.
- Dashboard indicators can be color-coded to indicate how close the actual measures are to the target. For example, green may indicate it is being achieved, whereas orange shows that the goal is not yet within reach and red would indicate a failure. The computerized dashboard enables users to click on the prime box to uncover the underlying boxes, each of which is similarly color-coded, quickly and on an ongoing basis, monitoring strategic performance.

The strategic performance measurement becomes as interactive and current as the organization chooses. Whereas some measures may be collected repeatedly, others may be required less frequently. The dashboard framework provides continuous feedback, as executives can use it to decide what they want to measure and how much each measure contributes to the key drivers of business success.

As an overview on variations of business measurement frameworks, the balanced scorecard has had a significant impact at senior executive levels, principally in formulating strategy. It has helped executives move away from running their businesses just on financial measures. This has led to the development of a *rapid strategy deployment* model. This is a strategic framework which has been successfully applied in the utilities, electronics, and white goods manufacturing sectors, as shown in Figure 2.8.

In effect, by using a structure tree, an organization's critical success factors, strategies, measures and goals can be summarized and communicated to employees. The framework enables changes in the marketplace to continually feed back into business strategy through strategic performance measurement. Some parts of even the soundest strategies can become irrelevant quickly, given the pace of change. Organizations need an additional capability in the form of a self-correcting measurement mechanism to be able to respond. As detailed in Chapter 5, this form of measurement focuses on process indicators to establish the root causes of variances in strategy.

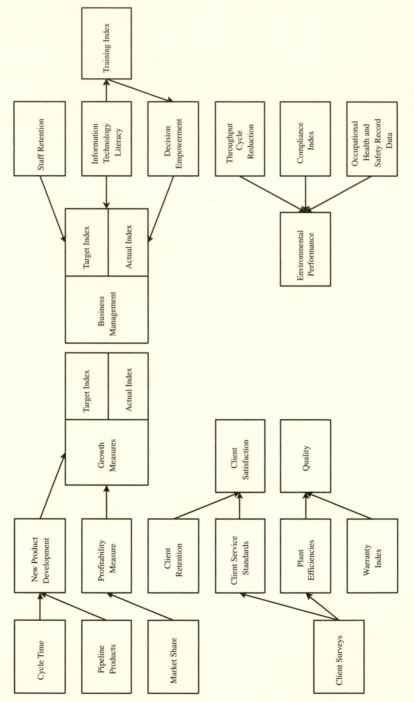

Figure 2.7 Detailed "Dashboard" to Track Strategic Measures

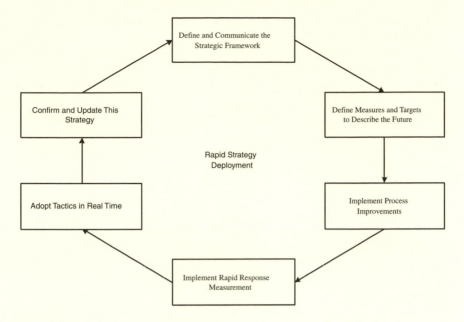

Figure 2.8 Rapid Strategy Deployment

CONCLUSION

As a broad overview in positioning the business measurement frameworks considered in this chapter, three tiers are evident. First is the balanced or dynamic scorecard, plus corporate dashboards, as generic frameworks for other methodologies or systems. These are followed by business excellence and self-assessment methodologies and then the more specific variation noted previously or others from consultancies. Certainly, in terms of impacts, at whichever links these measurement frameworks operate, wide organizational effects will occur, the most dramatic of which can be grouped around cultural change. Introducing and deploying strategic performance measurement frameworks has its difficulties.

It is worth emphasizing that it took Cigna P&C four years to address cultural and behavioral issues and that MichCon put maximum effort into aligning individual and business objectives, deliberately planning communication strategies, and tying in compensation. All such changes require significant executive consideration.

Organizations should expect skepticism and resistance to these changes because change may be perceived as yet another backdoor approach deriving from management. Key, then, are transparency, communication, and education, especially for finance professionals. These experts will see their source of power being eroded as nonfinancial indicators are introduced or if traditional financial measures become used and owned by other executives as part of their scorecards or dashboards. By not winning over staff, two competing measurement systems may well develop, so their cooperation is a make-or-break issue.

The need to convince others of the need for change raises the issue of strong leadership, again a crucial aspect of all frameworks and alternatives or, indeed, any major change program. This issue, which involves obtaining *sponsorship* and commitment, was a critical success factor in deploying the balanced scorecard at Royal Insurance. Leadership can be interpreted in two ways: as an overt leader or a champion. The need for consensus among senior levels of management should be emphasized. This consensus will be needed in setting business objectives and targets and must lead the organization's *new language* of change. Driving the scorecard process means those wanting it will have to lobby hard. Expect a range of responses from executives, including those keen to champion its principles as well as those who are unsure or prefer not to play ball. Plan for setbacks, recognize the leadership issues, and appreciate that implementation takes time.

Introducing a business-wide framework is more than adopting a cut-and-dried measurement system. It involves people, values, emotions, and attitudes, which can only be met or changed by being passionate and inspirational. There are four important factors to success with scorecards:

- Involvement and buy-in, which comprise an iterative, participative process
- Purposefully driving change, clarifying strategy, and aligning the organization
- Targeting different levels of activity in organizational layers to specific business-wide or strategic goals
- Understanding the crucial corporate and operational linkage

Building and deploying scorecard or other strategic frameworks will be a major, long-term undertaking and, perhaps, long term in payoff. No state of organizational readiness must really be assumed or in place before the balanced business scorecard can be considered or the undertaking begun; strategy is the key word.

PRACTITIONER GUIDES

1. Business is experiencing a significant change in performance measurement with the significant moves toward more strategic, macro

approaches. Examples include balanced and dynamic scorecards, corporate dashboards, and business control methodologies. A wide choice of alternatives exists, but methods should be selected with care so they suit each organization's particular situation.

2. Key questions include, Do current performance measures align or integrate with business strategies? How is this demonstrated? Where are the links to front-end or individual performance? Are these connections understood across the organization? Could a line operator describe how daily measures relate to strategy and financial performance? (Is such information ever communicated to the lower levels of an organization?)

3. Clarity over strategy is a first principle. If this is not evident, a review is critical, followed by a descending strategic analysis of capability, performance, measurement, and systems. Without succinctly interpreting these key words, there is little basis for considering a strategic measurement framework. A measurement audit of existing metrics is useful.

4. Consider the key words used where frameworks are effective, focused, balanced, integrated, flexible, and specific and also the fact that leadership and cross-functional participation are essential in drafting or prototyping a framework.

5. Examine the information technology (IT) implications of any move toward a balanced measurement framework. Ask questions, such as, At which levels should it operate? Who has access? Is an organization-wide system appropriate? How will developments impact on the executive information system?

6. As with any major change program, if building and deploying a framework, you must be prepared for the long haul, along with resistance and negative responses. Some practitioners report a three- to four-year time-scale, with eighteen months being a minimum for benefits to emerge.

7. People issues appear to be significant factors in success; deliberate, targeted, and ongoing communication strategies are crucial, along with education and reinforcement of a central question: How does individual effort relate and contribute to business strategy?

CASE STUDY—CIGNA P&C

Cigna P&C had discovered, to its cost, by late 1992 that risk can be an uncomfortable partner in business, especially if unmanaged. Claims for catastrophes, for example floods, hurricanes, riots, and environmental cleanups, led to US$1 billion in losses between 1990 and 1993. The organization's primary business measure, the combined ratio, had risen to 140 percent; that is, for every dollar in premiums they were paying out US$1.40 in claims.

Risk management and claims problems were compounded by an outdated, unfocused business strategy. Although this had served Cigna well at one time, the strategy was far past its replacement date in the 1990s. As a general insurance company, premiums came from any source or market to boost volume business. This led to specific risks not being clearly understood by underwriters at a time when markets were being driven by customers requiring more specialist needs and an integrated, one-stop service.

Apart from being in poor financial shape, relations with agents and brokers, who worked with customers on selecting policies and assessing risks, were deteriorating and morale was low. Effectively, Cigna P&C had lost its underwriting discipline, which was critical because the quality of underwriting directly correlates with payouts on losses.

From March 1993, however, strategic redirection began to transform the ailing business into a lean, focused, and aligned specialist insurer, based on three underwriting divisions:

- Commercial Insurance Services
- Speciality Insurance Services
- Special Risk Facilities

The new vision was to achieve top-quartile sector performance, In practice, this new focus meant, for example, that instead of workers' compensation policies being sold in all states and industries under the generalist approach, future portfolios would be based on far fewer territories. The territories that were the focus of activity might have more favorable regulatory environments, perhaps two or three fruitful sectors, or companies of a certain size.

The management team undertook a searching ten-week business analysis and conducted over one hundred in-depth interviews with employees while also talking to and surveying customers, field staff, agents, and brokers. The key question was: How does this business work? One important step soon after analysis started was to hire staff who could drive the transformation process by adopting the BSC approach to reengineer and improve business performance.

Three years after the process started, Cigna P&C started to see the benefits. Total operating income topped US$100 million from eighteen separate business for the first half of 1996, against a loss of US$31 million for the first half of 1995. Its combined income ratio was also heading in the desired direction. The organization has a near-perfect planning tool and management system in the BSC, which is tailored to the specific needs of each business unit. In effect, 18 separate scorecards evolved from one master scorecard for the entire organization. Each of the eighteen scorecards has four common quadrants: financial, external, internal, and learning/growth.

Strategic Issues

Cigna P&C saw this change in measurement techniques as a four-year process to build, deploy, and amend the scorecard process, with the first stage, in Cigna P&C's experience, taking about eighteen months. The process began in late 1993 with the top management team deciding how to convert the organization into a specialist insurer and to achieve top-quartile status. They were responsible for the vision, along with the process and performance measures, that would help determine this change. The key was to fully understand the business and its attendant risks and to make accurate assumptions about markets and customers, or variables such as business strategy, process/organization, people/skills, and information technology, in order to drive operational decisions. For each variable, the executive team perceived the transitions to be:

- Strategy: from general commercial products to specific products in niche markets and territories
- Process: from efficient task processing to effective decision making
- People: transforming latent knowledge into active knowledge flows
- Information technology: moving from data transaction systems to performance support systems

The BSC became the means of managing transformation by integrating the variables with the business vision and a seamless service among field offices (for sales, underwriting, and claims) and agents or brokers as the distribution channel and then on to the customer in the form of policies or special accounts. To do so, the scorecard was used as a tool in four applications: strategic direction, business planning and process redesign, aligning the organization as a management system (see Figure 2.9), and for strategic reviews.

Strategic Framework

First and foremost, the scorecard became a tool to articulate strategy, to translate the strategy into operational decisions and practice, and, in turn, to communicate the strategy throughout the organization (hence its use as a strategic framework). The scorecard clarifies what is meant to be a specialist instead of a generalist insurer for Cigna P&C at the corporate, division, and business unit levels. It assisted in assuring that

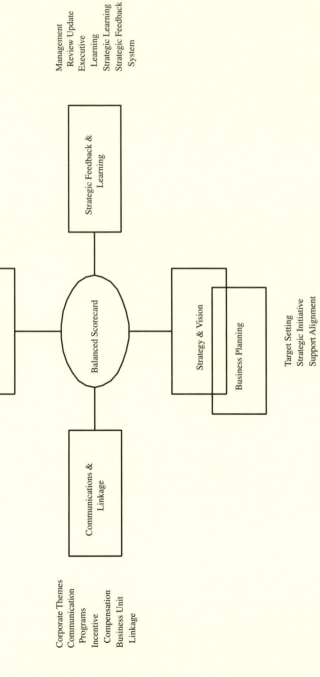

Figure 2.9 The Balanced Scorecard Role as a Management System

Cigna's vision and strategy were aligned with what its business units and people do.

Fourteen applications drove the strategic objectives, which are grouped into the scorecard's four quadrants or perspectives, each of which achieves focus by posing a critical question. These questions interrelate and, with strategic objectives, are the following:

- Financial perspective: If we succeed, how will we look to our shareholders? The strategic objectives are shareholder expectations, operating performance, growth, and shareholder risk.
- External or customer perspective: To achieve our vision, how must we look to our customers? Objectives are producer relationships, policyholder relations, and satisfying regulatory requirements.
- Internal or process perspective: To satisfy customers, at what business process must we excel? Business growth, underwriting profitability, claims management, and operating productivity are strategic objectives.
- Learning and growth perspective: To achieve our vision, how will we sustain innovation, change, and improvement? Objectives are to upgrade competencies, provide information technology support, and align the organization.

With its flexibility and alignment of processes, people, and technology, the scorecard allows a business to deliver value at the front end. For example, a business unit will relate its own strategy to corporate strategic objectives and decide which combination of those is most critical for that business. Each of these units has to consider what top-quartile performance looks like in its own area and assess its current position. Together with being clear on these points, business units will need to set strategic priorities and key initiatives for the business, along with local operating objectives, targets, and measures, that should be adopted and deployed. Each business identifies its own unique leverage points, using the scorecard process.

As an example of applying the external perspective, a business unit might decide to open a new sales channel or introduce a different product, as measured by productivity, profitability, cycle time, and service quality or seek to increase business with a particular agent or broker. Measures in this instance would concern quotes and revenues received.

Scorecard and Business Planning

A second application of the balanced scorecard at Cigna P&C is as a business planning and process redesign tool. As such, the BSC helps achieve two corporate priorities: to focus and fully integrate the planning process and then to define the transformation path for business units. The BSC is an aid to business planning because previously the planning process was related to financial budgets. Now, through the scorecard, planning highlights the capabilities the business unit needs and ties in management systems and decision making. The process encourages leaders to focus on how and in which direction they should be moving, allowing them to select their top three to five initiatives to be developed. As a planning tool, the scorecard changes or adds different dimensions to the process, as only one of its quadrants is financial.

Market selection and underwriting are examples of these initiatives. A strategic objective for the internal perspective is to implement the specialist insurer strategy in selected markets where an advantage exists. The planning attributes in this case are selecting profitable business lines, identifying key producers (the agents and brokers), and attracting customers. Achieving targets in these areas feeds back to, or impacts on, the external and financial quadrants of the model. Given the high risk and claims noted previously, it has been critical to reestablish underwriting as a fundamental business discipline and a profitable process, in order for it to drive specialist, rather than volume, income from premiums. Key planning considerations are to identify hazards or exposures, accurately price risks, and decide how technology can be used innovatively.

Again, the link to external and financial quadrants is evident, along with alignment with learning and growth; skill development and upgrading underwriting competencies are a crucial factor in risk management. The scorecard helps to explain Cigna P&C's risk appetite. Managers can tell from reviewing underwriting performance whether Cigna is achieving the right balance of risk for a particular business. If successful, the planning based on the BSC has a direct impact on operating income and the combined ratio. Cigna P&C converted a half-year loss of US$31 million in 1995 to a profit of US$100 million in 1996, and the figures for pretax catastrophe losses were down from US$41 million to US$31 million. Earnings per share against operating income rose from US$4.62 million in June 1995 to US$6.13 million in June 1996.

As a transformational tool, analysis of performance against the balanced scorecard's fourteen strategic objectives helps to create a transformation map. An example is shown in Figure 2.10. This guides business unit users in selecting their strategic priorities, the vital initiatives, annual objectives, and appropriate milestones as measures of performance.

Measurement and the Scorecard

Despite the use of more focused planning to improve business results, Cigna P&C is still learning about measuring performance after adopt-

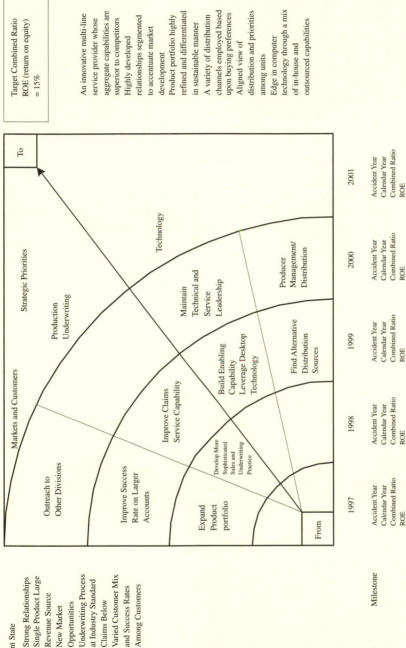

Figure 2.10 Sample Transformation Map

ing the scorecard. It is challenging to address the crucial question, How is a set of measures that articulate the results a business unit wants to be defined? The important point here is that measurement must be regarded as an indicator for implementing strategy and a control system; in other words, it is crucial to understand measurement in the context of business strategy because it is possible to achieve lower-level targets yet still fall short of meeting strategic objectives. In effect, Cigna P&C was grappling with the issue of measurement for two reasons. First, the most effective measures are not necessarily financial, and second, in the past, there had been a tendency to have too many measures at too low a level of detail.

In evaluating measurement, the emphasis is now on reviewing non-financial performance measurement, which is leading to, for example, a rethinking of how organizational learning impacts on the business. For example, if the new business requires stronger underwriting competencies, there are obvious implications for training and development, performance management, and how the underwriting process is reviewed. The reemphasis is possibly one of the largest challenges an organization will face because financial indicators are the language that business would normally use to talk about the insurance business but also because changing the tool of measurement means changing behaviors and cultures.

Aligning the Organization

As shown in Figure 2.9, a third application of the scorecard is as a tool for aligning the organization around the specialist insurer strategy. At Cigna P&C, this process is formally called "Communications and Linkage" and relates to four areas:

- Business linkage rosters to facilitate alignment or to pull together people in different processes and operating units so that business performance, rather than functional performance, is maximised; in effect, rosters are lists of all people who support or work in a particular business and therefore replace organizational charts
- Communication plans and programs
- Incentive compensation
- Stakeholder surveys and workshops, including employees, agents, brokers, and policyholders

Both alignment and communication are essential aspects of transforming any organization, as they are related to the point made earlier on changing behaviors and culture. People have to know where you want to go and the eventual outcomes, the difference between what you want to do and how to get there. If the vision is clearly articulated, people can change or make changes. For Cigna P&C, the vision to become a specialist insurer and to achieve top quartile status was clear but, despite new strategies to shape operational practice, mechanisms were not originally introduced to translate the vision into front-end goals or to align effort.

Business rosters have addressed this issue. For example, though a stand-alone business, the workers' compensation unit relies heavily on support from finance, human resources, information systems, and so on, none of which are direct reports. Therefore, it is the specific business unit manager's responsibility to communicate key initiatives, objectives, and measures being planned or used to all individuals on the roster. The communication helps them focus and facilitates understanding. The scorecard has helped realize alignment, which is also significantly reinforced by compensation. Cigna introduced a unique incentive plan in 1994, broadly based on the principles of goal sharing or performance share plans, which operates at the three levels of corporate, division, and business unit.

Each year, all employees start with a fixed number of so-called position shares, depending on job roles and responsibilities. When given, the shares have a par value of $10, which, at the time of payout, may have risen or dropped depending on progress against the scorecard most relevant to their work. Throughout the year, supervisors can award additional shares if an individual's performance exceeds expectations. In one payout, the most successful business, according to its scorecard and performance against the fourteen strategic objectives, paid $14 per share, against $6 for the lowest performer. Individuals in those units cash in their shares as a bonus and then values are reset at $10 for the following year. The idea has been well received. Position shares focus employees on business performance, getting them aligned with their unit in relation to the corporate whole, and the scheme is also a powerful motivator. People strive to be at the top of the payout, even if their share value was low the last time.

Review Process

An important contributor to the incentive program is Cigna P&C's scorecard review process. This operates annually, quarterly, and monthly to assess performance against strategic objectives. Monthly feedback from reviews affects share values, though the review process has far greater organizational significance. It is the cornerstone of the implementation efforts, a significant challenge in deploying the scorecard. The critical question concerns how implementation is monitored.

The review process relates to the strategic feedback and learning element of the management system in Figure 2.9. This is supported by a computerized strategic feedback system, in effect, an electronic scorecard, introduced through desktops in 1995. Although this system provides executives with an instant view of where critical indicators are going, it also feeds into communication by facilitating dialogue between top managers and process owners if a problem is revealed.

A particular innovation of the system is electronic data capture and display where results against the scorecard can be checked at any time and graphically portrayed; those on target appear in green on computer screens throughout the entire organization, yellow represents those close to target, and red represents those below target. Real-time analysis like this through the virtual signalling system means that action can be taken instantly if a strategy is not working, or performance is below expectations. The system helps to assess and drive performance, along with financial results. Using the tool or applying the whole review process is an exercise in continuous learning. There will always be new or different ways to drive performance because of changing business conditions or fresh strategic issues on which to focus.

The strategic review and feedback process is being rethought to identify further potential. Two developments that emerged are monthly self-assessments by business units against their scorecard objectives and taking one strategic objective each month, for example business growth, to examine cross-organizational performance.

Six benefits from the scorecard reviews for Cigna P&C have been the following:

- Act as an executive forum focused on the highest points of leverage in the business.
- Create opportunities for strategic learning at executive levels.
- Improve cross-business and support organizational coordination.
- Refine the measurement system on the basis of regular performance feedback.
- Improve or facilitate employee communication.
- Help define agendas for the business management group, which comprises business unit managers immediately below the executive team.

There has been a potential downside to the electronic feedback system, too. When a manager keys in his or her figures, the results are available to everyone in the organization at the touch of a button. This can create fear, a lack of trust, and resistance, as no one wants to publicly share poor performance figures with everyone.

Critical Success

The implications of such transparency are inescapable. Along with implementing the business scorecard and changing management systems, the organization's climate, culture, and behaviors had to change, too. In a sense, implementing the family of scorecards has shifted power, which was previously centered on the holders of pure financial results but now resides with the actual generators of those returns. It changed Cigna P&C into an organization of business managers rather than financial experts. In retrospect, the real work comes with implementation, when the ensuing changes to processes, systems, and so on, occur. It has been a three-year thinking and rethinking process, with the ultimate impact on the transformation unit being on organizational learning.[8]

NOTES

1. As indicated in the Preface, *strategic* and *strategy* are used in the context of long-term objectives and success of the organization.

2. Nolan Norton, *Performance Measurement in the Organization of the Future* (Boston: Nolan Norton and Company, 1991).

3. R. S. Kaplan and D. P. Norton, *The Balanced Scoreboard: Translating Strategy into Action* (Boston: Harvard Business School Press, 1996); R. S. Kaplan and D. P. Norton, "The Balanced Scorecard—Measures That Drive Performance," *Harvard Business Review*, 70(1) (1992): 71–79; R. S. Kaplan and D. P. Norton, "Putting the Balanced Scorecard to Work," *Harvard Business Review*, 71(5) (1993): 134–147; R. S. Kaplan and D. P. Norton, "Using the Balanced Scorecard as a Strategic Management System," *Harvard Business Review*, 74(1) (1996): 75–85; R. S. Kaplan and D. P. Norton, *The Strategy Focused Organization: How Balanced Scorecard Companies Thrive in the New Business Environment* (Boston: Harvard Business School Press, 2001).

4. Using the Balanced Scorecard as a Strategic Management System Conference, Sacramento, CA, 1996.

5. M. A. Milgate, *Alliances, Outsourcing and the Lean Organization* (Westport, CT: Quorum Books, 2001).

6. Using the Balanced Scorecard as a Strategic Management System Conference, Sacramento, CA, 1996.

7. C. K. Brancato, *New Corporate Performance Measures* (New York: The Conference Board, 1995).

8. P. M. Senge, *The Fifth Discipline: The Art and Practice of the Learning Organization* (Milson Point: Random House Australia, 1992); C. Argyris, *Overcoming Organizational Defenses: Facilitating Organizational Learning* (Upper Saddle River, NJ: Prentice Hall, 1990); C. Argyris, *On Organizational Learning*, 2nd ed. (Oxford: Blackwell Business, 1992); D. A. Garvin, *Learning in Action: A Guide to Putting the Learning Organization to Work* (Boston: Harvard Business School Press, 2000).

3

Self-Assessment and Business Excellence

Unlike some contemporary routes to business excellence, self-assessment, principally through the frameworks, methodologies, and criteria of leading international awards, is increasing. This is partly because it is a proven approach[1] to strategic performance measurement but also because it is a potential contributor to superior, and sustainable, business results. There is also the recognition of awards, although most winning exemplars stress that this is never a primary driver. After all, once introduced, self-assessment becomes an endemic part of business management.

Consider, for instance, that over 1 million copies of the Malcolm Baldrige National Quality Award guidelines were distributed from 1988 to 1997, compared to just over 600 applications for the award. Or consider that the methodology of the European Foundation for Quality Management (EFQM) has been adopted in South Africa, India, and parts of Eastern Europe. Are organizations implementing quality on their own without external assessment or reliance on self-assessment? Do they see what is required yet do not proceed with it? Although the latter suggestion may appear cynical, a reality associated with such programs is that many organizations cannot afford to implement them. Much of the cost is associated with taking people away from their normal duties, which may impact productivity, and so on.

In this section, these methodologies are considered in terms of their links to business strategy, the self-assessment rationale, and its process. For readers unfamiliar with the models discussed, a glossary is a pro-

vided at the end of the book and recent changes to criteria and termi-
nologies are explained. First we must consider a key question: what
strategic approaches are used by advanced exemplars of the pursuit of
business excellence through self-assessment?

One such exemplar, Corning Telecommunications Products Division
(TPD), adopted the Baldrige framework in 1989 and eventually won the
award six years later. The criteria acted as a continuous improvement
route map and systems approach to total quality, in addition to serving
as a foundation on which to build TPD's key leadership, strategy,
planning, human resources, and customer management processes. The
Baldrige criteria became their standard of excellence.[2] These criteria, in
themselves, require the organization to grow and continually improve
through assessment against the standard. Organizations know the performance bar will continue to rise, so they use a combination of Baldrige
criteria and their "Plan to Win" strategy to run their business.

Many of TPD's processes were a direct result of feedback from
Baldrige examiners. These include process management, integrated
manufacturing, supplier total value, and customer response with leadership, making sure the division stayed the course. By contrast, the
EFQM business excellence methodology adopted by Texas Instruments
in the mid-1990s was a crucial tool to evaluate structures and processes
in order to launch a radical restructuring initiative. Instead of thirty-one
business and support units, five European centers were created. Adopting the model changed the way organizations were structured and
operated, but more important, it helped Texas Instruments turn itself
around. It helped address fundamental competitive issues that were
institutionalized via annual planning. The model has the potential to
be a catalyst for change.

As an example, annual self-assessment reveals a few vital few excellence gaps that relate to the TI-BEST business process. This is integrated
with the EFQM framework and sets business excellence standards in
four areas: customer satisfaction, operational excellence, annual improvement, and performance metrics. The company's European Strategic Leadership Team is the process driver through eight quality teams
that champion the model's different categories.

Attaining business excellence was the first of four key strategies in a
five-year plan when ICL High Performance Technology (HPT), an independent computer systems group business unit in the ICL federation,
won the 1995 UK Quality award. The others are:

- Supplying existing products
- Opening new product streams and channels
- Structuring resources and skills to effect continued transition in
  the ever-changing IT sector

The EFQM model was an ideal tool for measuring performance when HPT was faced with the challenges of innovation and added value in a declining market sector.[3]

Self-assessment was the fifth in a series of quality focuses at ICL, and HPT had implemented it since the 1980s. Self-assessment was introduced in 1993 and followed the U.K. Ministry of Defence quality conformance program, Quality Through Leadership, in 1985, ISO 9001 three years later, and the Customer Focus process in 1991. Though self-assessment actually began in 1993 with limited internal exercises using Baldrige criteria, the EFQM methodology was chosen by HPT based on its more comprehensive scope and focus on business results.

These exemplar vignettes illustrate the following key points:

- In each case, business excellence through self-assessment is a central objective, usually used as a varied route map for continuous improvement; competitiveness is an important issue here.
- Self-assessment becomes normal business practice rather than a one-off or bolt-on set of initiatives and is a trigger for beneficial change.
- Organizationwide outcomes have been experienced, including process improvements, greater customer focus, better strategic performance measurement, and enhanced business results.

However, in all three examples, the self-assessment process took time to be effective. This involves an underpinning theme of adviser comments and research findings, as explored in this chapter.

RESEARCH INDICATORS

A U.K. study by a team at Bradford University supports the assertion that self-assessment is increasingly regarded as a contributor to the formulation of business strategy.[4] Findings from over 150 respondents in thirty-six European organizations in nineteen countries show that the methodology is becoming established corporate practice; around 37 percent said this was so, and 50 percent expected it to be a future intention. Twenty-one percent indicated that self-assessment is normal business practice (knowing details about industry sector breakdowns helps to make this more relevant to managers). According to the study, the three major improvements experienced by organizations since the introduction of self-assessment were in:

- Processes (77.3%)
- Policy and strategy (75.7%)
- Customer satisfaction (75.6%)[5]

Of note is that an increased customer focus was identified as a benefit of self-assessment by 82 percent of respondents, with 66 percent rating this as extremely important, primarily because the linkages between enablers and results were seen to improve customer satisfaction. In terms of the U.K. experience, the British Quality Foundation's annual member survey has revealed 40 percent of respondents conducted self-assessment in 1997, versus 33 percent in 1996 and 31 percent in 1995.[6]

For these organizations, self-assessment led to clear and concise action plans being developed for almost 70 percent of members, with more focused leadership resulting for 68 percent.[7] Other outcomes cited included perceived better policy and strategy for 50 percent of respondents and improved process improvement in 56 percent of organizations.

A 1995 Australian survey of self-assessment in 213 organizations reported by Cowan and van der Wiele[8] gave five reasons for its adoption:

- Finding opportunities for improvement
- Directing the improvement process
- Linking quality with strategic planning
- Focusing on a total quality management (TQM) model
- Managing the business

The survey noted that self-assessment provides the basis of a holistic TQM model, giving managers a coordination tool to direct improvement activities, increase organizationwide quality awareness, and improve business performance. In practice, key characteristics include gathering and scoring data, determining strengths and weaknesses, and linking improvement planning to business strategy.

By contrast, a 1996 EFQM membership survey provided pointers to future self-assessment needs by asking respondents to list potential hot topics for consortium business studies.[9] Typically, a consortium benchmarking study is instigated and sponsored by ten to fifteen members with a shared desire to improve a specific business or management process. It is common EFQM policy to use this means for establishing best practice. The top six issues, ranked in order of importance, were:

- Corporate performance measures
- Customer loyalty
- Knowledge management and the internal transfer of best practices
- Corporate strategy development and review
- Self-directed work teams
- Strategic use of information knowledge

The EFQM Business Excellence Model has stimulated interest in self-assessment, performance measurement, and the integration of total quality measures into strategic business thinking. However, this growth among both private and public sector organizations has raised three key issues:

- How self-assessment can be conducted efficiently and effectively
- How outputs from self-assessment can be integrated into business and action plans
- How self-assessment aligns with benchmarking, business score-cards, and total quality–based improvement activities

All of the respondents to the above mentioned Bradford University survey perceived self-assessment as delivering hard business benefits. The practice was integrated into mainstream business activities. The hallmark of success was seen as a balanced performance concept. There are very few organizations with high-scoring business results but low people and customer satisfaction ratings. The BSC model fits well with the EFQM model. Norton and Kaplan's original ideas broadly reflect the measures and results side of business, while self-assessment can be used as a diagnostic instrument to trace known results back to enabler-type factors. Taking up this point of linkage at a strategic level, I would argue that executive teams can be confused over how so many contemporary initiatives, frameworks, and models all fit with each other. What is missing for many is an overall inclusive framework pulling everything together – the EFQM Business Excellence Model does achieve this.

There are three dimensions of inclusiveness:

- Total quality, which provides the overarching business management ideology focused on satisfying stakeholders
- Underpinning this is the business excellence framework on which the five enabler criteria are causally related inputs to value creation as the foundation for managing the business on a daily basis
- Monitoring all four results criteria through a form of balanced scorecard as a scanning mechanism to shape what an organization does within the enablers to effect results, and as a predictive tool

In this context, the business excellence methodology acts as a strategic framework and is a genuine business model. Its greatest strength is visibility as a business measurement map, which gives the big organizational picture in one frame.

Another way of looking at the model is as a *dashboard* of performance measures to identify strengths and improvement areas across all business activities. In this sense, self-assessment is a complete and holistic concept, helping to chart results and determining their links to the model's enablers. It highlights capabilities and weaknesses, but does not directly provide solutions, or drive strategy and planning. Organizations will need other tools to work in parallel with the EFQM model to achieve the latter, for example the balanced scorecard. This takes elements from self-assessment and incorporates them in a wider framework of financial parameters, market environments, economic growth rates, and so on. In that sense, the scorecard is the umbrella under which self-assessment operates. However, the real strategic issue is that it must include the vital few excellence gaps identified by self-assessment. The framework gives a structure here, enabling an organization's most important success elements to be identified.

When the redesign of the Baldrige framework was announced in 1997, a new name for the process (Criteria for Performance Excellence) and a reordering of categories (covered in the Glossary), the National Institute of Standards and Technology (NIST), which runs the National Quality Awards, touched on the following various strategic issues in its mission statement: "The foundation on which the criteria were built, helping organizations enhance competitiveness through adding value to customers and improving organizational performance, remains as firm and solid today as it was in 1988."

The new framework, called Customer and Market Focused Strategy and Action Plans, effectively creates a different kind of umbrella to that proposed by the EFQM. It provides a better and more integrated systems view of performance management, which highlights the importance of customers and markets to business strategy, the role of information and analysis, and the goal of superior business results. All are now related through the new framework with, significantly, the weighting for business results being increased from 250 to 450 points, about half the total Baldrige score. All the criteria now rest on two primary building blocks. One is that quality is customer driven; the other is that organizations must continually improve their performance and capabilities. These principles are woven throughout all the Baldrige criteria.

In a NIST article, C. A. Reinmann, who is widely acknowledged as the architect and driver of Baldrige since the late 1980s, and H. S. Hertz, who took over from Reinmann in late 1995, addressed twin strategic issues in relation to self-assessment, quality, and business and the links among them.[10] For the first, a successful quality strategy has three elements, which:

- Integrate with business strategy
- Tie organizational learning processes to all other corporate requirements and responsibilities
- Contribute multidimensional results to business improvement and competitiveness

"The Baldrige criteria address an organization's overall objectives, including financial performance, through several mechanisms," the article explained. "These include the integration of quality into overall strategy development, business decisions and innovation across all company processes and operations."[11]

Reinmann and Hertz cite three examples of how this works in practice:

- Management of information is used in business decisions and strategy, in terms of scope, validity, and analysis
- Quality requirements are set for niches, new business, and export target markets, leading to market-drivern quality
- An analysis is conducted of societal, regulatory, economic, competitive, and risk facotrs that affect the success or failure of business strategy

The article concludes, "[T]he the criteria, therefore, encourage companies to demonstrate linkages between quality, operational performance improvement and financial performance."[12]

To summarize, advisers experienced in both Baldrige and EFQM methodologies use certain key words to explain critical strategic considerations:

- Alignment in terms of business management
- Integration of systems
- Balance among methodologies
- Linkage across performance measures
- Focus on imperatives

Effective self-assessment can address several of these factors, including competitiveness, customer retention, total quality achievement, and continuous improvement, in addition to hard business results. The 1996 Baldrige winner, ADAC Laboratories, has related these issues to self-assessment for a number of years.

ADAC LABORATORIES: SELF-ASSESSMENT AND BUSINESS PLANNING

Global change in health care markets and information systems, demanding customers, mission critical service, and the need for rapid innovations were four factors that convinced ADAC Laboratories to adopt a system of self-assessment against Baldrige criteria in 1992. These imperatives compelled ADAC to establish systematic processes where none existed before, strengthen business planning, and increase the focus on continuous improvement through employee involvement. The driver was, and continues to be, customer value.

Founded in 1970, the organization employs over 700 people at its U.S. sites. It designs, manufacturers, markets, and supports products for health care customers in nuclear medicine, radiation therapy planning, and health care information systems. Since 1990, revenue has tripled against industry averages of 50 percent and ADAC's nuclear medicine market share has grown from 10 percent to over 50 percent in the United States and from 5 percent to over 25 percent in Europe.

Structurally, ADAC Laboratories is guided by ten corporate values and a TQM philosophy. This shapes business practice through its Four Revolutions Framework, which consists of mutual learning, continuous improvement, total participation, and customer focus. A key to meeting objectives under each is the DASH business planning process, which establishes goals and measures in four areas:

- Finance
- Customer satisfaction
- Operational performance
- Regulatory compliance

The DASH process involves all employees and uses both annual and quarterly meetings to review progress and trigger self-assessment. It starts at the beginning of each fiscal year with a meeting to set objectives for the coming year, which are tied to a three-year business plan. At these sessions, participants look at what they are doing, what they want to do, and how they are going to reach their goals. They then condense their many objectives into a vital few that can be realistically achieved.

The quarterly meetings are, in effect, progress checks when mid-course business plan changes can be made in the light of recent performance against corporate visions, intentions, and objectives. Quarterly milestones are set relating to customer satisfaction, the ADAC service matrix, new or lost clients, and many other target areas. In addition, over one hundred customer and operational measures are reported in bi-weekly meetings, which are open to employees, customers, and suppliers. They look for trends, and if they discover that something is not on track, they can make appropriate adjustments.

During DASH meetings, people from each functional or process area examine performance against plans and determine corrective actions where required. In this way, a unit develops its own plan of specific goals or actions for the following fiscal quarter, in line with the business master plan and its performance matrix for profits and costs. All employees are invited to these DASH groups to make their own observations or comments, especially if the plans of other areas are not aligned with their own or in cases where facts or analysis does not support decisions. About 10 percent of staff attend at any one time, depending on specific areas of interest, with around 25 to 30 percent of employees being directly involved in the business planning and self-assessment process.

Related to the ADAC core value of *customers come first*, executives are expected to spend 25 percent of their time with customers, personally taking their calls and inviting them to attend weekly quality meetings. Over a five-year period, customer satisfaction results have shown improving trends for:

- Postsales technical support (up 10 percent)
- Customer retention (up from 70 to 90 percent)
- Service contract renewals (up from 85 to 95 percent)

A primary ADAC measure of service quality is service cycle time, the total time for getting a system back in operation after failure, which is critical because customers often cannot treat patients until a problem is fixed. Since the organization began tracking this measure in 1990, the average cycle time has dropped from 56 hours to shorter than 17 hours.

Reward schemes are also linked to group and individual performance. For example, management bonuses are based on achieving so-called *individual most important tasks*, and bonuses can be paid out twice a year to employees on variable pay. Staff objectives are linked with the vital few priorities established during the annual DASH planning sessions. These are the basis for determining incentives.

This link and the emphasis on performance reviews and participation has brought business rewards, too. For example, revenue per employee rose US$130,000 over a five year period. On this overall measure of productivity, ADAC Laboratories has achieved 65 percent greater efficiency than its closest competitor. Another measure is the number of direct labor dollars required to build cameras that detect and diagnose health problems. Through more efficient processes and technological improvements, the number has decreased by 40 percent over a three-year period. Despite the gains, feedback from examiners and the formal Baldrige report, which all entrants receive, will continue to improve an already effective improvement cycle.

On the examiners' recommendation, the organizations are analyzing how processes are measured. Though ADAC was good at measuring what the firm knows, it was less effective at predictive measurement. Self-assessment means being able to face weaknesses honestly through management by fact.

THE SELF-ASSESSMENT RATIONALE:
WHY SELF-ASSESSMENT IS ADOPTED

H. A. Bradshaw, president of Armstrong World Industries Business Products Operations (BPO), made this point on hearing of his organization's Baldrige award; anticipating the examiner's feedback report, customarily received by all the entrants two months after the results are announced, he said: "We'll start using recommendations to improve processes the day we get the report. We're by no means perfect and are never satisfied with just how we're doing."

BPO started self-assessment against Baldrige criteria in 1990 for three reasons:

- To help accelerate process improvement
- To ensure that systems are actually driving results
- As a source of rapid, incremental learning experiences that lead to internal action

For example, the organization's first Baldrige application in 1993 was unsuccessful, but the feedback report spelled out that improvements in process management, supplier relationships, breakthrough strategies, and strengthening goal deployment would enhance performance. Addressing these issues resulted in the eventual award in 1995. The firm received its feedback report on December 14, 1993, and started work the next day. It entered, not necessarily expecting to win, but more for the quality of external assessment. The firm ultimately reached a point where assessment itself had become a routine business process.

In 1992, Brisa, the Turkish tire manufacturer, adopted self-assessment. The decision was made, not only to strengthen total quality and business management, but also as a deliberately unifying influence on its 1,325 workforce and a catalyst for change in workplace behaviors. Significant strikes in 1988 and 1990 had led to adversarial industrial relations becoming embedded into the organizational fabric. In 1996, Brisa won the European Quality Award on the basis of four steps toward business excellence:

- An emphasis on changing working practices among management and employees
- Achieving "peace at work" by rethinking industrial relations; collaborative initiatives included participative goal setting, suggestion schemes, new employment conditions, and joint agreements for productivity
- Deploying continuous improvement by cultivating TQM through quality circles, problem-solving teams, total productive maintenance groups, Kaizen,[13] and TQM committees

- Active employee involvement by delegating responsibility to the line, introducing 40 hours per year of training for each individual, and encouraging innovative communications including closed circuit television

Addressing the 1997 British Quality Foundation conference, Ahmet Piker, Brisa's president said: "Respect for people became the most supportive pillar of our business excellence approach, based on the principle of 'the one who knows the job, knows it best.' The human factor is our competitive advantage."[14]

Research Indicators

The examples also show that there are sound business or organizational reasons for introducing self-assessment. In parallel, too, are heightened expectations among all who adopt the methodology concerning the eventual concrete and intangible outcomes. For example, a 1996 member survey by the Northern Ireland Quality Council provided pointers to the latter. For 75 percent of respondents, the awards application process, and therefore self-assessment, had broadly helped improve business performance in four areas:

- Customer service, 42 percent responding positively to the overall question
- Improved profits, 42 percent
- Better staff relations, 30 percent
- All areas of business, 20 percent

The most positive aspects of self-assessment were cited as:

- External evaluation, 40 percent
- Staff involvement and "bonding," 25 percent
- Adopting a customer focus, 17 percent

An important point is that members cited two factors for considering self-assessment in the first place: external evaluation and opportunities for benchmarking against similar organizations.

An Australian self-assessment study in 1995[15] found that the two most significant outcomes for 213 organizations postimplementation were, broadly, better customer focus and improved organizational performance. Broken down, respondents cited specific improvements such as greater line management understanding of TQM, fewer customer complaints, and reduced nubers of defects.

By contrast, the Bradford Management Centre self-assessment study asked respondents to list their original objectives prior to introducing the methodology, followed by those that had been most effectively met. In decreasing order of importance, these objectives were:

- Identifying areas for improvement
- Getting a baseline measure of the organization
- Identifying strengths
- Analyzing the value of self-assessment
- Increasing line management involvement in self-assessment
- Increasing employee involvement in continuous improvement

Among key benefits experienced by respondents were improvements in:

- Customer focus
- Top team awareness
- Knowledge about business processes
- Identifying key performance indicators
- Business planning

Of interest, overall responsibility for self-assessment rested with senior management for nearly 60 percent of organizations, including board-level involvement for 31 percent. However, the realization of benefits or of meeting objectives can take time, as was discovered in a 1996 research project on whether business excellence works. The project revealed that senior directors responsible for business excellence initiatives in almost sixty European organizations believe they have to wait four years or more before fully realizing the benefits.[16]

The project findings are not altogether surprising since one third of the organizations surveyed had only been implementing business excellence for less than three years and over 50 percent for only four to seven years. However, the conclusion was that the longer organizations continue the practice, the more successful they are in achieving its objectives. Measured over time, the incidence of total or near total success against objectives was most marked in eight areas of business performance:

Performance Area	1–3 years	4+ years
Higher employee productivity	10%	43%
Reduction in employee turnover	0%	33%
Better service quality	29%	57%
Improved customer satisfaction	21%	49%
Greater shareholder value/improved stock market performance	0%	27%
High rating within the financial community	6%	31%
Enhanced profit margins	0%	21%
Reduced costs	11%	31%

One finding is worth highlighting. Of these organizations, not one currently in the first three years of a business excellence program considered that it had achieved *total success* in reducing employee turnover, improving stock market performance, or enhancing profit margins. Yet after four years or more, these criteria were scored at 33 percent, 27 percent and 21 percent, respectively.

The issue of improved financial results and stock performance is becoming significant in self-assessment circles, at both awarding body and participant organization levels. For example, new investment portfolios are beginning to be launched using performance against business excellence criteria pointers, and some portfolios include only prominent high achievers in this area. A crucial question thus arises as to what extent there is a causal relationship between self-assessment and financial results. Although there is no conclusive proof that such links exist, there is strong evidence to indicate they do. Performance improvements in different business areas can have a positive effect on bottom-line results. Traditional measurement systems based on financial accounting criteria do not respond to the factors that drive business results. Traditional bottom-line accounts give us a financial picture but do not clearly show the drivers, so, in contemporary approaches, it is impossible to pinpoint what causes the bottom line to rise or fall. An organization can check margins, but not what produces those margins within these traditional measures.

New measurement systems, including business excellence criteria, are now being recognized as drivers of business results. For example, decisions made in customer satisfaction, process management, resource management, and people satisfaction can often lead to an impact on performance and, therefore, results. The key is the quality of management in relation to the process of creating and delivering value. For example, if you change by 1 percent any factors impacting in combination on key business decisions, prices, sales volumes, pay rates, efficiency, and materials or service costs, this has a leverage effect on the bottom line of 26–34 percent.

Texas Instruments European division, the 1995 European Quality Award winner, had an impressive record over the previous three years, with sales up 21 percent, compound growth up 63 percent, and a rise in profit margins from 5 to 12 percent. These improvements indicate well managed business excellence criteria on customer satisfaction, processes, and resource management, together with people management and satisfaction. These characteristics indicate how the theory and structure of the EFQM criteria drives business results. The three most influential attributes are leadership, clearly understood policies, and focused strategies. The emphasis should be on key results and performance targets to drive customer satisfaction by delivering perceived value, as defined by customer-specified measures.

A 1995 study of 25 organizations by the European Centre for TQM at Bradford University and a similar survey undertaken in the same year by the London Business School indicated positive correlations between the intangible aspects of stakeholder performance and bottom-line business results. All the TQM organizations that were studied outperformed industry averages on a range of metrics including financial performance, customer satisfaction, employee satisfaction, and training levels. Although it is not possible to prove a direct causation between these factors and business results, there is a strong association. If there were no links between the two, these would be very strange results.

As a contrast to these findings, NIST in the United States has researched two issues, the business effects of quality management and whether investments in these, or business excellence, lead to bottom-line returns. An initial study of five Baldrige winners between 1990 and 1994 (Eastman Chemicals, Federal Express, Motorola, Solectron Corporation, and Zytec Corporation) showed that they outperformed the Standard and Poor's (S&P) 500 Index from the date of their recognition to late 1994 by a ratio of 6.5:1. In addition, 41 organizations that had site visits under the scheme during this period achieved a 94.5 percent return on a hypothetical investment of US$1,000, compared to 40.6 percent for the S&P 500.

This quality of financial performance has allowed Texas Instruments to use the Baldrige criteria even after winning the award in 1991. It has helped the firm to build a quality organization and return substantial value to shareholders. From 1989 to 1994, sales increased from US$130 million to US$1.46 billion and net profit rose from US$4 million to US$56 million. Solectron's stock price had an average growth of 82 percent each year over the same period, and the number of customer awards for quality and service increased from 14 to 63.

NIST cited a study of twenty organizations by the U.S. General Accounting Office to support the point. The study found that nearly all the organizations using TQM practices achieved better employee relations, higher productivity, greater customer satisfaction, increased market share, and improved profitability. A follow-up NIST stock study published in 1996 and using the same hypothetical investment of US$1,000, showed that the sample of 14 Baldrige winners outperformed the S&P 500 by more than 4 to 1, achieving a 248.7 percent return compared to their 58.5 percent. NIST concluded that Baldrige wins achieved outstanding results in customer satisfaction, product and service quality, and overall organizational performance.

MORTGAGE EXPRESS: SELF-ASSESSMENT AND PROCESS IMPROVEMENT

This type of outstanding performance is exemplified by the UK mortgage lender, Mortgage Express, although in 1995, the organization did not appear to have much of a future. It was hit by recession, a plummeting housing market, and bad debts, and it had posted cumulative losses of £100 million for 1991–1992. Customer satisfaction was low, at 50 percent, with employee satisfaction as low as 25 percent. As a result, the firm's parent company decided to cut its losses and absorb the business by 1994. In short, Mortgage Express was to close down.

By 1997, however, the business was flourishing; £38 million in yearly profits had been posted twice in succession, customer satisfaction was up to 85 percent, and employee satisfaction was at 80 percent, about 30 percent higher than the sector's norm. In 1996, Mortgage Express was a joint winner of the UK Quality Award, after having adopted self-assessment four years earlier.

In between, a remarkable turnaround had taken place, driven by a new board of directors appointed in 1991. The organization's four values of teamwork, integrity, recognition, and quality had been identified, and the following strategic goals established:

- Recognition as a total quality organization
- Providing a first-class competitive service
- Enabling employees to achieve their best through training and career development
- Creating long-term shareholder value

The leadership's vision helped to determine these goals, to be achieved by strategic initiatives, key actions every year, and personal objectives, which are also the basis for performance review and pay. First used in December 1992, self-assessment has proven to be an invaluable business management tool, linking results to actions through the integration of the criteria. Self-assessment enabled the entire organization to be involved in an improvement process focused on service excellence. The model is easy to understand, and staff can see how the different initiatives conect to the achievement of common goals.

Each year, self-assessment reveals that improvement opportunities outweigh strengths. The firm's leadership prioritizes action from them and generally finds it useful to launch just a few, but significant, programs. This approach helps concentrate resources while aligning self-assessment to the annual operating plan and individual or team objectives for that year.

Given the organization's strategic position between 1991 and 1995, it was impossible to justify major investments in teamwork and reengineering to trigger process improvements, which are often a feature of self-assessment. Instead, in this case the approach was to:

- Simplify the processes of the way work was done
- Understand how good performance was achieved
- Measure performance
- Improve by implementing ideas identified through measurement processes

An example of process simplification is the rationalization of computer systems. The organization had two operating platforms, eight application systems handling mortgage processing, and twenty-seven separate mortgage providers, each with its own set of procedures. After four years, however, there was one platform, one application system, and one best practice procedural database.

In 1991, the firm used only rudimentary process measures restricted to simple time standards. Now a comprehensive range of measures for all operating processes covers:

- Process performance measures: time and quality standards
- Business performance measures: management information quantifying the impact on financial results
- Customer perceptions: event-based survey data providing satisfaction ratings and improvement ideas

These measures enabled Mortgage Express to direct and prioritize improvement activities. There have been radical improvements in performance across the whole spectrum of operations, and productivity increased by 26 percent over the period 1992–1995. Other process improvements include:

- Finance: monthly bank reconciliation errors 100 times lower than five years earlier
- Customer retention: success rates 10 times higher than when this unit was set up in 1995
- Litigation and property: the time taken for repossessing property was cut in half

Improvement activities have also targeted customer satisfaction levels, with 700 ideas being implemented from 1994 to 1997. One example is the use of weekly call-recording feedback sessions, in which the call center team identifies a number of difficult customer telephone calls from among the calls that are taped. They are played back at these sessions to discuss problems and agree on solutions. In 1995, over 300 people attended, including all company directors.

A further example of process improvement developed directly from annual self-assessment. The effort identified considerable scope for strengthening process management, which led to a cross-functional project being set up called Process, Review and Management (PRAM). Through PRAM, processes have been redefined and classified as key or support, the former being those that provide Mortgage Express with sources of competitive advantage. Process ownership has been introduced, and the firm is reengineering the way in which new customers are taken on. PRAM is already providing a more systematic basis for managing processes to help achieve targets.

Integrating the self-assessment process into "business as usual" is vitally important as it eliminates any risk of total quality being regarded as a separate project, unrelated to the business. Adopting the European Foundation for Quality Management (EFQM) model encourages quality management and business management to be viewed as one and the same. In effect, each year, the total quality program is relaunched. In this way, everyone knows how new performance imperatives fit into the corporate plans for the business.

THE SELF-ASSESSMENT PROCESS

The example of Mortgage Express illustrates that, in practice, self-assessment has countless variations and dimensions. Some of these are worth detailing; indeed, self-assessment is not a one-stop, one-solution-for-all methodology. At Ulster Carpet Mills (UCM), a 1996 U.K. Quality Award joint winner, self-assessment was deployed in three phases. First came the launch to strengthen the impact of TQM, which had been adopted three years earlier to improve customer service and product quality. This was followed by updating, after site visits to EFQM and British Quality Foundation (BQF) member organizations to better align the process with business planning. The third stage led to the introduction of UCM's Bridging the Gap program.

This program focused on the difference between customer perceptions and organizational performance, especially in terms of productivity. Now seven managers coordinate annual self-assessments against targets in the business plan, while organization wide briefings covering financial and nonfinancial results (for example profits, orders, performance strengths and weaknesses, improvement opportunities) are held monthly. Employee feedback is formalized and contributes to any new business plan. Cost of quality is down by one third, equating to an annual savings of over £4 million; delivery is now 24 hours instead of 2 weeks; and productivity has increased from 26 carpet rolls an hour to an average of nearly 40.

The Business Excellence Model is not an inert structure. It is a tool for assessing and enhancing performance, with external feedback from assessors being used constructively to improve every area of business activity. Another example is French semiconductor manufacturer SGS-Thomson Microelectronics. This firm has required different generations of self-assessment. It adopted the EFQM model in 1992 after considering the Baldrige approach. The Baldridge approach helped identify performance gaps, but internal shortcomings were revealed over policy deployment as the guidelines were too generalized and follow-up actions too loosely defined and implemented. These issues were addressed in two further phases between 1993 and 1996.

Now, self-assessment is undertaken annually by nearly thirty dedicated teams; criteria owners have been appointed, internal assessors trained, and self-assessment kits produced. Clear goals and measures for these results criteria have been established, and computerized self-assessment and a detailed scoring matrix are recent innovations. The results, that is, policy deployment, self-assessment, customer and employee surveys, process improvements, and team activities, are either mechanisms of, or inputs to, the five measures.

This *total approach* is also how 1995 Baldrige winner Corning TPD interprets self-assessment. Its so-called integration model incorporates stakeholder requirements into four functional strategies: commercial, technology, manufacturing, and human resources. These measures are then converted into four annual strategic initiatives through the strategic planning process, and on to strategy deployment. Under the Baldrige self-assessment framework, leadership is the driver of systems, processes, human resources, strategic planning, and information and analysis. Business results are the measures of progress toward the goals of customer focus and satisfaction, which also are relative to the performance of competitors. These measures are:

- Product and service quality
- Productivity improvement
- Waste reduction or elimination
- Supplier performance
- Financial results

The integration model is a completely aligned business framework that allows the firm to look at the same factors and characteristics and concentrate on the same priorities. Baldrige criteria are used annually to measure progress toward the goal of continued world-class performance.

The Baxter-Alliston plant in Canada, which has been manufacturing a complex range of health care products since 1957, won a Canadian Award for Excellence in 1996 and has been conducting self-assessment for several years, since the 1990s. The process has been aligned with the company's quality principles and related improvements within an environment of teamwork, open communication, and continuous learning. Incentives are also provided for those individual teams exceeding quality improvement objectives. However, self-assessment is multi-sourced. Baxter uses the Baldrige criteria in addition to stringent assessment against the Canadian Awards Quality Fitness Test and criteria for:

- Leadership
- Strategic direction
- Customer focus
- Improvement planning
- People
- Process optimization
- Supplier focus
- Organizational performance

Internal and external ISO 9001 audits and regulatory audits for Canada's Health Protection Board occur on a regular basis and are linked into an overall measurement framework. Results from audits and assessments are used to initiate corrective actions that feed into the improvement planning process. This is deployed to all functions, with quality improvement objectives being assigned to teams or individuals. Over fifty teams are active, involving over 70 percent of employees in quality initiatives.

An emerging problem for some organizations is the risk of information overload when considering the self-assessment process and implementation issues. In applying self-assessment, some organizations discover literally hundreds of areas for improvement and so have to decide which area to drive forward. Then they must assign responsibilities to function or process owners. Many alternative initiatives align well with the EFQM model, such as Investors in People, involving employee satisfaction, or ISO 9000, which mostly matches processes but touches on other areas as well. These programs are very compatible, so they can be used as components in a larger overall program.

Self-assessment should be viewed as a four-step process:

- Define and tailor business excellence to the organization
- Introduce a tailor-made self-assessment program
- Select areas for improvement
- Establish and manage breakthrough improvements

Only by engaging in all four steps will competitiveness be substantially improved. Tool sets are available for the first two stages and being developed for the others. Existing approaches like Kaizen and functional deployment fit well with the model and can be continued if already introduced.

The dangers of *initiative overload* can be overcome by mapping frameworks like ISO 9000 onto the EFQM model to see how they impact or to discover where potential synergies, interactions, conflicts, and needless repetitions exist. Particular confusion might occur if the model identifies areas for measurementand assessment, but does not specifically prescribe how to manage processes or enhance skills. This can be achieved by introducing or aligning complementary initiatives like Investors in People. Problems may also arise with the resource requirement for collecting data or the sheer complexity of amassing information in nine areas. Assessing data is less of a problem, as both the EFQM and Baldrige processes have given rise to an army of assessors equipped to help.

Integrating the results into business actions can be a further problem, whether using a top-down approach, which is used in a sophisticated way by leading organizations, or by a bottom-up approach, where results are used in localized reviews. The latter is recommended, as it gives a more structured approach to quality improvement and typically aligns with business requirements. Making effective use of model outputs is a major *pending* issue to be addressed by most organizations using self-assessment. It is the least satisfactory and most difficult part of the process.

"Excellent" organizations, which are regarded as exemplars in business excellence methodologies, do two things that make them stand out. They focus on creating value for stakeholders above all else and on making the right decisions to create that value. They are also able to differentiate between basic good management practice and TQM, the latter being customer-driven, concerned with process improvement, and focused on people.[17]

There are a number of shortcomings in adopting and deploying self-assessment, which may be taken for granted as just another framework, rather than a contributor to value creation. There are three common failings:

- Self-assessment is seen as another initiative acting as a quick scanning mechanism (in this case, users do not understand the model).
- Management displays an obsession with quality award scores and focus on achievement against a 1,000 point benchmark where weightings are irrelevant.
- Improvement priorities tend to be set against quick and easy to attain objectives to boost scores, which can make sustaining the direction and effort of self-assessment especially difficult.

All these failings help to create negative perceptions, which can be exacerbated by top-down imposed arbitrary targets. It is important to first understand the model and how value is created; second, get executive team buy-in; and third, make it crystal clear throughout the organization that self-assessment is the way the business is managed.

A realistic and thorough self-assessment involves an analysis of three elements:

- All strategic and business requirements, what influences them, and how they are changing
- How requirements are communicated throughout the organization
- How well requirements are being met

Effective self-assessments should demonstrate four characteristics:

- Educational value
- Completeness in addressing requirements and their deployment
- An integrated way to collect information so it may be meaningfully evaluated
- Results indicators that address how well requirements are met

A related observation is worth highlighting for any organization wishing to pursue, or indeed strengthen, self-assessment. All awarding bodies publish guidelines on how criteria break down into key actions or considerations that, at minimum, can be used as a checklist or as a noncostly access to a best practice framework.

Significantly, in the period 1988–1998, over 1 million copies of the Baldrige handbook were disseminated, predominantly in the United States (entrants must be an American organization) but also to organizations in other countries that are interested in applying the concept without the formal assessment aspects for consideration for the award. The information was reinforced over the same period by more than 30,000 national winners' conferences or state roadshow presentations.

Texas Instruments Europe: Aligning Self-Assessment

Texas Instruments Europe (TIE) has been an EFQM exemplar at workshops and conferences since winning the European Quality Award in 1995. In doing so, the electronics and software manufacturer mobilized all of its employees in sixteen countries by using the methodology as a common language to bring together multiple businesses, cultures, nationalities, and functions. EFQM also previously served as a unifying framework for aligning diverse quality initiatives after adoption in 1993 and as an evaluation tool to guide the restructuring of thirty-one business and support units into five pan-European centers in 1994.

Despite much progress on site-based total quality, the building of a stronger, more competitive business structure meant that TIE needed a harmonized approach that could also accelerate the rate of improvement. TIE announced its intentions at the June 1993 *L'Accord de Paris* meeting, at which all its European businesses and functions formally committed to the methodology. The first stage of self-assessment involved a total of 7,000 hours of input for 150 senior managers to kick-start the process, in addition to training for TIE's top 30 executives. Starting self-assessment was a salutary experience, and few senior managers doubted it was a worthwhile exercise. However, it requires that one ask difficult questions of oneself and is therefore humbling.

The TIE 75 page criteria reference and scorebook, which serves as the corporate guidebook for the whole organization, was designed, produced, translated into six languages, and shipped within two months of the Paris meeting. It was driven by the European Strategic Leadership Team and eight Quality Steering Teams, each of which was responsible for one or more of the model's nine criteria. All business units had a specially trained EFQM facilitator.

Achieving business excellence has become a central corporate objective, facilitated through the TIE-BEST process. This integrates with the EFQM methodology and features four elements:

- Customer satisfaction through total quality
- Operational excellence
- Annual improvement
- Key performance metrics

All units conduct self-assessment exercises annually, with scores being loaded onto a secure database. Based on points lost when compared with others, each unit priorities areas of improvement into a *vital few excellence gaps*.

The self-assessment process gives critical, comparative feedback on areas for improvement and helps transfer best practices across Europe and worldwide, supporting the principles of organizational corporate learning and continuous improvement. The continuous improvement process loop is therefore closed when priorities are redefined every year. These feed into annual policy deployment and directly impact on the organization's Development and Performance management process and individual objectives in the personal development plan. The EFQM methodology accelerates integrated self-assessment and has had a significant unifying effect on the organization. Applying the self-assessment process has also brought a very powerful collateral benefit as it is among the very best business excellence tools that are not confined just to quality.

Along with those others mentioned earlier, the TIE example highlights crucial strategic issues for organizations reviewing or rethinking business performance measurement or considering self-assessment.

- Its use as a unifying framework for aligning any initiatives focused on superior business performance, which harmonizes existing measurement systems and helps accelerate the rate of improvement (a closed-loop process is crucial)
- The visible involvement of senior executives supported by training and immersion in the methodologies, such that in successful organizations, they make business excellence a central corporate objective; the use of self-assessment champions is also important here
- Mobilizing the entire organization around the practice of self-assessment rather than just a chosen few, with awareness, education, communication, and, if possible, direct participation from employees being essential considerations
- The integration of self-assessment methodologies into business management processes and systems, including alignment with approaches such as balanced business scorecards

When considering self-assessment, an executive agenda will focus on the issues of business strategy, business management, leadership, human resources, and performance measurement. Naturally, vision is crucial, along with having a picture of what the organization can realistically achieve, bearing in mind the potential constraints of organizational capability and the pitfalls involved when deploying implementation.

Decisions resulting from the agenda will be underpinned by some semblance of TIE's virtual spiral, the Golden Circle program. If successfully applied, as in that organization's case, better business results are certain.

What is less certain for many organizations is putting self-assessment into practice. There are implementation problems that are common to all routes to business excellence and not just self-assessment. There are three critical steps for applying self-assessment to overcome the problems:

- Have a clear view of objectives and be able to answer a key question: Do you want a quick overview of the organization as a kind of health check or performance snapshot, or is the intention to apply the methodology for ongoing use in sophisticated business planning? The answer will guide implementation.
- Take a balanced, objective view of the process, fully considering resource requirements because the framework does not have to run

to the now traditional seventy-five pages that many organizations use. Short cuts are available that still allow the informed debate and dialogue so essential at executive levels.

- Do something with the data, because self-assessment has to produce action or improvement; there is a danger of doing nothing, either because measurement has become an end in itself, or because the complexity of what is collected is unmanageable.

Organizations might have to live with pain when doing self-assessment for the first time. The second time around and in successive years, however, the process will become easier and the results more evident.

CONCLUDING GUIDELINES

1. If a business excellence methodology or a self-assessment program is being considered, a crucial decision has to be made. Is the idea to have a quick overview or health check every year, or will its adoption result in more sophisticated business planning and management? If rigorously discussed, clear objectives should emerge.

2. Consider other key points. How will self-assessment align with business process? How might systems be integrated? Can a balance be achieved with other methodologies, such as scorecards? Where will the linkages with existing measures be? From which source does focus come?

3. Appreciate that the effects of self-assessment will be far-reaching, from organizationwide awareness and education to executive *immersion*, managing complex data and using any findings or analyses. It is critical that results feed into the improvement process.

4. Ask the following: Who articulates, instigates, and drives the self-assessment process? Research indicates that senior executives, board directors, and quality professionals are involved, but exemplar organizations tend to have *organizationwide ownership*. Self-assessment champions, criteria owners, and mentors can perform constructive roles in this matter.

5. Appreciate that any business excellence model does not have to be adopted intact by an organization. In fact, some consultants and organizations indicate that it should be tailored to your own business environment, organizational structure, and processes.

6. Be patient about results and outcomes: while some will be evident after a year or so, real success or significant improvement take two to three years and sometimes as long as five years. It is important to publicize gains to help sustain organizational motivation.

7. Recognize that the self-assessment process is not easy, particularly in achieving alignment and integration but also in the practicalities. Data management, analysis, using feedback, and regularly reviewing the process are four examples of challenging areas.

CASE STUDY:
CORNING TELECOMMUNICATIONS
PRODUCTS DIVISION, USA

When formed in 1983 to compete in the global optical fiber markets, Corning Telecommunications Products Division (TPD) was unknown in the USA and around the world. It had no customer base or market share and was threatend by a host of established competitors with first-class reputations. TPD did have business prospects from one outstanding advantage. Over a decade earlier, Corning invented the first low-loss, commercially viable optical fiber which, the firm perceived, would revolutionize global communications by replacing wire and coaxial cable. It has subsequently done so.

From zero sales in 1983, TPD has achieved world leadership in a market that has grown by over 25 percent each year from 1988 to 1997, and it will continue to grow given explosive business and domestic demand in telecommunications, cable services, and computing. Since 1990, TPD has won Corning's premier award, the Houghton Quality Award three times. It also won the U.S. Commerce Department's National Medal of Technology in 1994 for life-changing and life-enhancing innovation, and in 1995 it won a Malcolm Baldrige National Quality Award in the large manufacturing category.

Given these competitive realities, total quality has been a given requirement from TPD's first day in business. It was not the result of a wake-up call, but simply the admission price to the industry. As the newcomer, TPD had to be better in quality, product performance, service and manufacturing. It was clear from the beginning that if TPD tied with the competitors, it would lose.

TPD's Plan to Win philosophy, embracing the corporate values of "People, Process, Technology," was the firm's approach to obtaining a seamless integration of total quality and critically focused strategy. These elements allowed TPD to enter and outperform the market and now are the foundation for sustaining competitive advantage. A win-win tenacity was bred into the business early on.

What Baldrige Means

The 1995 Baldrige Award was a milestone in TPD's track record of winning. It recognized the division's world-class position, but also vindicated a twelve-year process of continuous improvement, customer focus, and, since 1989, self-assessment. In that year, however, TPD was unsuccessful in its only previous application for the Baldrige Award, although at that time, winning was secondary to experiencing the awards process for the first time. It was a stake in the ground. TPD expected to make a good show but knew that receiving the feedback report would serve as a major learning experience by revealing improvement opportunities. In effect, examiners' site visits and the official Baldrige feedback report for 1989 became a TPD road map for the 1990s by highlighting four broad areas for improvement:

- Managing customer relationships more systematically
- Building supplier partnerships
- Integrating process discipline with business systems
- Aligning the strategic planning process

TPD had to become more focused on the critical drivers of business performance. Continuous improvement is not just a good intention or a random walk: you have to understand your own personal and organizational capabilities and know the steps to be taken to deploy them.

Continuous improvement had been established in the 1980s by TPD's executive leadership team (ELT) well before business and support processes had been introduced. The continuous improvement process model is shown in Figure 3.1. Baldrige feedback also formed the basis for many business refinements, including process management and control, integrated manufacturing, and quality in improvement.

Many of the TPD's world-class processes were also a direct result of that feedback. Among these are Supplier Total Value, the Customer Response System, and Customer Total Value, which are examined later. Significantly, Baldrige criteria are still used to measure progress in process improvement toward the broad goal of achieving world-class performance.

The early 1990s were years of significant continuous improvement. The Baldrige criteria were used as a systems approach to total quality and to conduct internal self-assessments in 1991 and 1993, followed by a third-party assessment in 1994. The criteria also served as the framework on which TPD built its key leadership, strategy, planning, human resources, and customer management processes.

Leadership was perceived as the driver of systems (processes, human resources, strategic planning, and information and analysis), with business results being the measures of progress toward the goal of customer focus and satisfaction. Specially, the measures are product and service quality, productivity improvement, waste reduction or elimination, supplier performance, and financial results. There are also two customer-related goals: customer' satisfaction and customer satisfaction

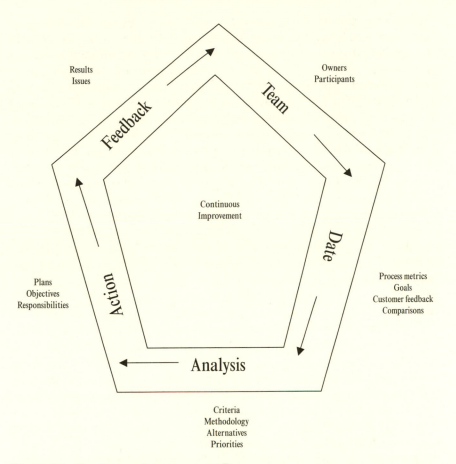

Figure 3.1 Continuous Improvement Process

relative to competitors. It is TPD's belief that total quality performance against these goals and measures means understanding the customers and their requirements, and meeting those requirements better than anyone else, without error, on time, every time. To accomplish this, quality is seamlessly integrated into the way the business is run, provided the following conditions are met:

- Stakeholder requirements are included in strategies, plans, goals, and objectives.
- Responsibility for meeting these requirements is shared across the organization.
- Processes are in place to enable these requirements to be met.
- There is an active, continuous culture of improvement for processes and performance.

As depicted by TPD's integration model, shown in Figure 3.2, quality integration is achieved by incorporating stakeholder requirements into four functional strategies, commercial, technology, manufacturing, and human resources, which are then converted into four strategic initiatives through the strategic planning process. The critical success factors for the strategic initiatives are determined annually by the ELT around the themes of customer satisfaction, markets of choice, affordable capacity, and lowest-cost producer, which relate to any new or continuing investments deemed necessary for the People, Process, Technology values. Business goals and objectives, along with those for departments, units, and individuals, are further aligned through the strategy deployment process. Compatibility among values, total quality, strategies, goals, and targets is thus achieved. The integration model provides a framework around which plans, goals, objectives, data, analyses, and results are aligned to ensure a critical company-wide focus and understanding. It means that all in TPD have the same focus and are concentrating on the same priorities.

Business Results

There are two main examples of integration and alignment, which are the linkages among continuous improvement, performance, business results, and customer satisfaction. First is product returns, followed by TPD's responsiveness in meeting customer-requested shipping dates. Both measures have improved significantly over the last fifteen years, 92 percent of customers rating TPD as *excellent* or *very good* and 80 percent citing it as best overall supplier.

Since 1992, process capability for 220 critical manufacturing parameters such as glass diameter, chemical durability, strength, fatigue resistance, and fiber curl has improved yearly, whereas productivity, as measured by miles of fiber produced per employee, doubled from 1987 to 1994. The following factors have been of key importance: reducing the number of manufacturing processes, introducing new equipment, and technological innovation.

Product consistency is an imperative. For example, ultra-pure raw materials are measured for impurities down to the parts per billion level. As the fiber is drawn, its diameter is measured hundreds of times a second and computer controlled to within a fraction of a micron. Before making a commitment to making improvements in the quality of its processes and customers service around 60 percent of TPD's customer promises used to be missed. This is no longer the case. TPD has a tremendous record, with three digits in parts per million product returns being the norm. It achieved this improved result in customer service by examining and tracking critical product attributes and by

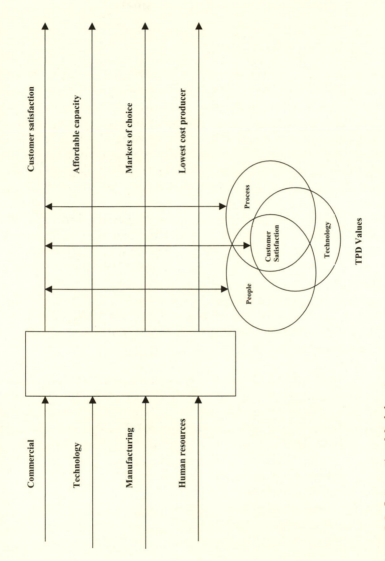

Figure 3.2 Integration Model

insisting that product and service quality drive the business. The Baldrige criteria had become the standard of excellence, which of itself required TPD to grow and continually improve as through assessment against this standard. Continuity comes from the firm's own values, and drive from its Plan to Win. A combination of Baldrige and Plan to Win describes the way TPD has run its business.

Process Management Systems

Plan to Win also defines the way in which TPD continues to sustain worldwide leadership in its markets. It emphasizes the firm's three core values (People, Process, Technology), is strategy driven and customer focused, and uses the Baldrige criteria as measures of progress. Two further elements of Plan to Win are managing the business through processes and ensuring continuous improvement. In these two areas, the organization has few equals. The ELT, comprising senior leaders across the business, has determined a hierarchy of processes, as follows:

- Four leadership processes to provide business direction: strategy development, planning, strategy deployment, and business priority
- Six vital processes, so called because they are critical to business success in having competitive leverage or new performance capability
- Around 50 cross-functional, core business processes, which have strong links with the four strategic initiatives and corporate values
- Over 800 processes and subprocesses that support day-to-day business operations

The majority of what TPD does is process focused, which means it is seldom in a reactionary operating mode. Process management is a disciplined, proactive process in its own right, which makes TPD focus on what is truly critical and what is important to the business through the process management system. The system has five elements:

- Designating a process owner
- Documenting every process
- Defining standard operating procedures
- Managing change control
- Ensuring continuous improvement

Production and delivery are two examples of critical business processes that relate to world-class performance. They are literally surrounded by other supporting systems and sub-processes, including process documentation, training and certification, process audits, engineering monitoring and analysis, materials management, and quality architecture, among others. Two key processes in production and delivery are the Products and Data processes and the Inventory Management and Production Scheduling process. The key requirements, each with metrics, for Inventory Management are:

- Deliver product quality
- Make product available when customers request it
- Maintain process control
- Manufacture product to specification
- Achieve process performance to standard
- Achieve financial plan
- Provide order and shipping accuracy

There are four requirements for Production Scheduling:

- Ship on time and error free
- Schedule right product for inventory
- Schedule most cost-effective equipment
- Provide fiber characterization data with shipment

All told, over 220 process variables are measured, which generates extensive reports to maintain process control and develop root-cause solutions when process problems occur. A special purpose Process and Equipment Improvement process is used to continuously improve the Products and Data process. This makes extensive use of process analysis and research, process optimization, alternative technology utilization, benchmarking, and customer feedback to ensure continuous improvement.

Continuous improvement is not a random walk; it has been embedded into TPD's culture for some time and certainly before process alignment and the Baldrige criteria were introduced into the business. A capability for continuous improvement has resulted from this historical foundation, but it is also strengthened by core process documentation, as there is little sense trying to improve if you do not know where you are. Continuous improvement is ensured through five steps:

- Process owners have twin responsibilities, for process effectiveness and its improvement
- Metrics are established to measure process performance
- Process performance is evaluated annually using stakeholders as members of a review team that analyzes appropriate data against performance criteria

- Action plans are formulated by taking business unit and individual objectives into consideration
- Closing the loop by regularly reviewing process performance improvement results and implementing corrective action steps as required

In addition, TPD had introduced its parent's variable compensation program for all employees, which is based on the continuous improvement of a business unit's key result indicators. These are critical metrics in performance and financials. If targets are reached, the program yields a bonus on top of a basic pay. In 1996, the formula for this *pay for performance* bonus in each of TPD's business units related to the following six goals: corporate return on equity, 25 percent; contributed operating margin, 25 percent; total unit costs, 20 percent; net sales, 10 percent; shipped miles of fiber, 10 percent; and customer returns, 10 percent. The program gives direct line of sight between individual or team effort and business unit performance. In effect, it relates the bonus to a team's ability to be successful in these six areas of performance.

Human Resource Management

In order to appreciate the link between business performance and human resources (HR), it is worth recalling that TPD's ELT is responsible for ensuring an integrated strategy-driven and customer-focused management system that directly links vision, mission, strategy, plans, and goals with employee objectives.

The Baldrige criteria are used to drive and track continuous improvement efforts through self-assessment from this business and HR performance perspective. An essential aspect of HR strategy and employee contribution, therefore, is alignment with the Baldrige criteria for HR development and management:

- Planning and evaluation
- High-performance work systems
- Education and training
- Employee satisfaction and well-being

At TPD, a HR strategy integrated with functional and business strategies established the essential directions for improving employee and organizational effectiveness, related to the first corporate value of *People*. An aligned annual HR plan then links activities to the division's short- and long-term goals. First introduced in early 1995, after being articulated by the ELT, the strategy hinges on a model of three interlinked circles, each of which demonstrates a critical business need:

- The first is to value people, as demonstrated by leadership and measured through bi-annual business climate surveys and more regular feedback
- Second is the need for employees to be effective, as shown by individual skills and training
- The third need is for organizational effectiveness, which ties HR strategy and structure and individual or team performance to business results, hence, the importance of the bonus scheme

This model is a template to structure and focus all HR activities and link them to business strategy. It is also used to apply the principles of continuous process improvement to HR.

Although HR uses different methods of feedback to measure employee satisfaction, its principal tool is the TPD-wide business climate survey conducted every two years among all employees. The survey measures levels of general satisfaction as well as those relating to specific issues. The data helps determine employee attitudes and beliefs and, ultimately, how they impact on employee contribution or performance toward achieving business objectives.

A key task for HR is to assess the drivers of the attitudes and beliefs that are identified and, should they be widespread, to design and implement improvement action plans. Then it must follow through with customized surveys and feedback mechanisms to measure the effect of any actions on targeted factors or the problems that always occur. For example, a recent climate survey revealed that employees felt management was not listening enough to their ideas and that there was a growing perception of technology threatening job security. As a result, more emphasis was put on training and skills development and the TPD hiring process was improved.

In regard to education and training, employees have access to over 200 courses for broad-based competency building, along with over 140 modules in specific job skills. HR has devised a formal training model for three levels of skill and competencies.

- Basic: those required for assigned jobs, as determined by job competency plans
- Those needed to achieve TPD, unit, and work group goals and objectives
- Others required for anticipated growth in responsibilities and for cultural change

As with the annual HR plan, training is related to TPD's strategy and values through business plans and goals, individual objectives, and each employee's personal development plan. The Performance Development and Review process is used for salaried employees, and an Annual Performance Assessment process is used for the other employees.

In terms of performance appraisal, one innovation from the ELT concerns 360-degree feedback that the team imposes on itself, plus one management tier below as a pilot study. This form of appraisal is expected to be distributed throughout TPD if successful. This technique is being used to encourage a different leadership style, focusing on the attributes of leaders and how they treat people within their sphere of influence. The belief is that more effective leadership will eventually translate into enhanced competitive advantage.

High-Performance Systems

In achieving business objectives, employee contributions are usually made in the context of teamwork. Improvements are initiated, implemented, and evaluated by cross-functional teams representing all organizational levels. Teams organize their own work areas, define multiple job tasks, facilitate training, and design pay-for-skills programs. For example, at one TPD plant, which employs 1,200 people, operations teams are organized into self-contained communities of production, engineering, and information services, which have full decision-making authority for their process areas. Teamwork and inter–business unit cooperation are now standard working practices, with four common operational results: improved information sharing, more rapid decision making, operational gains, and a climate of continuous improvement.

A four-stage, high-performance work system (HPWS) model has evolved since TPD was founded in 1983, which emphasizes building a foundation for employees or teams at each of the three stages before achieving the ultimate of HPWS implementation:

- Basic foundation, 1983–1991: process control and discipline; adherence to work rules; process simplification and complexity reduction; safety and housekeeping
- Readiness, 1991–1993: selection process, certification process, and line performance measurements
- Advanced work systems, 1995: managers are coaches, not supervisors; multiskilled flexible teams are employed
- High-performance work systems, 1996 and beyond

TPD recognizes the direct link between the satisfaction and well-being of employees and the organization's capability to achieve excellence in customer satisfaction and business performance, a key aspect of the Baldrige criteria in HR. This is demonstrated by ensuring a safe and healthy environment, providing an array of employee support services, and measuring and continuously improving employee satisfaction. A practical example is the health and safety initiatives, which are integrated into the planning process by establishing specific goals and objectives for improvement activities. Employee involvement is used extensively in this area through cross-functional and multipayroll category teams.

Compensation, reward, and recognition systems are designed to complement team and high-performance work designs. Apart from the goal-sharing bonus for all staff and pay-for-skills for production and maintenance employees, performance-based cash awards are used for all. The point of recognition programs is to strengthen the link between performance, reward, and recognition, whereas team recognition emphasizes interunit cooperation and individual collaboration.

Customer and Supplier Measurement

At the heart of Corning's TPD mission to *listen and learn from customers* is the division's Customer Response System, a unique combination of processes to identify, collect, and address customer expectations, as shown in Figure 3.3. Customers are cable manufacturers, their end users, and other organizations in joint ventures or alliances, and all data gathered about them is held in a customer database.

The area of performance also aligns with the Baldrige criteria, although the award scheme's major element is customer focus and satis-

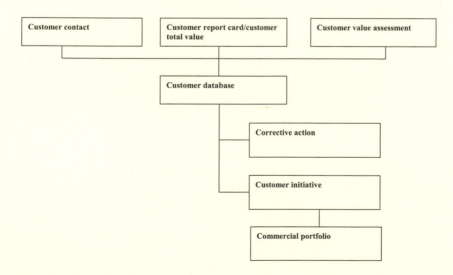

Figure 3.3 Customer Response System

faction. As noted earlier, TPD applies this by determining two goals: customer satisfaction in terms of its own performance and customer satisfaction relative to competitors. Through performance judged against these goals, it is reasonable to suggest that TPD has perfecte the satisfying of customer requirements. Three approaches are used to determine customer satisfaction and, therefore, performance improvement, if required. They are the Customer Report Card, Customer Total Value Process, and Customer Value Assessment.

The Customer Report Card is a quarterly rating system through which TPD is evaluated on each of seven primary customer satisfaction criteria:

- Product technology leadership
- Responsive commercial support
- Knowledgable technical support
- Simple, reliable ordering process
- Consistently improved reliable product quality
- Responsive supply (on-time delivery, adequate supply, etc)
- Price and value

Customer Total Value is a comprehensive feedback method to obtain detailed satisfaction data in four value areas:

- Performance
- Quality
- Business contribution
- Supplier value

The interactive Customer Total Value process was developed as a special measurement tool for larger strategic customers, who account for over 70 percent of sales. Customers prepare feedback and share it face-to-face with cross functional account teams at TPD, which then identify corrective actions in the most critical performance areas.

The Customer Value Assessment is a third-party assessment of customer satisfaction performance. In separate studies, cable buyers and end users are interviewed and asked to evaluate products, services, and customer contact functions relative to competitors. The survey results identify customer expectations, as well as their perceptions of TPD performance compared with their expectations. Both the Customer Value Assessment and the Customer Total Value processes solicit competitive comparisons on products, services, and support. Some TPD customers also have their own supplier evaluation processes, from which, where possible, TPD obtains data to give competitive comparisons.

Managing supplier performance and evaluation is also a crucial concern for TPD, given its potential impact on business success. TPD has segregated supplies into three levels, according to the impact each has on its customers and performance:

1. Direct input because they supply critical raw materials or components that have a direct impact on TPD's products
2. Important or large suppliers, but not necessarily critical suppliers, such as information management and construction contractors who are managed by functions
3. Providing commodity products focused on price and delivery

As a direct result of Baldrige award feedback from their application in 1989, TPD introduced its Supplier Total Value process for Level 1 organizations, which ensures close, collaborative working relationships. Suppliers are measured in the four categories of performance, quality systems, technology contribution, and value/price.

Specially appointed cross-functional teams manage these relationships and provide performance feedback through report cards and a formal quarterly report. Based on this system, suppliers are allocated ratings on a scale of 1 to 5, with the highest ratings receiving preferred supplier status. This provides a significant competitive advantage for TPD.

Critical Success: Integration and Alignment

Since 1983, TPD has consistently displayed attributes that have sustained the market leadership it achieved. This has been confirmed by three Corning Inc. awards and the Baldrige award in 1995. First are values and total quality, which are taken for granted since they have been embedded into TPD from day one. Further, the entire organization is aligned to superior customer performance; its process management system is world class; and there are strong linkages, whether as drivers or support, among vision, business strategy, and front-end performance. Integration and alignment are key words.

These attributes stress the crucial importance of information and analysis, along with the role and performance of TPD's information services (IS) organization. As with the business itself, IS has a vision, and its Information Management process is a core business process. IS personnel are represented on cross-functional teams, and the unit's data management systems are built on the principles of customer satisfaction and continuous improvement, for both IS and TPD.

As an example of the latter, continuous improvement in IS over the years has led to implementing electronic data transfer with customers, introducing a state-of-the-art customer database, employing real-time manufacturing data, and devising the Navigator Systems Series™ software design methodology. Extensive analysis is used for transforming data into critical information to support decision making and long-term planning. The Information Management process aligns data, analyses, and decision making with the strategic initiatives and values. This creates an effective road map for analysis.

All analyses are further aggregated into higher-level analyses that quantify critical impacts for the business. These include, for example, relationships among:

- Quality, price, customer satisfaction, and retention
- Market growth, new products, market share, and sales revenue
- Process capability, employee and process productivity, and unit costs

These higher-level business analyses are crucial determinants, for example, for product and customer initiatives, market choice, expanding capacity, deciding on breakthrough improvements, and testing plans for affordability. TPD has strategic significance. As IS is vital for making business decisions, TPD continuously improves its capability for aggregating data and analysis. It is important for TPD to ensure that this capability meets present and future needs and that everyone at the firm understands its contribution to competitive advantage. The latter point indicates where more can be achieved. Although there is already a wide appreciation of the tactical benefits from IS processes, the strategic potential of the linkages and their importance have not yet become clear to some employees. The message is that if TPD has the metrics in place, users must look for the right signals.

The right signals underpin the main outstanding attribute for TPD: leadership through the ELT and its leadership system. The responsibilities of ELT team members are to ensure linkage among the seven elements of the leadership system:

- Vision
- Mission
- Strategy development process (which balances the external environment and internal capability)
- Planning process, driven by critical success factors and key results indicators
- Strategy deployment process through shared goals and objectives at the business, department, unit, and individual or team levels
- Execution using the "plan, do, check, act, implementation" approach

- Review results, which links the data collection, analysis, and decision-making process with the business priority process and annual projects defined and sponsored by the ELT

Leadership was rigorously involved in the Baldrige process, and the applications of 1989 and 1995 helped to ensure that TPD stayed the course. The key was to unite people around a common set of understandings about what is important in the business and TPD's will to win.

NOTES

1. The success of self-assessment in the measurement approach is in terms of the results achieved from self-assessment in quality awards such as the Baldrige National Quality Program.

2. See Baldrige National Quality Program, *Getting Started with the Baldrige National Quality Program: Criteria for Performance Excellence—A Guide to Self-Assessment and Action* (Gaithersburg, MD: National Institute of Standards and Technology, 2001); Baldrige National Quality Program, *Criteria for Performance Excellence* (Gaithersburg, MD: National Institute of Standards and Technology, 2001); and for a Web-based self-assessment tool, see www.quality.nist.gov/ebaldrige/step_one.htm.

3. United Kingdom, Department of Trade and Industry, *90s News*, April 1996.

4. Bradford Management Centre, *Self-Assessment in Europe: A Report on Current Practice*, University of Bradford, U.K., 1996.

5. The term *customer satisfaction* is vague. For it to be meaningful, it needs to be qualified with a definition of how it was described or the research.

6. European Quality Publications, *UK Quality* (London: Author, 1996).

7. Again, this is a very vague term and needs to be clarified by those doing the research to make it relevant to readers. Such clarification should allow readers to make comparisons between the results and their own organizational situation more accurately.

8. A. Cowan and T. van der Wiele, *Self-Assessment* (Bedford, U.K.: IFS International, 1996).

9. European Foundation for Quality Management (Brussels), *Quality Links Newsletter*, 8(44) (October 1996).

10. C. A. Reimann and H. S. Hertz, "The Malcolm Baldrige National Quality Award and ISO 9000 Registration: Understanding Their Many Important Differences," *ASTM Standardization News* (November 1993), pp. 42–53.

11. *Organisational Excellence*, 3(2) (December 1995).

12. British Quality Foundation, Winning Through Excellence Award Winners Conference, London, February 1997.

13. Northern Ireland Quality Centre, *Evaluation of Northern Ireland Quality Awards and Awareness Events* (Belfast: Author, 1996).

14. Cowan and van der Wiele, *Self-Assessment*.

15. Bradford Management Centre, *Self-Assessment in Europe*.

16. Total Research, *The Benefits of Total Quality and Business Excellence Programmes*, London and Manchester Business Schools, 1996.

17. D. Lascelles and R. Peacock, *Self-Assessment for Business Excellence* (Maidenhead, U.K.: McGraw-Hill, 1996).

4

Benchmarking and Strategic Performance Measurement

BENCHMARKING AS A BUSINESS DRIVER

James Straker revealed the double-edged wisdom and danger of benchmarking when speaking on the subject: "Benchmarking is not a fishing expedition."[1] This is a refreshing insight, in contrast with jaded phrases, such as *stolen with pride*, still cited frequently by die-hard benchmarkers, who often demonstrate further pride in seeing benchmarking studies collect dust on their bookshelves.

Benchmarking is neither tourism nor passive comparison. Signs are that newer waves in the process will consign this approach to corporate history as benchmarking takes on greater significance for strategic performance measurement. For example, Rank Xerox applies benchmarking to business growth in its lean,[2] decentralized organization; it is an integral element of strategic reviews at the U.K.'s Information Technology Services Agency; and at least six leading British organizations are benchmarking community involvement in relation to corporate governance, public expectations, and their image.

Of critical importance, and discussed later in this chapter, benchmarking is evolving strongly into managing the wider field of best practice rather than purely comparative projects. Accelerated improvement and superior performance are the issues, driven by five executive questions:

- What is the benchmark?
- Where are the best practices?

- How do organizations do it?
- Are their best practices solutions for us?
- How fast can they be deployed?

As to the benchmarking practitioner, a different breed swims in the new waves, who is strategically astute, advanced in electronics literacy, fast moving, results driven, and usually office based, in contrast to the industrial tourist of old. As this chapter finds, the era of virtual benchmarking, with virtual networking, studies, and missions, has dawned, through different phases of evolution, exemplified over more than fifteen years by Xerox Corporation and its subsidiaries. Faced with going out of business when Japanese competitors entered the global copier market after Xerox's patents expired in 1978, benchmarking as a competitive strategy was born at the corporation two years later. It was then that an executive mission to Japan learned how Xerox's competitors did it. Crucially, the practices discovered by the mission were rapidly deployed within the corporation to regain its reputation and lost market share.

Benchmarking evolved throughout manufacturing in 1981, followed by its implementation in nonmanufacturing units, engineering, logistics, sales, service, and field operations, and integration into the Xerox Leadership Through Quality strategy, which was launched in 1983. By the end of the 1980s, benchmarking was completely internalized throughout Xerox and all its subsidiaries, with cost reduction being a significant outcome.

The Japanese mission represents a common application of benchmarking for many organizations: response to a specific business threat. For Xerox, it served a strategic purpose in waking up the corporation to business realities and alarming performance gaps and in helping shape a survival strategy. However, the organization's subsidiary, Rank Xerox (UK), recognized that, as a restructured, decentralized, and lean organization, benchmarking can more proactively shape growth strategies by being fully integrated into the management review and planning processes. In this capacity, benchmarking helps improve market share and revenues. Similarly, benchmarking is central to strategy at the Information Technology Service Agency (ITSA), which provides IT support for the U.K. social security program. It is a key element of strategic business management and a predictive tool for establishing targets. ITSA has formed partnerships in the public and private sectors for both functional and generic benchmarking. Areas for benchmarking are identified during the annual strategic review, which includes an assessment of stakeholder expectations, cultural and people issues, sourcing strategy, the business process model, and process performance. The change program for ITSA has included improvement projects using all types of benchmarking.

The strategic context of benchmarking has three elements:

- Strategic review: corporate objectives and performance, as shaped by stakeholder expectations, values, culture, resources, and capabilities
- Strategic options: identifying and evaluating options to select appropriate strategies
- Strategic implementation: identifying and prioritizing projects, allocating resources, and managing strategic change

Strategic considerations are also implicit is selecting benchmarking partners. The need to identify how different business and performance drivers vary among organizations and sectors in order to achieve an appropriate fit should be continually emphasized. By doing so and then recognizing the resulting differences, one can adapt and deploy the processes of benchmarking partners from other sectors to introduce competitive benefits for the organization.

A third example illustrates an unusual but significant application of strategic benchmarking in community involvement by the London Benchmarking Group. This has six members: BP, Grand Metropolitan, IBM UK, Marks & Spencer, NatWest Group, and Whitbread, who unveiled a new technique for measuring corporate inputs, outputs, and impacts of community activities in their 1997 report.[3] In effect, this technique is a template used to put hard figures on the profit contribution and assess whether organizations or beneficiaries receive value for money. Group members who have combined community budgets of over £30 million have tested it, and partners are being sought to benchmark the measures and practices. In addition to addressing corporate governance issues and the effects that public perception of a business can have on financial markets, corporate support in the community is a growing requirement. The template produces greater transparency and recognition of organizational roles in contributing to society. For the first time in the United Kingdom, a formula has been developed through which the business world's commentators and politicians can see a total corporate picture for three broad types of intervention:

- Charitable giving
- Community investment
- Commercial initiatives

Among impact measures in the template are financial leverage, social impact, and business benefits. These business benefits include enhanced reputation to attract quality recruits, and increased market share arising from cause-related marketing campaigns.

Taking an overview of strategic benchmarking, it has been successfully applied to technological leadership, market segmentation, competitiveness, organizational structure, and the strategic planning process itself. In practice, only in about 5 percent of organizations is the application of benchmarking widespread. The light has yet to dawn in terms of revealing benchmarking's strategic significance to others, who are still focused on it as merely a tool to improve work processes or operations.

Significantly, and where strategic benchmarking is established, organizations have usually also adopted self-assessment through business excellence methodologies. A key finding from Baldrige award examiners supports this point: directly or indirectly, benchmarking accounts for between 20 and 25 percent of the total 1000 point score. The inference is clear: without benchmarking, an organization has no chance of winning this type of quality award. Concerning what should be benchmarked at a strategic level, productivity, customer processes, and business growth are three possible areas (which Rank Xerox see as critical), which confirms the emphasis of Rank Xerox (UK) described previously.

It is increasingly difficult for organizations and benchmarkers to keep up because the performance bar is being continually raised, so they have to couple benchmarking with business issues like competitiveness, rapid market change, innovation, and new product development. In sectors such as pharmaceuticals, electronics, and software, organizations that are getting results from benchmarking understand that it is no longer just a tool, but rather a continuous learning process. It identifies and measures performance gaps in business processes and then seeks solutions from ever-widening networks of partners.

Two trends are evident in strategic benchmarking. First, it is being used to help facilitate business growth. The focus is not on pure costs and financials, which give only historical and nonpredictive data. Second, it is being used as a critical element of self-assessment against business excellence models. For both situations, the real potential of benchmarking is being discovered, revealing powerful strategic applications. The key is for executives to make a conscious decision to understand and deploy benchmarking at these levels.

Benchmarking produces the discipline for translating strategies into tangible outputs to benefit the customer by referring goals to processes and process capability. It places great emphasis on what to do, how to do it, when to do it, and, more important, on performance measurement and the output. Strategic benchmarking has several essential elements. It will:

- Address internal business needs or issues as they arise and define performance gaps
- Design a framework that clearly integrates the process with strategic objective
- Ensure that benchmarking is a continuous learning and improvement process

The point to appreciate about benchmarking is that it should have the flexibility to be adapted or rapidly deployed within the context of the shifting sands of business conditions, where change is the only constant.

BENCHMARKING AND COMPETITIVE ISSUES: IMPROVING PERFORMANCE CAPABILITY

Apart from a natural alignment with business strategy, benchmarking can be issued focused, adding another dimension, which extends from a higher-order framework. In this capacity, benchmarking builds or repositions strategic capability within the context of competitiveness. Three aspects of this process are establishing new standards for competitors to chase, protecting a known competitive advantage, or, for laggards, frantically catching up. This responsiveness of benchmarking is important because competitiveness may not necessarily be an annual or quarterly planning issue, whereas for some issues it is a constant reality.

A central question is: What should be benchmarked that has a capability or performance impact, either as part of a predetermined strategy, or in response to arising competitive pressures and issues? There has been a fundamental shift in benchmarking applications. It has evolved from initially focusing on specific problems like cycle time, error rates, or cost base to examining cross-functional processes that are critical to an organization's success in directly supporting mission, goals, and objectives. Example include customer satisfaction, performance, targeted marketing, order fulfilment, technology transfer, and supply chain issues. The following examples illustrate some of these applications and others in practice where benchmarking addresses competitive issues and therefore improves performance capability.

Rank Xerox (UK) recognized that its 112-day invoicing process was a customer dissatisfier and an internal inefficiency with substantial financial implications, so it benchmarked this area with American Express, an exemplar in the field. The revised process now takes 2 days, saved over £3 million in interest charges per annum, and vests invoicing authority with processors at source. Benchmarking has evolved into process benchmarking at the company and has included:

- Inventory management with retailer L.L. Bean
- Employee involvement at Cummins Diesel
- Service visits to customers compared to Hoover
- Distribution with TNT Express, which, led to this process being completely outsourced to its former benchmarking partner

Shell UK Exploration and Production (Expro) also sought enhanced competitiveness in benchmarking its Tern Alpha platform in the North Sea with Norske Hydro's Brage facility in 1995. From initially being perceived as an operational issue, this project had strategic significance for the company because of its results amid constraints not normally associated with best-in-class benchmarking. First, management approval insisted on the proviso of project completion in 12 months; second, except for man-hours and flights between Tern and Brage, no resources were budgeted, and finally, those involved had never benchmarked before.

The Expro staff knew their jobs, understood offshore performance figures, and had open minds. Benchmarking was more than an academic exercise or consulting methodology: if it did not improve performance, it was a waste of time. This action orientation involved benchmarking with Norske Hydro in four areas of offshore platform operations:

- Maintenance
- Support services
- Production systems
- Use of technology

Expro sought answers to the key question: How can we do things differently to improve the business? A post-benchmarking action plan included reducing personnel, introducing new maintenance standards, rationalizing reporting and responsibilities, and conducting equipment reviews, all of which have had major outcomes. Annual operating costs have been reduced by over £3.5 million, the initiative has triggered more extensive benchmarking to improve North Sea performance at Expro, including a strategic review of administration offshore; and Expo won the 1996 European Best Practice Benchmarking Award.

At Hewlett-Packard Finance (HPF), service quality and customer response were the primary business issues for benchmarking with First Direct in three areas: training, complaints handling, and recognition systems. HPF was strong in systems and technical skills but needed a more interpersonal and process-focused capability in customer care.

The benchmarking project was a initiative under the 1995–1996 development plan after the organization's annual review of its Ten Step

Plan in late 1994. This revealed performance shortcomings at two levels in the all-important first two steps:

- Customers/channels and competition in terms of current capability
- Future performance gaps projecting these steps to meet anticipated business needs in three years' time

The U.K. division was underperforming against other HP units in the order fulfilment process. Benchmarking with First Direct, for many years the U.K. exemplar in full-time, responsive telebanking, led to significant changes and results:

- An administrative/technical focus was redesigned into a customer care process.
- Eight-week staff inductions have corrected training gaps.
- Customer-focused behavior was rewarded through innovative recognition schemes.
- Complaints were traced and resolved, leading to improved ratings in customer satisfaction surveys, which now operate on a more dynamic and rolling format.

HP reinvented customer care, so benchmarking has led to sustainable business improvement. Internally too, HP found the process was very motivating, creating attitudinal and behavioral change in customer relations.

In each of these examples, the results outweighed expectations. The benchmarking process was triggered by perceived capability gaps: cost, quality, service, or response issues were the drivers of business improvements with benchmarking helping to provide the solutions.

SUSTAINING COMPETITIVE ADVANTAGE

As noted, benchmarking is also applied to protecting competitive advantage or setting new standards for a given industry or sector. This may be achieved independently or, more frequently in recent years, by joining benchmarking consortia of like-minded organizations run by networks, associations, and consultancies. The London-based Benchmarking Center's network, the American Productivity Quality Centre through its International Benchmarking Clearinghouse, and management consultants Pittiglio Rabin Todd & McGrath (PRTM) are three examples of these forms of networking.

Key to consortia participation is deciding on the business imperative, that is, the potential source or driver of competitive advantage, and the performance issue deemed critical to address this, as three following case reports show. They cover new product development, employee involvement, and organizational learning, all of which are considered as performance enhancers in leading organizations.

In a 1997 Benchmarking product development study on European technology-based organizations, PTRM found these organizations represent sectors such as aerospace, defense, automotive, chemicals, applied materials, computers and electronic equipment, medical equipment, semiconductors, and telecommunication equipment. Such a study would typically look at over one thousand projects and measure and analyze critical attributes, as defined by the benchmarking participants and the consultancy. Concerning outcomes, PTRM would disseminate detailed analyses by industry segment, including product development effectiveness measures, such as:

- Time to market
- Time to profitability
- Project goal attainment
- Revenue from new products
- Research and development effectiveness
- Wasted spending

As is common with such studies, organizations analyze their sector's results to facilitate performance benchmarking, set improvement goals, and rethink internal strategies.

Faced with tough business pressures and conditions in the United States (with deregulation between 1997 and 1999), New Haven, Connecticut–based electric utility United Illuminating used strategic benchmarking to prepare for change. This involved rethinking or building processes and positioning itself to sustain a home advantage on its territory of over 300,000 customers, or extending its reach. The organization's business imperatives are multifaceted with four examples being:

- Lower energy prices
- Cost reduction
- Greater competition
- Profit pressures

These imperatives were addressed in 1996 by means of three benchmarking studies with the Houston-based International Benchmarking Clearinghouse, in power generation, cost and reliability in transmission and distribution, and employee involvement.[4] Resulting from these developments, benchmarking was institutionalized and is run by a cross-functional team, which meets monthly. It is also action oriented. United Illuminating began implementing ideas immediately after benchmarking and, because all departments were running on a minimal budget, they did not have a year to do a study. It was a real-life process, which gets results.

United also chose to benchmark employee involvement as it was seen by the chief executive officer (CEO) as a competitive differentiator that helped United to run better and smarter. This is more of a necessity today than at any other time. Employees best understand the way their jobs work and how they can be done better, so United sought ways to tap their creative minds about some of the organization's complex issues. Benchmarking employee involvement programs were the chosen route, using partners like IBM, American Airlines, General Electric, Motorola, and Toyota over a six-month period. The coordinating team created a matrix of best practice, which led to the utility's Unlimited Ideas initiative, an organizationwide suggestions scheme, which was recognized as an essential contributor to tackling the critical issues.

United has averaged 51 implementable ideas per 100 employees against the benchmark itself, General Electric which scores 53, and sector norms of 23. A notable learning point in this case is that the catch-up partner may well outperform the benchmark in the future. Benchmarking can provide the quantum leaps to surpass the competition. United's process is integrated with strategic goals and can benefit employees, stockholders, and customers.

By contrast, a 1996 KPMG study, *Learning Organization Benchmarking*,[5] involved ten organizations, including Compaq, BP, BMW, and Standard Chartered Bank, in measuring their practice toward this ideal. The study revealed a conviction that becoming a learning organization was of great strategic importance, though participants had experienced difficulties putting the concept into practice. To stay in front, they must acquire knowledge at a greater rate than their competitors.

However, all ten organizations believed that they had a strong capability in learning, but most struggled to overcome inertia and internal resistance. This reveals a major outcome of strategic benchmarking, that significant improvement gaps or opportunities can be revealed even though an organization might consider itself to be best-in-class.

IDENTIFYING, MANAGING AND TRANSFERRING BEST PRACTICE: BEYOND THE BENCHMARK

There are several dimensions of benchmarking, in terms of what should be compared: performance, process, or strategic. There are four common approaches, competitive, functional, internal, and generic. Regardless of which is adopted, a fundamental question faces any leading organization: When maturity or benchmark leadership is achieved, what follows in terms of performance? Though most organizations simply aspire to this status, the benchmarks themselves usually recognize that leadership has to be sustained or that there are steps beyond the plateau of maturity. Rank Xerox (UK) and Texas Instruments are examples. Since 1994 a new quest has emerged in these and other high-performance organizations to identify, manage, and transfer best practices. Some experts believe that today this process is more significant for revolutionizing performance than has been the case with benchmarking over the last fifteen years or so. Best practices are crucial to improving business processes. The mastering of best practices has become the strategic performance issue and is far more than a casual initiative, when the principles are applied to business growth. Through their transfer, continuous improvement becomes a way of life.

For example, at Rank Xerox, best practices have two broad interpretations: internal comparisons and special intradivisional projects. All the European operating units benchmark performance against each other, followed by sharing best practices, as one unit's exemplary performance is another's improvement goal. The result of doing this is that the bar is continually raised because every unit seeks out and implements internal best practices to exceed previous performance. This is the essence of continuous improvement.

The second interpretation concerns dedicated businesswide projects. Faced with a struggle to make the mandated return on net assets in 1994, a strategic performance indicator, Rank Xerox's Office Documents Products Groups (Europe) instigated a pioneering initiative to identify and share best practice. Over forty were examined by a team of executives, from which ten were selected for transfer. They were validated at this top level and, prior to introducing any in a unit, two-day awareness workshops were run. Monitored over a two-year period, the initiative saved US$105 million in 1994 and a further US$300 million in 1995. Top management commitment and infinite patience by managers were critical success factors. It was not easy: translating and transferring best practice is one of the most difficult processes on which this unit of Rank Xerox has worked.

COLLABORATING ON BEST PRACTICES

The collaborative process can be industry specific, for example, the UK oil and gas sector's Cost Reduction Initiative for the New Era (CRINE) Network was launched in 1993 to reduce costs by 30 percent among volunteer members so that their collective expertise could become more competitive on global markets. CRINE is now seen more widely as a best-practice working group. Over 1,300 organizations and 30 major projects contributed to its work in its first five years.

In contrast, the World Class Standards Network (WCSN) is an electronic consortium of fifteen European centers of excellence and partners committed to accelerated performance improvement for subscribing organizations by using advanced communications and information services. It is partly funded by the European Commission's Best Business Practice Network. WCSN's services include:

- An on-line thesaurus of approaches, processes, and methods related to world-class business performance
- Electronic services featuring models, case studies, process tools, and guidance notes
- Access to eleven best business practice networks, over seventy technology projects, and a best-practice database.

WCSN sees itself as a supporting process for transformation or change management related to world-class standards of performance.

The benchmarking databases are part of an organization's tactical armory, but to be effective they have to have global coverage. Local best-practice networks were useful but quickly exhausted their potential, so national and international sources are now of significant importance (providing language and cultural differences are overcome). Internally, intellectual awareness is a crucial prerequisite for transferring best practices, along with a determination to follow through, implement improvements, and close performance gaps. Its is worth noting that there is no single best practice for any aspect of business performance.

When considering the definition of best practice, it should be emphasized that an organization should not literally strive to find out who, what, or where is the ultimate best. The point of best practice is to discover and close performance gaps, so defining *best* might be as simple and subjective as what a manager instinctively feels it is, based on the business and its competition. Adopting this process does not necessarily mean aiming for world-class status.

In effect, the best practice process represents an early phase in knowledge management, where the key is to motivate others to search for best practice as a business imperative, the leadership management issue, and aligning their deployment with employee objectives and compensation. The starting point is for organizations to put a stake in the ground and then determine how to embed best practice.

Building on the leadership and management issue, managers have to be clear on levels of best practice, considering different dimensions, such as strategic, operational, external, and internal for four critical areas of performance:

- Customers
- Operations
- Product development
- Innovation and knowledge creation

The corporate emphasis has been on the external side, building databases for instance, which can be too confining in practice. The dilemma is whether best practices are tacit or explicit and the degree to which internal sources can be leveraged. This is the most interesting and challenging trend because it involves issues such as cultural change and organizational learning.

TEXAS INSTRUMENTS: OFFICE OF BEST PRACTICES

Texas Instruments (TI) have been the trendsetter, having established its Office of Best Practices (OBP) in late 1994. It was founded following remarks made by the late Jerry Junkins, the former president and CEO: "If only we knew what we knew." Following the leadership of Junkins and in line with TI Business Excellence Standard (TI-BEST), a four-step continuous improvement process, OBP has become a catalyst in meeting the 1994 imperative.

OBP is an electronic, manual, and meetings network for best practices worldwide. These are identified, captured, cataloged, and disseminated using dedicated facilitators who represent every operating unit in TI. Sharing is two-way, from OBP outward and incoming from the corporate business, the latter generally directed by three key management questions:

- What is the benchmark?
- What are the best practices?
- How do others do what they do?

The emphasis is on quickly obtaining low-cost solutions. Best practices at TI are part of an integrated framework, which aligns with, and then distributes, its total quality strategy as the guiding force of business excellence. This is:

- Achieved through a commitment to customer satisfaction by customer focus, continuous improvement and people involvement

- Supported by operational excellence in customer satisfaction, process focus teamwork, and diversity
- Implemented through the annual improvement process of policy deployment, benchmarking, best practice, and evolving goals
- Measured by key performance metrics: meeting customer commitments, cycle time, Six Sigma quality,[6] training hours per employee, and financials

The best practices process is a facilitator for achieving business excellence as it has a matchmakers' role in deploying tools for people to use, in addition to promoting knowledge transfer, providing the infrastructure, and communicating the information potential of what business units see, hear, or hold.

Particular challenges that OBP have faced include uncovering hidden knowledge in order to reduce learning cycle times and free resources, as well as helping potential users move from an attitude of *I must solve my own problem* to more proactively approaching others for proven solutions. At the same time, all employees need to be willing to share what has been learned, but this transition to a more open culture is not easy as it requires many changes. Practical initiatives help awareness, as in OBP's awards, dubbed *Not Invented Here, But I Did It Anyway*, which were a recognition scheme for best-practice implementation ideas that have resulted in significant cost reductions.

Apart from emphasizing these strategic interpretations from case reports (in effect, integrating benchmarking with strategy to close performance gaps which addresses business issues), the critical issues are the process itself and its implementation. There are three points to be made:

1. Even though the focus and scope of benchmarking have changed, the basic approach is still the same:
   - Analyze the strengths and weaknesses of a process.
   - Identify the competition and industry leaders.
   - Incorporate the best of the best.
2. Senior management's role is to set the overall strategy and put appropriate programs in place to ensure that benchmarking is applied consistently and with measurable results.
3. An organization should approach benchmarking with the attitude that, as a result of the process, it will become the new benchmark, or even world class.

There are other variants or interpretations of these elements, which can be adopted to suit an organization's particular circumstances.

For the process issue, the basic model is:

- Plan against a strategic objective, business issue, or need.
- Analyze and define internal (and, to a lesser extent, external) processes.
- Select partners.
- Research and collect data.
- Analyze findings for improvement opportunities.
- Implement.

In seven out of ten benchmarking exercises, the findings sit on the shelves without follow-through, action, or process change. This is an incredible waste and misunderstanding of resources due, in part, to benchmarkers not being sufficiently aware of how important change is if benchmarking is to be useful or preferring to let others finish the project. Implementation is sometimes regarded as a chore.

In terms of critical success for organizations on the verge of benchmarking or those rethinking it as a strategic process, there are several stages that are imperative:

- Understand business strategy and needs and their alignment to benchmarking, which is far more than just an awareness issue.
- Integrate benchmarking and business strategies into a coherent framework.
- Consider resource and time issues, typically allowing an eighteen-month period for major projects.
- Appreciate that appropriate skills will be required for implementation, which as implications for training.
- Build links with business unit, line, and individual objectives.
- Maintain a commitment to change and communicate success and failure stories.

Above all, it is critical to secure and reinforce ownership for benchmarking at every level in the organization. This means positively selling the principles, not necessarily as benchmarking, but more as a continuous improvement project or process. Without this, buy-in will rarely occur.

RANK XEROX (U.K.)

The early to mid-1990s were good years for Rank Xerox Ltd., the European arm of the Xerox Corporation. Despite electronic alternatives, the document market in Europe was still worth over 20 billion euros per year and produces over 5 billion documents a day. It is estimated that 90 percent of information is still on paper, taking up 60 percent of office time. Small wonder the organization rebranded itself as The Document Company in 1994.

To reflect the changing marketplace for document production, business has shifted from office machinery to integrated products and services that deliver solutions, including workstations, printers, electronic printing systems, and color photocopiers. The year of rebranding also had significance for other aspects of Rank's business. Evolving from the European Foundation for Quality Management's Business Excellence Model, first adopted in 1991, the Xerox Management Model (XMM) was implemented across the entire organization worldwide. At the heart of the model is a customer and market focus which replaces the emphasis on product and quality of previous decades. This shift is the basis for the development of Customer Relationship Management (CRM), which is define as a

> Business strategy the outcomes of which optimize profitability, revenue and customer satisfaction by organizing around customer segments, fostering customer-satisfying behaviours and implementing customer-centric processes. CRM technologies should enable greater customer insight, increased customer access, more effective customer interactions, and integration throughout all customer channels and back-office enterprise functions.[7]

Organizational priorities are now customer satisfaction, employee motivation and satisfaction, market share, and return on assets. Underpinning performance across all four areas is shareholder value, an area in which investors have little cause for complaint.

The organization's emphasis is on growth through the two constant imperatives of value and productivity. This is being achieved by expanding the existing customer base through deploying more sophisticated retention and loyalty strategies and acquiring new customers. Rank Xerox management believes the firm will continue to reach annual growth targets by delivering better value at lower costs, thereby satisfying the customer expectations of value for money.

Although the future augurs well, the relatively recent past sounded a virtual death knell for Xerox when it almost went out of business. Phenomenal success and expansion throughout the 1960s and 1970s resulted in an unassailable 100 percent market share, created because Xerox machines were protected by worldwide patents. Competition was virtually nonexistent and it had become the fastest U.S. organization to reach US$1 billion in annual sales.

However, the expiration of the Xerography patent in 1978 allowed prepared Japanese imitators to rapidly penetrate Xerox's markets, which brought a dramatic turnaround in business fortunes. Within two years, market share had nosedived to less than 20 percent against competitors with cheaper prices, better quality, good delivery performance, consistent customer service, and less time-to-market.

Singular Benchmarking Experience

Rank Xerox noticed that the only part of the business that was prospering was the joint venture with the Fuji film company in Japan. At the time executives believed the dramatic fall in business was due to Japanese competitors dumping their machines on the market place as a spoiling strategy. The executives thought they were operating at little or no profit and would have to eventually pull out of the market. However, this did not happen. The executives then realized the Japanese competitors were doing something different. Moreover, they were doing it well and sustaining it. Acknowledging Japanese success led, in effect, to the world renowned firm's first benchmarking exercise in 1980 when the then chief executive officer of Xerox Corporation, David Kearns, took his first-line team to see what the differentiators were at Fuji Xerox. For example, they discovered the following:

- Xerox's product lead times were twice those of competitors.
- Defects per 100 machines were seven times worse.
- Assembly line rejects in parts per minute were ten times greater.
- Remarkably, machine manufacturing costs equaled the Japanese selling price.

The organization was finally convinced it has a problem. Following the executive visit, a benchmarking team was formed to work with Fuji Xerox in order to fully understand performance gaps but, more crucially, the processes, practices, and methods that were driving superior performance in Japanese organizations. Critically, the team's imperative was to see how these practices could be introduced in the Xerox Corporation to gain competitive advantage.

This fact-finding mission began a trend and subsequently led to a benchmarking process being developed based on applying knowledge or best practices gained from another organization. Benchmarking as a competitive strategy was thus born at Xerox. The philosophy first evolved in manufacturing with joint U.S. and Japan manufacturing studies being initiated in 1981, before benchmarking was formalized and implemented throughout the whole organization, including its European and U.K. businesses. However, in terms of the original benchmarking project, it is worth noting a key statistic. In 1995, Rank Xerox's market share was back to where it was in 1979, the year when Japanese competition began to have its savage effect on the business. The organization is regarded as being the only Western firm to regain market share in an industry deliberately targeted by the Japanese.

Benchmarking Evolves

The competitive benchmarking scenario just described is a commonly used application in many organizations. For Xerox, it represented a response to a specific business threat and served a strategic purpose in helping shape a survival strategy. Furthermore, it also alerted the organization to business realities and alarming performance gaps. As other organizations have found in similar circumstances, this motivates people toward improvement by demonstrating how competitors achieve outstanding performance.

The effects for Xerox were, first, strategic, in that the organization was successfully turned around, and second, performance related. For example, in six product classes based on the number of copies made per minute in 1986, competitors were best-in-class for all. By 1988, Xerox itself had achieved this in two classes, with three more being attained in 1990. By 1992, it had regained world leadership in all six product categories.

Following the initial U.S. and Japanese studies, which focused on establishing benchmark targets for the cost of manufacturing, cost reduction opportunities have also been a natural target for benchmarking projects and, to some extent, still are in the appropriate situations. Given Rank Xerox's early 1990s restructuring of field operations into small, self-contained Customer Business Units and dramatic reduction in central staff groups, the far leaner organization recognizes that, to remain strong, it has to significantly increase growth rates. These changes have led to a final phase in the evolution of benchmarking, involving its use as a tool for growth in the decentralized organization. This tool has been examined and will lead to benchmarking becoming more fully integrated into the ongoing management review and planning processes.

A key to this evolution has been a realization that, although identifying performance gaps is critical, exercises or projects are of little value if the comparator's processes and methods for delivering the results are not fully considered. This is the process view of benchmarking practiced at Rank Xerox, which involves identifying specific best practices not just restricted to competitors. The organization is keen to identify them worldwide for any aspect of business operations.

Best Practices

American Express (Amex) has been a partner in benchmarking the invoicing process, because preliminary research had shown it to have achieved excellence in the timely production of easily interpretable and accurate invoices. As one example of a post-benchmarking outcome at the time, in one Rank Xerox invoicing process for clients renegotiating standard terms and conditions, which accounted for approximately 40 percent of its business, Rank Xerox was taking 112 days to produce an invoice, mainly because of a lengthy internal checking and approval process. The revised practice now takes 2 days and saves over £3 million in interest charges alone. Authority and accuracy are now vested in the invoice processor at source. In broad terms, any organization is essentially carrying out the same basic procedures, whether they are selling information or manufacturing. One tries to reduce their work to step-by-step processes to make an effective comparison of how excellent performance is achieved. The key is to know how other organizations are functioning.

Over the years, the benchmarking process has been appreciably refined and projects extended beyond pure cost-reduction exercises. Time to market in new product introduction is an example where Rank Xerox benchmarked with competitors and other organizations both large and small, in the United States and Europe. As an outcome, benchmarking in this case contributed to a new product delivery process.

Integrating Benchmarking with Processes

As might be expected of a large, American-based multinational that has transformed itself, Rank Xerox (U.K.) has a well-defined and -managed structure. Following the Xerox Management Model, a holistic view of the business is assumed where the key words are balance and integration. Since 1990, benchmarking has been progressively integrated and managed across the organization. How this has been achieved is described next.

First, benchmarking is aligned with processes that are used to drive superior results in the four corporate priorities of customer satisfaction, employee satisfaction, market share, and return on assets. The Xerox business architecture, shown in Figure 4.1, is the organization's highest-level process model. It shows how all processes are linked and have a direct impact on stakeholders, from customers and suppliers to employees and stockholders. The model is common across all operating units and, as such, facilitates the effective comparison of approaches, methodologies, and also results.

This architecture provides an integrated framework for focusing any benchmarking activity. Its elements are:

- Manage for results
- Infrastructure

- Time to market
- Integrated supply chain
- Market to collection
- Customer services

From the self-assessment process, the business knows where it is going and what needs to be achieved. Most important, however, it has identified the processes or methods for getting the firm to where it wants to be. It is the *how to* part that is crucial. Benchmarking is one of many tools linked with strategy that helps them decide how to move forward. It is not just an exercise for the sake of it.

As an example, the higher-order process of customer services shown in Figure 4.1 progressively breaks down into fifteen more detailed subprocesses, which broadly cover:

- Service requirements, strategies, programs, and requests
- Consulting
- Implementing, maintaining, modifying, and updating solutions
- Technical solutions
- Operational services
- Training and education
- Customized services
- Performance assessment

These Level 2 processes, or subprocesses, ultimately map out step-by-step procedures, which are followed by employees and ultimately

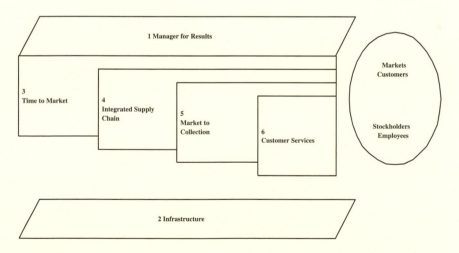

Figure 4.1 Business Architecture

affect the customer. As to their application for benchmarking, the Level 2 subprocess of solution maintenance, which covers the ongoing servicing of equipment supplied by Rank Xerox or its strategic partners, uses standard process measures to internally compare performance in this area across all operating units.

Integrating Benchmarking with Business Management

A second dimension of how benchmarking is integrated concerns the Xerox Management Model (XMM), shown in Figure 4.2, through which Rank Xerox assumes a holistic view of its business. Introduced in 1992, it is delivered from key learning related to the EFQM and Malcolm Baldrige Business Excellence Models. Significantly, the Business Products and Systems Division of the Xerox Corporation received a Baldrige award in 1989, the second year of the competition, and Rank Xerox Ltd. was a European Quality Award winner in 1992.

The XMM represents the organization just as it represents the business and is the framework against which every unit of the corporation perform an annual self-assessment. Its six categories break down into more detailed elements that describe how to achieve excellence in a category. Each element has a desired state, appropriate measures,

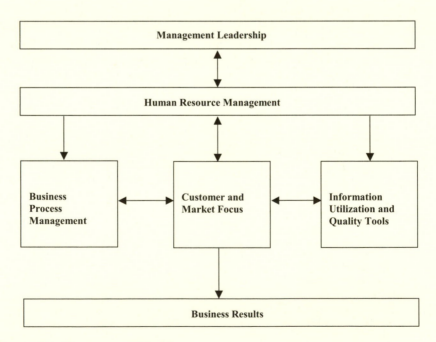

Figure 4.2 Management Model

guidelines, and rating criteria to indicate world-class levels of performance and enable accurate assessments.

Apart from identifying gaps or shortfalls in performance, self-assessment against the XMM also highlights best practices within a business unit, which can be potentially benchmarked with that benchmarking implemented across all units to raise collective performance. This latter point again reinforces the strategic significance of benchmarking to Rank Xerox.

Once gaps have been identified through self-assessment, they are prioritized and, if deemed crucial to the future success of the business, become what Rank Xerox calls *the vital few*. They are then disseminated through the organization using the policy deployment process, which links corporate vision, business direction, strategy, and goals for the coming year. Performance targets for *the vital few* are based on benchmark levels, so at this point the process of benchmarking is integrated in order to ascertain the best practices that must be adopted to achieve desired performance levels.

Business measurement is then aligned with business expectations through a three-level approach:

Level 1: Setting direction
- Vision, mission, corporate priorities
- Five year goals and strategies
- Annual; objectives and *vital few* actions

Level 2: Deployment
- Cascade objectives
- Agree on *vital few* actions

Level 3: Management process
- Implementation
- Regular review
- Annual diagnosis through self-assessment

Strategic intent thus becomes annual operating plan reality. The dissemination process ensures individual congruence with business objectives through each employee or team committing to a role, and responsibilities and objectives are documented each year, along with details of performance measures based on previously determined benchmarks. It starts at managerial levels, where commitments are likely to be strategic and related to providing resources for, or facilitating, the next level of employee to reach objectives.

All targets are extrapolated to the team and individual levels to ensure that the organization is involving those people who work and run the processes. Once individuals or teams are convinced that what is being asked of them has been achieved elsewhere, they will buy into the achievement of goals themselves.

A Benchmarking Application

In practice for any benchmarking project, the Rank Xerox process has evolved into four stages with separate steps prior to process maturity, be that for the managers, cross-functional groups called X *Teams*, or individuals involved:

Stage 1: Planning

- Identify subject for benchmarking
- Identify the best
- Collect data

Stage 2: Analysis

- Determine current competitive gap
- Project future performance.

Stage 3: Integration

- Communicate results of analysis
- Establish functional goals

Stage 4: Action

- Develop action plans
- Implement plans
- Monitor results
- Recalibrate the benchmark

Maturity occurs when a leadership position is obtained and maintained through the full integration of benchmarking results and actions into everyday business processes and practices. As noted previously, the Xerox Business Architecture for higher-order processes progressively breaks down into subprocesses, which direct employee and team efforts toward customer-focused outcomes. Naturally, under the customer services Level 1 process, efficient solution or equipment maintenance is a vital subprocess for customer satisfaction, loyalty, and retention.

Standard process measures are used to compare performance in this area across all European operating units and to internally benchmarking their performance against each other. In practice, one unit's exemplary performance is another's benchmark for performance improvement.

For example, RX Belgium in 1997 was the organization's benchmark of ten European operating units. Each engineer was able to handle an average of 77.8 machines, identified by figures from annual self-assessment against the XMM. While recognizing that RX Belgium had European leadership in this subprocess, the organization also pinpointed every other country unit as having a performance shortfall. This represents a lost opportunity, in terms of that business and also collective performance.

When the results are announced RX Belgium publishes its process and practices via an appropriate pan-European network. Units wanting to improve performance will arrange benchmarking visits so that teams, including engineers who work on the actual processes, visit the benchmark country to share in how it operates to best-practice standards. For RX Belgium, its task was to look for external partners to further push up performance standards. As a result, each unit is tasked to catch up internally, with leaders having to benchmark externally to further raise standards. As to the scale of this type of internal benchmarking at Ran Xerox, it is worth recalling that there are fifteen separate subprocesses for customer services alone. With five other high-level processes to consider, this gives an idea of corporate activity for both self-assessment and benchmarking. In essence, this is how the organization's internal and external benchmarking strategy is driven.

There is a downside of using the internal environment as both a measure and benchmark. The process can become introverted and may also lack an understanding of competitive reality outside the organization or in the marketplace. Internal benchmarking must always form part of an externally focused approach if maximum benefit is to be gained.

Corporate Measurement Overview

As previously discussed, the Xerox Business Architecture identifies processes or methods to deliver the right results, whereas self-assessment through the XMM ensures systematic continuous improvement against annual objectives. Both are related to the organization's four corporate priorities of customer satisfaction, employee satisfaction, market share, and return on assets.

Customer satisfaction, which has been corporate priority number one for over ten years, is one example of how business performance measurement is interpreted by Rank Xerox. Customer measurement covers four different areas, product, sales, administration, and service; and a range of tools is used to measure satisfaction levels, including sponsored and anonymous surveys for postinstallation support, customer relationships, and service experiences.

Feedback is also gained from the account management process, which measures market dynamics, suppliers, internal best practices, internal surveys and competitive benchmarking externally. For example, a benchmark of customer satisfaction might be that 98 percent of another organization's customers are satisfied with the service they get. While accepting this, Rank Xerox more critically will want to know how that has been achieved, whether, for example, the organization has given greater front-end responsibilities to teams or whether other processes have been put in place to meet expectations. This ownership is crucial to Rank Xerox and is reinforced by compensation, appraisal, and recognition systems. Customer focus is featured in individual appraisal criteria, bonuses are paid to both employees and managers, and a variety of recognition schemes operate.

Over time, customer strategies have been driven by the application of key performance metrics based on benchmarking. From once being content with a visionary goal of 100 percent satisfied customers back in 1987, now the key metric is not the percentage of customers who are very satisfied, because externally focused research has found that these customers are the most loyal.[8] This form of measurement is crucial for devising customer loyalty and retention strategies that focus on creating and delivering value or for their realignment. For example, the organization's original product delivery process effectively makes the product and sells it. This has been refined into the value creation and delivery process. Under this process, value is chosen on the basis of customer segmentation, market selection, or value positioning and is then provided through products or services. The final-process stage involves communicating any value to potential customers in order to make the value offer explicit.

The Benchmarking Lessons

In taking an overview of the critical success factors for benchmarking, the one that stands out the most is the importance of working with suitable partners. Most often, the best partners for Rank Xerox are organizations of similar standing: American Express, L.L. Bean, and Cummins Diesel. However, partners do not necessarily have to be of a like status, as shown by benchmarking with the London Ambulance Service. Those with established quality processes and, for example, accreditation to ISO 9000 can be appropriate because they have formalized procedures.

This level of documentation enables an organization to compare processes easily and highlights differences or those best practices that drive superior performance. However, organizations that have followed TQM for some years and have a defined process model are, for many, a dream to benchmark against, assuming that their processes are delivering world-class results. Organizations do not have to operate in a similar marketplace to Rank Xerox, as most work in any organization can be broken down into common processes, which may reveal different levels of performance because of different approaches or methods. Virtually any element of business performance can be compared.

There are benefits that often result from benchmarking. Both partner organizations should focus on and review what they are doing, which can reveal unseen potential for process improvement. The most profitable benchmarking partnerships are based on the assumption of mutual benefit. Focus is another key word if valuable resources are not to be wasted. In the past, some organization have seen benchmarking as a costly exercise because there has been much uncoordinated, frenetic activity under its name. This can lead to a duplication of effort and a feeling that the organization is only paying lip service to continuous improvement through benchmarking.

In terms of strategy and methodology, organizations should know what to benchmark and why, for credible performance comparisons to be made or how best practices can be identified and introduced. Essentially, this includes an understanding of what drives performance and the setting of realistic targets. Boundaries have to be drawn to determine where any benchmarking project starts and ends, giving a contained situation that helps participants focus on what they are trying to achieve. Even if a task seems too large, it can be tackled by dividing it up into small, separate components that can be measured within short defined time scales.

Finally, and probably most important, as with any successful change program, management commitment in terms of time, people, and funding is essential. Without this commitment, it will be difficult to accurately diagnose best practices and virtually impossible to implement them. As a result, business as usually tends to prevail until it is often all too late. As Asian philosopher Sun Tzu said: "If you know your enemy and know yourself, you need not fear the result of a hundred battles."[9]

NOTES

1. Oak Business Developers P.L.C., *The Fourth Annual European Benchmarking Forum* (London: Gerrards Cross and The Benchmarking Centre, 1996).

2. For a discussion of what constitutes, and how to create a lean organization, see M. A. Milgate, *Alliances, Outsourcing, and the Lean Organization* (Westport, CT: Quorum Books, 2001).

3. The London Benchmarking Group, *Companies in Communities: Getting the Measure* (London: Author, 1997).

4. American Productivity and Quality Center (Houston), *Benchmarking in Practice* (1), 1996.

5. KPMG Management Consulting, *Learning Organisation Benchmarking* (London, Author, 1996).

6. For a discussion of Six Sigma, see M. Harry and R. Schroeder, *Six Sigma: The Breakthrough Management Strategy Revolutionizing the World's Top Corporations* (New York: Currency, 2000); and P. S. Pande, R. P. Neuman, and R. R. Cavanagh, *The Six Sigma Way: How GE, Motorola and Other Top Companies are Honing Their Performance* (New York: McGraw-Hill, 2000).

7. S. A. Brown and M. Gulycz, *Performance Driven CRM: How to Make Your Customer Relationship Managepment Vision a Reality* (Ontario: John Wiley and Sons, 2002); see p. xv.

8. For detailed discussion on loyalty in business, see F. F. Reichheld, *Loyalty Rules! How Today's Leaders Build Lasting Relationships* (Boston: Harvard Business School Press, 2001); and F. F. Reichheld, *The Loyalty Effect: The Hidden Force behind Growth, Profits, and Lasting Value* (Boston: Harvard Business School Press, 1996).

9. Sun Tzu, Liang Zhuge, Liu Ji, Thomas F. Cleary, *The Art of War* (London: Shambhala Dragon Editions, 1988).

5

Process Measurement

PROCESS MEASUREMENT AND BUSINESS STRATEGY: QUESTIONS AND ISSUES

Is process measurement a process, function, or both? Deciding which framework to guide, coordinate, and push organizational activities into different dimensions of success, competitiveness, market leadership, outstanding customer service, and so on is a difficult executive dilemma. Resolving this decision, or at least being clear on which approach best suits the organization, will determine how performance is to be measured.

One consideration in resolving this choice is results. Functional effectiveness can be incrementally enhanced; efficiencies, productivity improvements, and cost reductions are three examples. However, there is usually a point beyond which a function and its organization cannot proceed. On the other hand, as many case examples in this chapter will show, process-oriented activities can bring superior results, in addition to parallel gains in customer satisfaction, retention, and loyalty. This cannot be done, however, without pain. This chapter will opt for process because transition to processes has wider effects than simply the way work is conducted and measured. A second consideration is impact; impact on culture, structure, and human resources are three examples, Questions may arise, such as: What does process orientation mean for organizational capability? Are there special effects on individual competencies? How does training or education change in response?

The latter questions are significant because process creation, management, and measurement are little understood, even where first attempts at all of them have been introduced. Education, awareness, and communication are other considerations. And what of business performance measurement itself? While best practice in process measurement is demonstrated by case reports, there are things to watch out for. Some organizations adopt a process focus yet still use functional measures, others measure historical performance, which is of little use for predictive measurement. This is a critical quality for process measurement, in addition to enhancing organizational capability to outperform the competition.

Measuring the "voice of the process" is measuring capability and consistency and, therefore, enabling the organization to define the parameters of its competitiveness and that of its competitors. The Ritz-Carlton Hotel Company certainly practices the "voice of the process" principle. The organization has service delivery as its core process, which is supported by others, including:

- Six personal service processes: employee satisfaction, orientation, training/certification, daily line-up meetings, three steps of service (warm welcome, anticipation and compliance, fond farewell), and pacification of customers who have complained
- Nineteen critical work processes: these produce or have a direct impact on customer needs from registration, housekeeping, and breakfast to facsimile delivery and billing
- Six quality and cost reduction processes: inspection, cost of quality, benchmarking, quality improvement, problem-solving process, and error proofing

Critical performance attributes of quality, cost, and timeliness are measured at different levels against goals established by Ritz-Carlton's Executive Leadership Team. Strategically, measurement is through the leaders' inspection process, for example, daily quality reports in real time and the line-ups, plus quarterly reviews of guest and travel planner satisfaction. It is also done operationally, through process control tools. Performance against influential external hospitality ratings of customer satisfaction is an additional critical differentiator. Continual process improvement is the rationale. It is directed at retaining customers, attracting new ones, providing a return on investment, reducing the cost of quality, and measuring the gains or losses in revenue per available room compared with competitors.

IBM Canada Customer Service (CS) in Ontario listens to the voice of the process and those of customers, too. It has become one of Canada's market-leading support enterprises in computer hardware and software maintenance and is widely known as a customer-focused organization delivering world-class standards of satisfaction. This and other attributes won the organization a Canada Award for Excellence in 1996, which is equivalent to a Baldrige award.

In 1995, IBM CS handled over 320,000 service calls for hardware and over 125,000 for software, achieving customer satisfaction levels of 96 and 90 percent, respectively. It employed over 1,500 people, operated out of 70 locations in Canada, and expected growth to outstrip the industry in both revenue and market share. The organization's process approach is to take a customer, rather than a product view in order to protect its business from the complexities and vagaries of hardware, software, and defect or nondefect interrelational problems.

Service processes are well documented with the emphasis on prevention to guarantee high service availability. Numerous indicators track performance over time in service and efficiency and the organization periodically recertifies key processes by reviewing existing systems to encourage their refinement. Service improvement is an integral part of IBM CS's strategic planning process, through which the full deployment of improvement goals and systematic process measurement is a way of managing market-leading business performance.

Integration is a critical principle at information products company Hewlett-Packard, with all operating units using a comprehensive business management process. There are five interrelating elements between stakeholder inputs and results or outcomes:

- A medium term, ten-step plan based on three questions: Where are we now? Where shall we go? How shall we get there?
- The tenth step and second element is the annual business plan for all units.
- Plans are focused through six processes: customers, product generation, product fulfilment, order generation, employee development, and planning, with annual breakthrough targets being established that are significant to the business, as in improving customer or employee satisfaction.
- Process measures or *business fundamentals*.
- A review process to check that performance is on track.

These elements interrelate in a continuous loop, and each process has a range of process-specific and financial measures, which are the bedrock of the measurement system. This is because the measures are all linked to process targets and thus provide a means of tracking client data. Reviews are crucial here; they are conducted once a month on a selective basis, with a full review of all process measures every quarter. This provides trend analysis over time.

These examples raise some important insights:

- Effective process measurement is driven buy the principle of continuous improvement against critical success factors and performance attributes.
- There are different dimensions, or tiers, to this form of measurement, from strategic reviews to operational and process detail. Systemic deployment of goals, targets, and indicators is a key issue here.
- The integration of process measurement with business planning and management is a critical success factor in itself.

However, even if these are current arrival points at most leading organizations, the route map to get there is varied and uneven.

In considering the extent of process orientation, more traditional structures are still common. Organizations are not clear on how to move away from functions or, where they do work on some processes, they tend to use functional measures. This occurs for two reasons. First, the dominant measure in most managers' mindset is to meet budgets on a monthly, quarterly, or annual basis, with no focus on process or process accountability and measurement.

Second, most organizational performance measurement continues to be backward and inward looking, which means it cannot be predictive or, indeed, help create a different, more competitive capability, which is crucial. The strategic issue of process measurement is that it has to build capability and deliver better market or customer positioning. This cannot be achieved by applying existing measurers to new processes. Rather it involves significant change with implications for organizational culture, structure, competencies, and behaviors.

Organizations are measuring the wrong things in the wrong way and using measures too selectively because they are the easiest to apply. The key words for process measures are:

- Capability
- Positioning
- Predictive, by looking forward and outward

Focusing on quality, cost, and timeliness may provide no more than business snapshots. Firms must focus instead on outputs rather than inputs and examine how areas like customer retention, loyalty, and customer profitability are measured. These are key process issues.

If you can master four steps, you can implement them in a few days and you will know more about setting predictive process improvement metrics than 90 percent of people in your organization. First, you must define the improvement goal. Vision, mission, strategy, and customer input are important, but five central questions should be asked to determine if an improvement goal is well defined and appropriate. Is this goal:

- What you want at the end?
- Specific?
- Quantitative? (though it could be asked, Why not qualitative?)
- Realistic?
- Customer driven?

Second, measure what gets the organization to its goal, making sure there is a causal link.

- Is the proposed metric likely to cause the goal to happen?
- Is the list of causal actions prioritized from, ideally, just three to five on which to focus?
- Are the causal actions correct and adequate?

Third, tier the items to expected levels of outcomes, with central questions being:

- Who is responsible for the metric?
- Do they control the process?
- Are the responsibilities formed in the form of a *dashboard* for clarity?
- Do lower-tier goals lead directly to upper tier actions?
- Are sufficient tiers established to manage the project?

The fourth step is to test the decisions for timing as all actions should be scheduled to help manage the improvement process. Ask the following:

- Does a proposed action precede the goal? If it is not, it might be a worthwhile result metric but not a good predictive one.
- Is it objective? Again, this could be debatable if you prefer a more qualitative approach.
- Will it cause appropriate organizational behavior?

What you have when you have worked through these four steps is a list of causal actions that have passed all the tests. It is a relatively trivial move then to translate these into a metric by asking of each action, *How much?* Another important question to consider is posed here in a rhetorical sense: Is metric all about quantity?

Despite the simplicity of this approach (albeit focused on crucial and commonsense questions), it does relate to process management, and measurement, in turn, relates to quality self-assessment methodologies. There are some very sophisticated process practices in leading companies such as Texas Instruments and Nortel, but process management overall represents the biggest variances of internal assessor scores in the EFQM. Many organizations are not clear on what key processes are, what they are supposed to be doing, and the place of a process measurement system. It is relatively easy to determine what constitutes a business process as practically every work activity may be organized as such.[1] The more difficult question is how many processes are absolutely critical to business success. These are complex and businesswide, acting as a hierarchy of interrelated subprocesses and sub-subprocesses, or work activities.

Concerning the integration of this process hierarchy with business management and measurement, all well-managed processes have five common characteristics:

- A process owner, accountable for how well the process performs
- Well-defined boundaries or a clear scope of activities
- Measurement and feedback controls close to the point where the activity takes place
- Customer-related performance measures
- Known cycle times

After completion of process mapping and agreement on performance targets for the process, policy deployment, there are three measurement steps as follows:

- Measure the actual performance of the process through process control.
- Determine how well the process is meeting customer requirements or process effectiveness.
- Take actions to improve process performance as necessary through continuous improvement or business process redesign.

With the emergence of the self-assessment methodology as a critical business tool, and bearing in mind the previous comments on process management and self-assessment, EFQM ran a consortium study of eight interested member organizations on this theme. Its report is a significant contribution to good practice.[2] In articulating an approach to process measurement that is shaped by experience, the EFQM report recommended several essentials for introducing measures, most of which are related to the external environment of customers and markets. These essentials define or identify the following:

- Business strategy, strategic objectives and a balanced scorecard of high-level indicators, being clear on cause-effect relationships to reach strategic objectives is vital
- Key processes and their critical success factors
- A few key performance indicators (KPIs) or measures for processes that match with balanced scorecards and verify their contribution in meeting strategic objectives: this is the cause-effect relationship

The KPIs should be measured on a continuous basis and in a systematic and timely manner, and converted into workable information with added value.

The report made two other observations. First, it is the role of process owners to review the effect of measured values on a periodic basis and check the suitability of measures. Second, if strategic objectives have changed, processes, critical success factors, and key performance indicators also have to be adapted to the new situation.

PROCESS MEASUREMENT IN PRACTICE: THE PERFORMANCE AND MEASUREMENT ISSUE

As shown in this chapter, there are many variations in good process measurement, although the best of these are integrated with business strategy, planning, and management. However, there are two key words: capability and performance. This chapters' case study, Design to Distribution Ltd. (D2D), a subsidiary company of ICL, now part of Fujitsu Ltd., demonstrates the importance of these words.

High-level process performance reviews are critical strategic measures for D2D. As a contract electronics supplier, every process at the organization supports the delivery of products or service to customers and is mapped by a flowchart or model. The most important processes are determined annually by management at strategic reviews, supported by quarterly updates and monthly business reviews.

Led by the managing director, reviews at D2D are used to analyze and discuss indicators for each of the EFQM self-assessment criteria that the organization has adopted. This gives the top team a systematic overview of progress against targets, improvement actions, and overall business performance. Both financial and nonfinancial (the possibility of qualitative measures alluded to above do come into the picture) performance are reported in these reviews, the latter including people satisfaction, customer satisfaction, delivery, quality, absenteeism, training, labor attrition, process yields, test yields, inventory, and similar factors.

The value of the review process is that it is self-sustaining. Any new targets determined by the reviews are agreed on the basis of an organizationwide understanding of what is required to improve performance. As the business measures would already have been examined at the supervisor and managerial levels before reaching the directors' monthly review, performance against a consistent, systematic and structured set of measures is subjected to a three-level review.

The Columbus Regional Hospital in Indiana is an example of an organization that uses cross-cultural and service contracts as a different form of process performance review since initiating a corporate transformation program in 1989 through continuous quality improvement. This transformation has taken over a decade to achieve. One year was spent on initial investigation and awareness followed by another for intensive planning, and two more years on the first phases of implementation. It was only then that the hospital had sight of its ultimate goal, integrating total quality and its processes into organizational planning, systems, and activities. The Columbus core process is customer, or patient, mindedness, which is supported by other processes for medical, HR, budgeting, administration, and quality. Traditionally in health care, many measurement activities have not been meaningfully linked to each other or to the core process. As Columbus's understanding of the core process deepened, it recognized the need for an integrated approach to measurement.

The hospital began the measurement integration process by developing a set of fifteen macrolevel indicators, known as the performance circle, which help assess core process effectiveness on a monthly basis. Indicators represent each major category of organizational goals, including:

- Quality of care and service
- Patient, physician, and employee satisfaction
- Financial and productivity measures
- Future growth

Results against the indicators are displayed on a spider diagram, a tool that allows users to determine if performance is balanced and to identify possible areas where suboptimization, or underachievement, is occurring. Although the performance circle provides an overall view of results along the core process, it does not measure activity within each component process. In order to integrate the measurement system horizontally and vertically, interdisciplinary teams are developed for these separate components, with each devising their own performance circle related back to corporate goals.

Process improvement activities are also integrated into this system. For example, the teams launch process design or improvement actions themselves and contribute to organizational development interventions. To support the integration of corporate quality initiative (CQI) activities, a quality resource group provides support for each department and component team as work is done within the macro processes of:

- Building customer knowledge
- Measurement activities
- Process improvement/design initiatives
- Clinical information, retrieval, and reporting
- Surveying

The Hoshin quality planning methodologies and software helped Columbus to understand how to link the efforts of each individual to the vision of the organization, and a tree diagram, one of the seven management and planning tools, provided a structure to help visualize these linkages.

Extending the issue of capability and performance, Glasgow-based TSB Homeloans has achieved much of its success by using process measurement and control. These tools allowed management to focus attention on the key performance drivers rather than the outcomes of processes, with the former being the cause and the latter the effect. To identify process measures, the processes were prioritized on the basis of impact and scope. Any deemed to have either high impact or wide scope were selected for monthly performance reporting. Typically, these processes relate to five critical success factors of TSB Homeloan's strategy:

- Employee satisfaction
- Customer satisfaction
- Process capability
- Resource deployment
- Creativity and innovation

Significantly, in terms of implementation, all processes were allocated a process owner, the role being perceived as crucial to process measurement in eight areas:

- Mapping the process
- Identifying a control system
- Establishing process capability, the key performance drivers
- Setting process outcome measures, the key performance outcomes
- Identifying and eliminating special cause variation
- Setting improvement targets
- Carrying out reviews
- Sponsoring improvement activities

The tools used to measure and monitor processes are extremely variable, but include:

- Statistical process control, to measure the capability of key business processes, along with supplier performance, though these are used daily, a capability index for reach process is compiled monthly
- Service-level questionnaires, to measure the perceptions of different types of customers regarding performance of TSB Homeloans
- Internal satisfaction questionnaires to measure internal customer service, with a satisfaction index being published monthly
- Monthly staff satisfaction questionnaires to gauge staff morale and any areas of concern, a staff satisfaction index is also published monthly

Other process measures used include: competence profiles to monitor the progress of learning in the organization, bar coding and light pen technology to measure productivity and process performance; and several cost measures, including a monthly cost-of-quality report.

Whereas the values for TSB Homeloans involve the way it conducts business, there is the difficult issue of the relationship between values and processes. This is based on describing behaviors that are the expected manifestation of holding a set of beliefs and then formalizing those behaviors into a set of business processes. A formal approach is essential because business processes need to be repeated, reviewed, and improved. As for performance, it is worth noting some of the achievements TSB Homeloans can point to as a result of its approach to process management and measurement: productivity has improved by over 110% since 1990, staff satisfaction is above 90 percent, and the organization won a Quality Scotland Award for Business Excellence.

In the United States, capability, performance, and client satisfaction are the business issues at a process-oriented law firm, Mays & Valentine in Virginia. Its case is important for two reasons: the sector is traditional bureaucratic and functionally or specialist biased; and it also highlights how process management is equally as applicable for knowledge-based organizations as for manufacturing or larger organizations.

Mays & Valentice was one of ten organizations to try continuous improvement through a quality improvement demonstration project run by the American Bar Association. The group of ten law firms listed ninety different activities that could improve their operations, including the broad categories of response times, administration, client service, employee satisfaction, and client retention. These were classified as critical issues, and each organization articulated them as five processes with related measures:

- Finance
- Client complaints
- Human resources
- Management information systems
- Office services

Emulating the balanced scorecard approach (see Chapter 2 for a detailed explanation of this concept), Mays & Valentine now monitors performance from three perspectives: financial, client, and internal business. Financial measurement covers net income per partner; operating expenses per lawyer; chargeable hours for partners, associates, and legal assistants; realization rates on its accounts receivables; and work in progress. The firm also tracks the speed of its billing and collection processes against established goals. Speed is regarded as a key business issue in process-focused client service.

The firm also tracks the client complaint process, analyzing complaints by type, using, not partners or lawyers, but secretaries, personal assistants, receptionists, and clerks to produce condensed data for the firm's managing partner. Lawyers seen to drag out a case to boost their personal billings (sometimes a common practice in law) are asked to explain the process data collected.

Since 1993, revenue generated from the top fifty clients has been measured, as it has become a key business indicator of client satisfaction. With greater internal effectiveness, satisfaction levels are increasing. Mays & Valentine also implemented a client manager system, with one person being designated as the responsible lawyer for every element of each case. This new process has been documented so that any lawyer can manager all elements of the client relationship. Financial indicators alone do not provide all the data you need to make sound decisions. You need to manage by fact, not by gut feelings, to make sure what gets measured then gets improved.

HEWLETT-PACKARD LABORATORIES: MEASURING THE NEW PRODUCT DEVELOPMENT PROCESS

The importance of measuring new product development and process performance at the California-based electronics and controls giant Hewlett-Packard can hardly be underestimated. On the one hand, approximately 40 percent of its sales come from new product launches, while on the other hand, research and development (R&D) costs run at approximately 10 percent of net revenue. Product development is decentralized, with over one hundred divisions worldwide.

Appreciably, control is a key word, for the discipline of process measurement and also because it is core business for the company. HP measures many things, though essentially it is an intuitively managed organization. It does not let measurement get in the way of good business decisions. It uses measurement to help the business decision-making process, not to perform it.

Most investments in R&D measures tend to yield intermittent or small improvements. Performance measures will be systematically effective only if they are:

- Implemented in the context of processes
- Well integrated with staff responsibilities
- Supportive of business decisions and objectives
- Aligned with desired behaviors
- Primarily aimed at improvement, not punishment

The key point is that process measures interrelate with business planning and organizational behaviors in an integrated management portfolio. There are critical success factors at Hewlett-Packard Laboratories where process measurement:

- Supports the achievement of business objectives, monitoring the performance of a critical few, which are focused on customers
- Promotes behaviors that improve performance, aligning with reward and recognition systems and linking results to improvements for all organizational levels
- Supports effective decision making and organizational learning
- Integrates with management systems to give balanced views of cross-functional performance, while providing value for all customers of the measurement system

In practice, process measurement for product development at Hewlett-Packard Laboratories operates through a three-tiered hierarchy. At the top is the business management system level, which focuses on strategic direction, alignment and strategic relationships. In the middle is the product generation process, or strategic management for R&D activities. At the bottom are project and program management systems.

The following objectives and measures for the top tier determine the organization's overall Hoshin or breakthrough goals and related measures:

- Market and customer leadership: market share, order growth rate, loyalty, and satisfaction

- Financial excellence: return on assets, net profit, inventory-sales ratio
- Strategic direction: scenario trigger status and new markets outlook
- Best place to work: employee satisfaction and retention, depth of strategic understanding among employees, and strategic alignment

Senior management then distills measures from its work and distributes them down to the middle tier, which is the basis of overall R&D effectiveness in three areas:

- Business results: financial performance, market performance, and customer results, the latter including competitive quality, new customer rates, and new market share
- Product generation renewal: technology distribution, platform renewal, and technical competencies
- World-class product generation: internal and external competitiveness, process predicability, and investment productivity

At the project or program management level, there are three areas of focus for objectives and measures:

- Clearly aligned deliverables: change control and product definition
- Efficient resource utilization: staff
- Project performance: predicability versus plans, and business and technical risk management

For each tier, desired and basic behaviors are defined, not just for individuals or teams but also in displaying successful corporate attributes such as customer understanding, fostering innovation, optimizing performance, and so on. Sixteen behaviors are expected across the three levels.

The bottom line on process measurement in R&D is to stay strategic, measuring too many or the wrong things makes as much sense as flying blind. Effective metrics have these three characteristics. They are part of something bigger; they support the behavior you are trying to foster; and they facilitate good business decision making, helping to get answers to critical questions.

PROCESS MEASUREMENT IMPLEMENTATION ISSUES: CORPORATE CHANGE AND IMPLEMENTATION

For all the strategic questions and links raised throughout this chapter, difficult enough issues in themselves to grasp or articulate at executive levels, implementation is a crucial make-or-break factor in effective process measurement. Operational by nature, it has strategic significance for board agendas if resources and effort are not to be wasted. The following case reports confirm this point, while also reinforcing the underpinning issues of capability and performance in relation to process measures.

The 653rd Communications Computer Systems Group (CCSG) at Warner Robins Airforce Base in the United States was once structured around functions and specialities, much in keeping with any traditional armed services unit. In the early 1990s, CCSG was completely reorganized around thirty-eight key processes over an eighteen-month period, following a U.S. government *reinventing government* initiative. For each process,[3] a cross-functional team was formed, headed by a process owner who made a flowchart of the system, identified and eliminated non–value-added steps, and analyzed potential obstacles to be monitored closely over time. The point of reorganization was to better service forty-seven customer organizations on the airbase.

Now process measurement and analysis is one of the cornerstones of CCSG's quality effort. Once processes had become clear, the teams identified key performance indicators and established procedures to routinely measure and report on them. The indicators were based on critical performance variables after interviewing base customers to determine their requirements. CCSG then drew up a hierarchy of indicators for each process to embrace all operations under which operating units, teams, and employees collect data on their own indicators and report them to the next higher organizational level. This is the primary basis for review by the group commander and the parent organization, the Air Logistics Center at Robins Airforce Base.

After process reengineering, on-time delivery of critical computer products to base customers rose to 99 percent. Computer on-line time reached 98.7 percent of capacity. CCSG's data systems management process reduced manpower requirements by half, and a seven-fold increase in new projects was achieved. As a result of its performance breakthroughs, the 653rd Communications Computer Systems Group received the President's Quality Improvement Prototype Award.

The experiences of CCSG raise the point that there are fundamental steps for implementing process management and measurement. As a snapshot, these are:

- Reorganization into processes: the key task is identifying processes and resolving support, facilitating, and subprocess criteria
- Process mapping: examining process flows through the organization and resolving interface or boundary issues

- Determining critical success factors or attributes for the business: quality, cost, and speed are examples
- Devising meaningful measures, goals, indicators, and targets for a given process and its key elements: this includes an integration of systems standards such as ISO 9000/14000
- Defining and prioritizing methods or process improvements such as incremental or breakthrough, including how process change is continually evaluated

Process mapping is crucial to devising appropriate measures. For example, Nortel introduced three levels of process map after reorganization in 1995, higher-level corporate, regional, and business units. These are based on value steps and decision points rather than tasks and procedures, which is often the case in process reorganization. Value helps focus people on outcomes, and the use of decision points has introduced a decision-making discipline by providing information to make decisions at these points rather than spelling out how decisions should be made. This helps to encourage self-determination.

A third issue is that implementation is not simply a matter of having good metrics, as D2D discovered in 1990, despite achieving gains in efficiency, effectiveness, and product quality against conventional manufacturing practices such as quality metrics and reviews. D2D ended up with an organizationwide perception of *If it moves—measure it!* This was not deliberate, but more a logical outcome of having to measure to improve as they discovered that people were not necessarily measuring usefully.

Despite achieving productivity increases of 10 to 15 percent each year, cost reductions of around 10 percent annually and 99 percent in first time deliveries and quality, the organization found that these improvements were increasingly difficult to sustain. As is common in measurement, improvement plateaued, so a new focus on business processes was introduced.

Through process reengineering, in 1992 the business was remodeled into six separate units, each acting as a profit center. The transition required sixteen major change or renewal projects, conducted by cross-functional teams, which were led by a business director and reviewed monthly by the top management team. These projects included sales and marketing, engineering, finance, human resources, and distribution, among others. They began to examine self-assessment as a way of moving them up from the plateau they had reached.

In fact, the first exercise using the EFQM methodology revealed that processes and procedures fully supported business direction only 60 percent of the time, encouraged by mainly functional measures rather than an integrated measurement framework, which self-assessment typically brings. Self-assessment is now an integral part of the management and improvement processes. It has also brought changes to critical processes by shifting priorities from procurement, testing, and inspection to product and service delivery, process improvement, people satisfaction, supplier partnerships, and cost reduction.

HONEYWELL MICRO SWITCH: CASCADING MEASUREMENT

It says much for the quality of process measurement as the Honeywell division MICRO SWITCH that it has won the Illinios State Quality Award, a Malcolm Baldrige award finalist and has been congratulated on its goals and measures systems by ISO 9000 assessors. All recognized a distinct attribute, however, that the division's framework and measures touch every one iof its employees, which is a crucial implementation issue.

The division implements and communicates measurements through a cascade distribution process. This results in every office and location having a continuous improvement control board, typically four by six panels of goals, measures, and results related to the organization's strategic priorities. The processes are the mirrors of activities on the line, in the service areas, and in boardrooms. Each measure is born of the strategic planning process. The process begins at the Honeywell parent organization and then is distributed to divisions and business or marketing teams and on to the lowest operating levels. It is the strategic planning team's job to identify key business drivers (KBDs) after analyzing customer priorities, supplier capabilities, competitive business designs, financial results, and operational performance. From this they generate the business issues, strategic issues, and KBDs. Everything they do is linked to the KBDs because they are the critical elements of the business.

As examples of KBDs in practice, those identified in 1996 were:

- Baldrige award improvement process
- World-class workforce
- Emerging systems and subsystems
- Quality
- Responsiveness
- Focus
- Organizational productivity
- Globalization

MICRO SWITCH's Goals and Measures Council is responsible for aligning measures and turns the KBDs over to each department as a framework to design work specific measures. To do this, measures must meet five strict criteria:

- They must measure something measurable.
- They must be simple.
- Data for them must be readily available.
- They must be broadly understood.
- They must continue to be relevant.

Goals and measures are posted throughout MICRO SWITCH by using the control boards, the primary method for communicating work-unit level goals and their relationship to division goals.

The goals are categorized in three areas with a total of six key measures among them. The classification is based on their being important performance indicators that focus attention on key customer and business drivers:

- Responsiveness: customer lead time and on-time delivery
- Quality: parts per million and errors per million
- Robust business: gross profit and sales growth

These measures are present improvement areas that can be influenced by the actions of virtually all employees on a daily basis and therefore link to the principle of continuous improvement. Also, any line suggestions for process improvement have to be put in context by meeting one of the six key measures. Primarily, control boards display measures to link employee actions on a daily basis to the KBDs through three sections: product, people and process, and the concept works for several reasons:

- Location is at the hub of the group or team activity.
- It is reviewed frequently.
- Management pays a great deal of attention to every board in the division.
- Supervisors use them as a showcase of team activities.

The key to success in goals and measures at MICRO SWITCH is its personalized and participatory process. People understand how their department is a little business, underpinning which is communication. There are three primary reasons why managers and supervisors do not clearly communicate business goals and measures:

- Failure to understand the goals and measures and why they are important

- A desire to avoid any confrontation associated with displaying goals and then being unable to achieve them
- The inability to communicate goals in simple, easy-to-understand terminology

Although goals should be positive and externally oriented, a crucial measurement and implementation issue most of senior management do not recognize is how closely employees monitor their behavior both on and off the job and how finely they dissect their messages.

CONCLUSION

In terms of a broad overview of good practice for implementing process management, or indeed, as a fundamental starting point, process is more than just breaking down functional barriers. Success depends on building a process culture, not dissimilar to experiences at process exemplars such as D2D and the Ritz-Carlton Hotel Company.

Apart from a clear process structure and encouraging people to *think process rather than function*, process management comprises several interlinked elements:

- Control and maintenance, which form the basis for process management
- Control, the systematic evaluation of process performance and corrective actions taken if performance does not conform to standards
- Maintenance, which assures the repeatability of processes, according to standards and procedures such as ISO 9000/14000

There are two dimensions for measuring and improving process capability: either on a gradual, incremental basis or through radical breakthroughs, as in the case of CCSG.

As noted earlier in this chapter, there are misgivings over the extent, quality, and effectiveness of process measurement because organizations continue to misuse inappropriate measures, partly because they are comfortable with the status quo, but also through rigid, backward-looking mindsets. That said, there are three considerations for implementation:

- Build an integrated process framework linking critical success factors, key performance indicators, and measures with customer outputs.
- Test all measures against the consequences of measurement (the issue here is coherence).

- Ensure that individual performance measures are aligned with processes and process measures.

The third point is crucial. There are very few organizations where personal performance and behaviors are a driver of success in the context of team-structured or process-orientated organizations. They fail to appreciate the linkage of human resource management to process management, which, in a sense, means they do not know what they do not know.

The word *process* is the key in the context of performance measurement. Taking this as a starting point, it becomes easier to design and implement performance measurement systems that measure what the customer wants, and determine incremental progress made.

- Measure the right things in terms of what customers perceive as important.
- Relate process performance to customer needs, internally and externally, for the voice of the process to reflect the voice of the customer.
- Determine appropriate measures for different parts of the organization.
- Compare the value of a measure with the cost of producing it in order to reflect high leverage points.
- Measure all critical parts of the process to facilitate easier management and control.
- Start with simple measures and progressively use better ones.
- Distinguish between measures for different purposes, in how they might variously apply to the different roles of shop floor personnel and management, for example,

Superior business results can be achieved by focusing entirely on process management, by measuring efficiency and effectiveness, consistency through process control, and competitiveness through continuous benchmarking.

CASE STUDY: D2D

A critical emphasis on business performance measurement has been at the heart of a multiphase change process at ICL's electronics manufacturing subsidiary, Design to Distribution Ltd. (D2D), for over a decade. The organization has changed radically from once being ICL's manufacturing division, an integrated part of the group and a captive supplier to its parent, to a global, stand-alone, sector-leading contract supplier of electronic components.

Customers include Sun Microsystems, Dell, PACE Micro Technology, with internal ICL business as well. D2D grew non-ICL revenues from £3 million in 1990 to over £200 million in five years. During the same period, the organization has won outstanding supplier awards every year from Sun Microsystems from 1992, an European quality prize nomination in 1993 followed by the premier prize itself in 1994, and the U.K. Best Factory award in 1994.

Registered as an arms-length subsidiary in the ICL federation in 1994, D2D operates from a number of manufacturing sites in the United Kingdom, the Netherlands, and the United States, producing over 1 million printed circuit boards (PCBs) each year, as well as bare boards, other electronic components, and integrated support services. In 1997 it was the world's sixth largest contract electronics manufacturer in a very competitive and fast-changing market. Their emphasis is added value in service to differentiate them from competitors and avoid setting unreachable standards.

The turbulent market place is also illustrated by product costs. Back in the 1980s as ICL's manufacturing division, D2D built parts for mainframe computers, with boards costing tens of thousands of dollars. Today, PCBs cost under $100 and the potential applications for advanced technology are expanding rapidly. The development of Internet access terminals or those for retail outlets are two examples of D2D expertise. The attitude on the sales operation was, "We will keep making it and if you cannot sell it, then that is your problem."

Business Change and Measurement

Recognizing that organizational change was imperative to adapt to business conditions, D2D embarked on a deliberate program of change in 1983. It began a shift toward becoming market driven, lean, and customer focused, driven by a three-phase recovery strategy: survive, profit before growth, and profitable growth. These imperatives have been achieved through TQM philosophies embedding into daily operations, substantial investments in training, business process reengineering, devolution of responsibility to six separate functional businesses, and an increasing focus on advanced team-based activity, which has replaced any semblance of hierarchy.

Rigorous measurement of operations, performance, and business outcomes has been central to the change process. The performance measures now in use have been designed within an overall corporate review process. When aligned with business requirements, they provide a complete, integrated framework but are no more or less than they need. However, the measurement process took eleven years to evolve.

Originally, the measures of the mid 1980s were those normally expected of any conventional manufacturing organization:

- Performance against production schedules
- Volumes of boards and materials produced
- Component use
- Assembly time
- Internal cost center budgets and control

Initially, these measures were refined through early quality improvement efforts as ways of reducing organizational costs were sought and served their purpose: efficiency, effectiveness, and product quality improved. However, quality then was a separate function and was not regarded as a business issue. D2D found quality metrics and reviews were insufficient to serve business needs.

During 1985–1986, a second change phase began with a quality improvement process based on the teachings of Crosby and the costs of non-conformance. Management realized that quality was a conformance to requirements rather than a measure of goodness and that finding root causes was more effective than fixing the same old problems. For the first time, the division focused on assembly line operators as internal suppliers or customers to each other in a productive flow system.

In practice, this approach had its limitations. One requirement was to measure all they needed to know, so everything and everyone was measured. Moreover, as nonmanufacturing staff were not used to conducting measurements, much time and effort was spent in sorting out problems. D2D ended up with an organizationwide perception that anything measureable must be measured. More positively, getting staff to analyze and measure performance marked a fundamental change in attitudes. People realized they had a measurable output from processes that could lead to improvements, thus establishing a climate for introducing goals and targets such as zero defects. This was backed by training in target-setting skills and processes, which brought about the first stages of self-directed measurement.

What evolved was a sequence that took people through the process. They examined any measures used, made decisions about their validity, and then created different and better measures. In practice, each department set its own goals, targets, and measures. It became common for results or progress to be displayed on the walls, underlining improvements and stressing their importance to the organization. This culminated in 1990 with a Zero Defects Day intended to recognize achievements but also as a focus point for further refining the measurement process.

Despite achieving productivity increases of 10 to 15 percent each year and cost reductions of around 10 percent annually and 99 percent in first-time deliveries and quality, the organization found that these improvements were increasingly difficult to sustain. As is common in measurement, it had plateaued, and a new focus on the process was needed. Measurement was becoming part of the D2D culture by this stage. It allowed benchmarking and structured review processes, but these functions were still not integrated with the main business processes.

Strategic Measurement Begins

D2D had a foundation for strategic measurement to emerge since its culture of measurement and those methods used for both manufacturing and nonmanufacturing functions or processes could be harnessed when remodeling of the business began in 1992. Most processes by then had been recorded as flow diagrams and were documented for ISO 9000 accreditation, which had enabled an understanding of key processes and where change was needed.

Through process reengineering, D2D was reorganized into six separate businesses within the organization, each acting as a profit center. The transition required 16 major change or renewal projects, conducted by cross-functional teams, led by a business director and reviewed monthly by the top management team. These projects included sales and marketing, engineering, finance, human resources and distribution, among others.

At that stage, D2D began to examine self-assessment as a way of taking them forward from the plateau reached. There was a perceived need for greater customer focus and business improvement, confirmed by an initial self-assessment exercise. It revealed that processes and procedures fully supported business direction only 60 percent of the time. A corporate weakness, therefore, was implementation of business strategy, encouraged by mainly functional measures rather than an integrated measurement framework which self-assessment can bring. As a result D2D adopted the EFQM model with its nine criteria. They in turn are divided into two categories, each with a 50 percent score weighting, as facilitators, including leadership, people management, policy and strategy, resources and processes; and results, including business results, employee satisfaction, customer satisfaction, and impact on society. This holistic, self-assessment approach showed management that, while the firm was doing well, a key question remained. If one particular business unit was successful, why were all the others not successful as well? Gaps in deployment were revealed, which meant the firm had been looking at the better performing areas through rose-tinted glasses.

Other questions and shortcomings were raised, too. By what or by whose standards was the business performing well? Which measures or benchmarks existed in different parts of the organization to reflect or prove these standards? Moreover, though functional measures were working well, there were widely differing formats for very different audiences, which lacked coherence. For example:

- Some measures were publicized on internal e-mail, and others as hard copy.
- Some use spreadsheets for recording, others use different formats.
- Access to some measures was by the management team only.
- HR measures were confidential, whereas quality measures were widely circulated.

The results of the self-assessment exercise helped D2D identify issues, problems and some points they perhaps had taken for granted, such as the effectiveness of the policy deployment or recognition process. D2D realized that scoring from the self-assessment process was not as important as actually identifying improvement areas.

Self-assessment is now an integral part of the management and improvement processes. Each business unit or functional area is responsible for its own assessment and for introducing corrective action plans through process improvement, self-managed or customer–focused teams. It is important that each of the EFQM model's criteria has a process owner or champion from senior management. A greater understanding of corporate strategy and business planning has ensued, with more active participation of employees in setting goals and objectives that relate to their own targets. Line of sight between individual effort and business outcomes has become clear.

Self-assessment has also brought changes to critical processes by shifting priorities from procurement, testing, and inspection to product and service delivery, process improvement, people satisfaction, supplier partnerships, and cost reduction. In support, all staff have received process management training and are aware of their place in the supplier-process-customer chain.

Performance Reviews

Every process supports the delivery of products or service to customers and is mapped accordingly by flowcharts or models. The most critical processes are determined annually by management at strategic reviews, supported by quarterly updates and monthly business reviews. Led by the managing director, the monthly review meetings analyze and discuss a full set of indicators for each EFQM criterion to the top team, giving it a systematic overview of progress against targets, improvement actions, and overall business performance.

Specifically, areas reviewed cover both financial and nonfinancial performance, the latter including people satisfaction, customer satisfaction, delivery, quality, absenteeism, training, labor attrition, process yields, test yields, inventory, and so on. The value of the review process is that it is self-sustaining. Any new measures or targets from the review are agreed based on organizationwide understanding of what is required to improve performance. Should performance gaps be identified, corrective action plans always result, monitored weekly for progress.

As an example of how potential problems are avoided, prevention based feedback loops are built into all process where operations are empowered to stop the line at any stage if they are failing to perform within required limits or targets. Proactivity in process improvement is also enabled by D2D's computerized quality modeling system, which helps users understand optimum performance levels compared with actual results. "What if" analysis demonstrates the effects of any proposed changes. As to specific line measures which have strategic dimensions, the costs of nonconformance is one example, particularly as profit margins in the electronics components market are relatively slim. At D2D, these costs were halved between 1989 and 1997 as a percentage of revenue, along with manufacturing set-up speeds and time to volume production. Total productive maintenance measures, such as overall equipment efficiency, are also used by manufacturing teams.

Another significant tool is statistical process control in building and assembly processes, which used a standard process capability index of targets of 1.6 in 1991. This implies a failure rate of less than 3 parts per million, which over 60 percent of business processes were meeting by 1997. Achievement of this order is as much a case of awareness and understanding as a business-focused measurement. Supervisors report on quality as much as they do for schedules, which helps drive responsibility, ownership, an understanding of the measures, and the requirement for corrective actions right down the line. Their teams appreciate the business imperatives of change.

Related to the people satisfaction criterion of the EFQM model, employee morale is also monitored through absenteeism, turnover, and teamwork involvement measures. In addition, an annual opinion survey allows staff to comment on their own performance, pay issues, manager's styles, the working environment, and the business itself. The results are compared with other organizations, with feedback being used in business planning. As one example, a staff perception that communications were poor (confirmed buy the comparative studies discussed previously) resulted in more frequent management-employee face-to-face communications and team briefings and better internal publications.

The EFQM's impacts on society measures particularly relate to D2D's environmental performance, which is accredited to BS 7750 and ISO

14001 standards. Measures ion this area include energy use, waste to landfill, recycling, precious metal recovery, and so on.

One final point is worth highlighting on the monthly management reviews, given business pressures and increasingly heavy executive workloads. Should a top-level meeting fail to take place for whatever reason, statistical handouts, which are always prepared in advance, are still published and disseminated, along with corrective action plans, which are recommended and ready for implementation. These can start without top team approval.

The Effects of Change

Despite the obvious gains already cited, embedding cultural change and creating a climate of focused performance measurement has been far from easy. It takes a long time and has to be sold to the workforce. You can pressure people to do things, but if these activities have no special value in their eyes, then most initiatives will die.

D2D has also found that setting of targets can lead to conflicts. In one instance, the managing director and the HR specialists agreed to a 100 percent increase in training provision for a particular department, yet a few days later the program's funding was agreed to with a limited and insufficient training budget. Issues like these can be sensibly resolved by assessing the business benefits and needs against what can actually be afforded. Policy states that D2D must have, on average, a certain number of days of training per person per year, which, if provided externally, would be very costly. Consequently, the firm must become innovative in training provisions to meet both policy and financial requirements.

The key lesson here is that there must be a will to achieve. If managers and employees value training, they will want it, not just because there are business benefits in terms of increased flexibility and commitment, but also for career progression, job satisfaction, and motivation. Getting to that level of understanding and commitment takes time but is fundamental to success.

Customer Scorecard

One specific set of measures with strategic dimensions, which has directly shaped D2D's business performance in recent years, has been the scorecard system for assessing and analyzing customer satisfaction. This derived from the division's original relationship with Sun Microsystems, the U.S. high-performance workstation supplier and D2D's first major external customer.

In 1990, Sun had begun to purchase PCBs from D2D based on contract standards already well articulated and understood within ICL. On-time delivery and quality are two examples of these standards. However, over time, it became clear that Sun was unhappy with other areas of performance, such as responsiveness to changes in product design, technological achievement, and service support. Sun insisted on its supplier scorecard being introduced, which went far beyond conventional performance measures in the electronics supply sector. Each quarter, a range of customer satisfaction requirements had to be met under its concept of total cost of ownership in five areas: quality, delivery, technology, service support, and price.

To comply with Sun's requirements, D2D reorganized its manufacturing into team-based operations and converted traditional production lines into customer focus teams. Each is dedicated to the needs of a particular client, coordinating closely to act as an *internal outpost* of that customer's operations in D2D's manufacturing plant.

Developing from this, the customer ethic has been substantially reinforced at the business and operational levels. First, D2D policy is to continually refine, review, understand, and manage customer relationships, using gap analysis between customer perceptions and actual satisfaction to drive performance improvement. As two examples, the organization has achieved a 99.8 percent delivery performance and customer complaints, as in a faulty part, for instance, are responded to within one day, 100 percent of the time.

Second, while quality circles, corrective action, and process improvement teams have operated for many years, a network of customer care or support teams was also introduced in the early 1990s. This concept was extended into two additional dimensions during 1994 and 1995: the customer focus team noted above comprising an entire production line, as in Sun's case, and a customer-focused factory that allocates time and space to process teams.

The effect of introducing the scorecard across the entire business has been all-encompassing and drives D2D's competitive difference. The firm has advanced failure analysis facilities on site that would be superfluous if they were a conventional contract manufacturer. Rapid and detailed analysis helps provide an added value service appreciated by customers, which more than pays for itself in the long run. For similar reasons, D2D has maintained a strong information technology infrastructure, the depth and extent of which enhances performance in areas such as inventory control, materials management, and analysis capability, which helps facilitate improved customer service.

Scorecard Developments

D2D uses individually tailored versions of the scorecard with all its major customers, even though immediate acceptance of the technique among them is rare. A common initial response has been for them to ask what they want it for, despite the competitive importance to business planning of customer feedback on pricing, delivery mechanisms, and future developments. They have to explain, persuade, and convince them of the business benefits to both parties. From D2D's point of view, if the firm only works on its perceptions of what the customer wants, mistakes can easily be made. With hard data from the scorecard, D2D can avoid these mistakes and be sure of adding value.

Given the strategic importance of the scorecard, D2D has developed a simplified version to use with its own suppliers. A vendor rating scheme was first introduced in the late 1980s, when the then division implemented just-in-time manufacturing processes. However, this developed as D2D accumulated more information and feedback from its close customer relationship with Sun Microsystems.

The scorecard adaptation is now called the Vendor Accreditation Scheme (VAS). All the organization's over 150 key suppliers have a VAS place, which is guided and supported by teams in D2D and, as with Sun, outstanding performance is recognized through an annual award scheme. Though minor suppliers rarely adopt a VAS, they are still monitored through its criteria.

This form of supplier alliance is essential to cost effectiveness and is an important element of D2D's continuous improvement process. Delivery quality today is to guarantee a failure rate below 10 parts per million, something that was not achievable fifteen years ago.

External Comparisons

Benchmarking has been widely practised within D2D for many years and at different levels. Pairing through benchmarking clubs and circles does not, however, tend to offer the most appropriate of matches. Nonetheless, it does not pay to be too choosy, as you can learn from anyone and the cost of a reciprocal relationship is not very onerous.

However, much effort at D2D is spent on developing more structured and selective pairing relationships, both to ensure the likelihood of a worthwhile fit and to accurately assess the type or level of information needed in the first place. This means asking searching questions. For example, if delivery quality is being assessed, D2D can share information with other organizations on, for instance, percentage failure rates. In order for external measurement to be meaningful in practice, D2D would insist ion knowing what was meant by *fail*, which tests were in place at which facilities, how an application was run, and the level of problem or difficulty that triggered a fail verdict. Similar questions would be posed if a potential partner sought to exchange data on the results of customer satisfaction measurement.

There is a certain level of understanding or differentiation that has to be made when trying to compare performance with competing or noncompeting organizations. Key factors include having baseline measures, knowing how they are calculated, and understanding the connections with your own measures. Measuring itself against external comparators is not something D2D can claim as a core capability. Like all process measurement over time, it has become endemic. The benchmarking process only becomes significantly noticeable if inconsistencies appear or if it is not done at all.

NOTES

1. D. Lascelles and R. Peacock, *Self-Assessment for Business Excellence* (Maidenhead, U.K.: McGraw-Hill, 1996).

2. European Foundation for Quality Management, *Being Leaders of Change: How to Move from Process Mapping to Process Management*, Working Group Report (Brussels: EFQM, 1996).

3. Federal Quality Institute, *High Performance Organizations in Federal Agencies* (Gaithersburg, MD: Author, 1994).

6

Customer Measurement: Strategic Issues, Best Practice, and New Dimensions

STRATEGIC ISSUES AND RESPONSE

Key Questions and Issues

Donald Peterson, former chairman of Ford Motor Company, could have spoken for any business leader worldwide whose organization is intent on customer homage when he said, "If we aren't customer-driven, our cars won't be either." A significant development was the QS 9000 world automotive supplier standard jointly devised with General Motors and Chrysler. Two imperatives of doing business with this type of customer are 100 percent just-in-time component deliveries and a maximum of 250 parts per million rejects. As the global giants reposition themselves to secure buyer loyalty, the customer is calling the tune.

The United Kingdom's financial services sector has similar pressures. Mike Jackson, chief executive of Birmingham Midshires Building Society, an exemplar in its holistic approach to customer measurement and performance, has his home telephone number on monthly customer questionnaires in case complainants wish to go to the top. Over a million questionnaires have been distributed in the last five years under two unifying catchphrases: "First Choice" and "Recognised for Excellence." Now, since a recent strategic review, Jackson's executive group is formally titled the Customer Relationship Team, which sends out strong internal signals. Monthly satisfaction, dissatisfaction, defection, and retention information lands on his desk, resulting in the following questions: What do they tell us? How will we respond? Who will take action?

Research in North America confirms the importance of customer satisfaction to senior executives, as shown in the late 1995 *Survey of American Business Leaders* by Deloitte & Touche.[1] Over 200 executives in Fortune 1000 companies were asked to name their biggest challenges. Global competition and workforce productivity were the top two, and 75 percent of executives cited customer service as the primary internal solution or critical success factor.

These examples provide the following valuable insights:

- Competitive pressures force a continual refocusing on customers as critical factors in mid- to long-term corporate success.
- The organization has to be aligned behind an easily understandable vision.
- Leadership personally and visibly drives the customer imperative.
- Appropriate customer measurement is a strategic issue.

Customer measurement cannot simply be considered in terms of effort or achieved by applying the best possible metrics, as believed and practiced by some organizations. This is demonstrated by a further example cited by Whiteley and Hessan.[2] A US$30 million office services client committed to "becoming the most customer-driven organization in its industry and world-class at understanding customers." A battery of 105 separate customer measures or research activities was rapidly deployed, engaging 200 employees in 17 departments and costing close to US$1 million. At the end of year one, customer retention decreased by 10 percent and satisfaction levels by 5 percent.

Analysis of these results revealed two problems. First, data collection was uncoordinated with repeated duplications and customers began to complain about being asked similar questions by different people (albeit for different purposes). Second, measurement infrequently triggered a response since only 27 percent of customer feedback was acted upon. Forty-three percent of the employees involved kept data to themselves. The story begs certain key questions:

- Why is customer measurement being used?
- What will change as a result?
- How will action be shaped?
- Who facilitates this, and has the organization the capability to respond?

The most crucial question, of coures, is the last.

Research Indicators

A 1995 benchmark research project by the then Coopers & Lybrand's Toronto-based Center for Excellence in Customer Satisfaction addressed the issue of how customer measurement helps create product differentiation and customer value. Called *IDEAS—Innovative Approaches to Deliver Excellence through Improved Customer Practice and Total Quality Service*, the study quizzed 1,800 organizations in the United States and Canada that were engaged in retailing, manufacturing, services, and hospitality about their philosophies, internal practices, external influences, and tools for improving customer satisfaction.[3]

After noting that in the 1980s, customers generally defined value as price and quality, the report reveals that value is now perceived in terms of supplier relationships, flexibility, and capability. Respondents surveyed customers in the following areas:

- Complaint-handling effectiveness, 84 percent
- Customer satisfaction, 74 percent
- Customer needs, 65 percent
- Conformance to standards and specifications, 50 percent
- New product ideas, 47 percent

Three quarters of those companies surveyed internally measured themselves against competitors, and 53 percent compared competitive performance relative to specific customers or their needs. Of the respondents who claimed that customer satisfaction had improved over the previous year, 45 percent benchmark with superior performers.

Significantly, the study found, this group was not satisfied with measuring just to confirm the customer performance status quo; indeed, 30 percent now focused on:

- Completely understanding customers, markets, and competitors
- Adopting process benchmarking and reengineering for customer-related processes
- Redesigning order fulfilment, billing, and complaints systems
- Strengthening account and sales force management

The center also found that the most successful organizations typically emphasized five points to create an internal service culture, improve customer satisfaction, and facilitate retention:

- Employee communication, needs assessments, skills reviews, and levels of job satisfaction, all of which contribute to customer well-being

- Senior management's visible commitment to a service culture
- Customer input to help set service standards
- Ensuring that employees actually apply best practices
- Backing the customer ethos through training, recognition, and incentives.

Underpinning these integrated, more holistic approaches to customer measurement is a fundamental belief that a causal relationship exists among customer satisfaction, loyalty, market share, revenues, and profits.

Reichheld and Sasser, researchers who demonstrated that a 5 percent increase in customer loyalty could improve profits by between 25 and 85 percent, first articulated this idea.[4] The implication, they said, was that quality of market share for customer loyalty is strategically as important as quantity of market share. European research reinforces the same point. A study by the European Foundation for Quality Management (EFQM) concluded that customer loyalty, but not customer satisfaction, was a key driver of bottom line performance.[5]

Over the longer term, customer retention significantly increases profits, in some sectors by 400 percent over a five-year period. Loyal customers also help generate new business because they act as advocates, the study found. In addition, some sources suggested that half of all new customers came from their existing loyal customers' recommendations. Significantly, however, the study argued that customer satisfaction may be no more than an important success factor and not be enough to guarantee business growth or profitability, contrary to a widely held view that it is a performance driver. EFQM's customer loyalty research team reasons that traditional, customer-focused organizations do not take account of customer reactions to market dynamics or competitor performance. To be effective, customer measurement has to become dynamic in itself.

The following examples support this point. Telecommunications giant AT&T experienced a loss of 6 percent market share, despite its customer satisfaction levels reaching 95 percent, and, as noted later in this chapter, Rank Xerox discovered that almost one-quarter of "very satisfied" customers may not necessarily repurchase. The organization has since deployed a range of innovative customer loyalty initiatives and measurements. Clearly, these findings imply the need for a strategic review of what drives customer value and loyalty. Guidelines come from Heskett, Jones, Loveman, Sasser, and Schlesinger in their Service Profit Chain model,[6] which highlights key relationships and drivers:

- Customer satisfaction drives customer loyalty.
- Value drives customer satisfaction.

- Employee productivity drives value.
- Employee loyalty drives productivity.
- Internal quality drives employee satisfaction.

In practice, these researchers say, leadership is the critical enabling factor (something that is easy to say but difficult to demonstrate) and in ensuring the drivers are effectively managed and resourced. A division of Corning Inc., which has introduced strategic and process-driven dimensions to customer measurement, exemplifies this approach.

CORNING TPD: STRATEGIC CUSTOMER MEASUREMENT

Corning Telecommunications Products Division (TPD), world-leading fiber optics manufacturer and Malcolm Baldrige Award winner in 1995, is driven by its Customer Response System. This is a unique combination of processes which identify, collect, and improve on customer expectations. They also align with 6 vital few processes, 50 core business processes, and about 800 more that support day-to-day operations.

As explained in the case study in Chapter 3, TPD's customers are cable manufacturers, their end users, and other joint venture companies. They benefit from two customer-related goals, high satisfaction levels and customer satisfaction relative to competitors. The division's measurement process focuses on three elements:

- Gathering customer requirements and measuring satisfaction levels
- Data storage, access and retrieval
- Analysis and prioritizing through corrective actions and special initiatives that provide feedback to customers

Three forms of measurement determine satisfaction, process or performance improvements and competitive comparisons:

- The Customer Report Card, a quarterly, internal rating system to evaluate TPD's performance against its seven customer satisfaction criteria:
  - Product technology leadership
  - Responsive commercial support
  - Knowledgeable technical support
  - Simple, reliable ordering processes
  - Consistently improved and reliable product quality

- Responsive supply, on-time delivery, adequate supply, and similar criteria
- Price and value

- Customer Total Value process, a more comprehensive customer feedback process for larger strategic customers, who account for over 70 percent of sales and require satisfaction in four value areas. Customers themselves prepare feedback and share it face-to-face with cross-functional account teams at TPD. Any shortcomings or new requirements result in corrective actions or process improvements in critical performance areas. The value areas are:
  - Performance value
  - Quality systems value
  - Business contribution value
  - Supplier value

- The Customer Value Assessments, a third party measurement using special techniques. Cable buyers and their end users are independently interviewed on behalf of the division to evaluate products, services, and customer-contact functions relative to competitors. Up to 300 of these surveys are conducted annually to accurately depict customer expectations and perceptions.

Using these means, TPD achieves outstanding business results. Product returns from reels of fiber optic cable are below 250 parts per million, 92 percent of customers rate the division as "excellent to very good," and in the last five years, it has never failed to provide customer requests for quotations in four hours or under. Managing and evaluating its own supplier performance is also crucial for TPD, depending on the supplier's potential impact on customers, performance, and business success. Suppliers are segregated into critical or noncritical levels under the Supplier Total Value process. Each is measured in terms of performance, quality systems, technology contribution, value, and price.

Total quality performance against our goals and measures means understanding who the customers are, analyzing their requirements, and meeting those requirements better than anyone else, without error, on time every time. Behind TPD's integrated customer measurement processes (developed over almost 17 years, it has to be said) are three strategic considerations:

- Only by meeting or anticipating customer requirements does the firm sustain global leadership.
- Regular, multisourced, and multimedia customer feedback determines whether performance expectations are being met.

- Shortcomings or opportunities for continuous improvement are addressed immediately through corrective actions.

Another important success factor has been a constant customer focus from the Executive Leadership Team to unite people around a common set of understandings, along with frequent internal reviews to ensure the focus remains sharp.

REVIEWING CUSTOMER MEASUREMENT

Shifting Internal Mindsets

Although not all companies may aspire to world-class leadership or a Baldrige award, most would benefit from at least a strategic review of customer measurement. At the minimum, this acts as a health check or is the first step toward a new customer focus.

Speaking at the 1995 Association for Quality and Participation annual conference,[7] Sharafat Khan, a consultant with Arthur Andersen's International Management Group in Michigan, suggested that a comprehensive road map of customer measurements is essential. It helps to manage service more effectively because traditional methods typically deliver disappointing results. Khan cited three reasons:

- Customer data is not used to improve business operations.
- Concepts, standards, measurements, and tools are often misunderstood.
- The connections between customer service and providing value are unclear.

A shift in attitude toward service management should have a systemic effect on the entire organization. Service is no longer the domain of a customer department but means every employee has to see the job through the eyes of the customers. This strategic orientation, with appropriate tactical alignment, will result in profitability.

On the same conference platform, Bruce Murray, principal of the Change Management Group, took a skeptical view of customer measurement based on his own experiences.

Most companies believe they are customer-focused, pointing to high marks from customer satisfaction surveys as proof they are meeting customers' needs. In fact, the number accomplishing this successfully is much smaller than it appears because leaders believe they know what customers want, what drives their buying decisions and what must be done to satisfy them. Often, they are wrong.[8]

Murray cited a striking example. An organization in the United States required nine to twelve days between order receipt and shipment of its semicustomized technology products. Management refused to believe that customers valued fast delivery, even though 25 percent of orders required response times of forty-eight to seventy-two hours. Because the organization could not meet delivery expectations, 20 percent of customers did not repurchase. The point is that what matters most to customers is not necessarily what the supplier expects or thinks is important. This is demonstrated by Milliken European Division, covered later in this chapter. The Larry Kishpaugh, manager of Customer Service with Corning Inc., catchphrase of "listening to and learning from customers" also applies.

Murray's view is that the business strategies of world-class companies are directed by an understanding of customer values, which shapes short-term operating plans and any customer-related projects. World-class companies determine:

- What customers themselves value
- Their buying motivations
- Why they are attracted to particular suppliers
- What makes them loyal

It asks that organization to visualize what they must look like in three to five years to satisfy those values. This leads to strategy development, which, in turn, focuses on the right places to devote resources for maximizing customer value. However, the key is that only customers know the right answers to what is of value. Customers need to have the opportunity to specify how they perceive value at the outset. This may allow the organizaiton to ask the right questions in the right way to gain greater insight into what customers see as value.

The kind of process organizations use when reviewing customer measurement is essential to understanding the whole evaluation process in the first place. You have to think like customers by examining the entire process from their point of view to see what type of problems or opportunities may emerge. However, deciding on, and then measuring, what is important to customers raises a potential problem because it entails negotiation. The first question to consider is whether satisfaction should be measured internally or by using an external agency. (Though in many cases, customers are insightful and will tell you if given half a chance.)

When reviewing customer measurement, it is crucial to get definitions right. For example, if a customer says it is important to deliver on time, what is meant by on-time delivery? If this is required by Tuesday and can only be delivered on Friday, is that on time from the supplier's point of view or three days late for the customer?

Textiles and fabrics manufacturer Milliken European Division experienced the problem of on-time deliveries after analyzing its first customer satisfaction survey over ten years ago. Assuming that shipping performance was good because quality requirements were usually met and no one had complained about delivery, only 77.7 percent of deliveries were, in fact, on time from the customer's point of view. After rapid corrective action, the figure reached 90 percent just nine months later and is now 99.9 percent. Until the first survey, the firm had not really asked customers what mattered to them.

More precise customer measurement followed which revealed that on-time delivery to customers meant when they actually received products, not when despatched. Also, Milliken found that the dates promised may not have been those preferred by customers in the first place.

An Aligned Customer Measurement Process

Gathering and using customer or organizational information to drive performance is an aligned customer measurement process. There are two critical issues:

- The first is measurement, because customer satisfaction is difficult to define and harder to measure.
- The second, often discovered by organizations that find reasonably effective ways to measure satisfaction, is that it is a weak predictor of customer loyalty and competitive advantage.

The underlying problem is that customer satisfaction is the wrong business objective because this analysis must be concrete, expressed in customer behaviors and not abstract customer attitudes. Practical examples include increases in customer retention, annual revenue per customer, customer referrals, and so on. However it is important that any objectives should be strong predictors of bottom-line business results. The key for promoting desired customer behaviors is the degree to which an organization meets expectations that build value for the customer, from the latter's point of view. This approach is an excellent strategy for obtaining superior business results such as improved profitability, increased retention, better customer acquisition, faster cycle times, and higher employee morale. This capability rests on accurate and detailed accounting of those expectations, which is woefully lacking in most companies because they do not capture and use the customer's voice on a systematic basis.

The need for a "laser beam customer focus" that is pure business strategy, avoids distractions, sheds noncore activities, decides which customer should or should not be serviced, and create a sense of purpose must be continually stressed. Relating this focus to the customer measurement process involves two initial stages:

- Gathering data from three sources: casual or anecdotal; formal as in surveys, interviews and research; and direct customer inputs from complaints or inquiries
- Accurately analyzing and integrating data as the basis for creating outputs

Customer measurement should then result in eight interrelated outputs:

- Set business strategy and policy.
- Evaluate, manage, and reward performance.
- Set improvement priorities.
- Improve processes and systems.
- Respond promptly and openly to customer problems and requests.
- Manage customer relationships.
- Develop and enhance products and services.
- Educate and train employees.

Customer measures should guide at least three kinds of decisions and actions: strategic, or what the senior team has to consider and act on; operational, what the firm should do more or less of or do better in terms of performance; and behavioral, how the firm should interact with customers to meet their expectations.

Solectron Corporation: Customer Measurement Process

Ever since 1985, Californian-based integrated electronics manufacturer Solectron Corporation has asked this question: How do we meet customers' expectations? That year, Solectron introduced dedicated customer satisfaction initiatives. Now, customer measurement is an integrated process of four elements:

- Customer Satisfaction Index (CSI)
- Customer Complaint Resolution Process (CCRP)
- Customer Expectations Program
- Thursday Morning Forum, a weekly meeting of one hundred executives, managers, and customers to discuss complaints

Solectron has eighty-four customers, including IBM, Apple Computer, and Hewlett-Packard, and has tripled market share between 1992 and 1994. Over the same period, customer complaints dropped from

958 to 460 and customer satisfaction rose to 92.44 percent, from 89.91 percent in 1992. Customer feedback has been used as an improvement tool since 1985, with the Customer Satisfaction Index (CSI) measurement and reporting system being redeveloped over a four-year period since that time. Apart from giving management essential data, this also helps to confirm the corporation's competitive positioning. Significantly, much preliminary work had to be done before a sophisticated index could be considered.

Solectron surveys all customers weekly, mostly via e-mail, and analyzes trends from the results. Customers grade a division with which they work in four areas, quality, service, delivery, and communication, and also give verbal comments. All feedback results in action if required. It is important that a customer interface group of sales representatives and project managers will network with certain customers between one and four times daily, or even ten times a day during specific projects. Remarkably, since 1991, response rates for CSI surveys have ranged from 96.18 percent to 97.28 percent, whereas the industry average is around 27 percent. Moreover, to help reinforce the importance of the CSI with customers, customer expectations meetings are held annually. This is all part of a Customer Expectations Program introduced in 1995, which sets expectations for performance and quality thresholds once a year using a cross-functional team of engineers, managers, and planners at the corporation, plus customers themselves. The team focuses on ten areas:

- Quality
- Delivery
- Communication
- Service
- Technology
- Technical support
- Price/cost
- Invoicing
- Cycle time
- Documentation

Customer needs are determined and evaluated at this annual meeting. Customers tell Solectron what they require, and Solectron tells them what its capability is. It is better to be honest regarding any capacity limitations there might be rather than disappointing customers later.

Solectron has tracked the number of customer complaints and grades since 1990, following the introduction of its Customer Complaint Resolution Process (CCRP) a year earlier. This is triggered whenever a division receives a C grade or lower or when a major concern is repeatedly revealed. The responsible project manager must then present a report, with root cause analysis and an action plan to rectify the problem, at the Thursday Morning Forum. The agreed plan is then presented back to the complaining customer within seventy-two hours. The forum is the centerpiece of Solectron's internal feedback system for disseminating customer information. Typically lasting an hour, it covers daily quality status reports, weekly CSI updates, and any CCRP presentations, including questions and answers.

Despite many national, state, and outstanding supplier awards, the corporation believes long-term relationships with customers are more important than recognition, as strong retention figures are its link between customer satisfaction and business results, it has supplied IBM for 20 years, Hewlett-Packard for 18 years and Sun Microsystems, Apple Computer, and Exabyte for 15 years.

The Solectron report concluded with the following key learning points for any organization reviewing customer measurement or related processes:

- Problems or complaints must be identified quickly, with customers being updated on the progress of any response.
- Senior management involvement is essential.
- Employee training and communication are critical to ensure that everyone understands the importance of customer measurement.
- Finally, continuity must be apparent for any customer measurement program; it cannot be something that is done once in a while.

Examining Customer Satisfaction and Feedback

While not all organizations will be as advanced as Solectron Corporation in its customer measurement processes (albeit from a small, 80-plus customer base), most will measure customer satisfaction and dissatisfaction in one way or another. At times, this practice can appear to be little more than checklists and crude ratings. However, in some organizations, customer feedback is a critical matter, definitely tied to business objectives and results. For example, customer feedback is a primary contributor to competitive advantage at the medium-sized European carrier, SAS Scandinavian Airlines, which flew nearly 19 million passengers to 105 destinations in 34 countries in 1995. With so many passengers, there is always a risk that a customer will become part of the mass. To avoid this problem, when measuring and recording data about travel patterns and issues, SAS uses an individualized, personal approach, knowing who the customers are, their experiences when traveling SAS, and how SAS can respond with the respect they deserve. The airline places great emphasis on measuring customer satisfaction using traditional survey methods. They are complementary measures to monitor performance rather than being used to originate action. Its principal tool is an annual performance survey, which helps compile the airline's Satisfied Customer Index.[9] This rates the relative importance of issues such as service quality, punctuality, reliability, staff welcomes, cabin efficiency, and aircraft comfort. In addition, customer panels and special focus groups discuss particular issues or projects and the airline's top one hundred executives each have a personal customer from the frequent flyer program whom they meet quarterly[10] for direct feedback on service quality and performance. A structured feedback tool is being devised to make more effective use of these comments.

By studying behaviors, SAS reasons that significant insights occur on how passengers should be treated, which will eventually have an impact on satisfaction and loyalty. Also, functional design for check-in areas, lounges, departure gates, and aircraft interiors can be reconfigured following this unusual form of feedback. Along with customer surveys, this technique contributes to small and large changes in service delivery that will, in total, create a positive impact on service quality and customer perceptions.

Birmingham Midshires Building Society takes a holistic approach to customer feedback, which is strongly integrated with corporate priorities and business strategy. Customer measurement is one set in a hierarchy of performance measures and is part of the society's Total Customer Management process. Eight sources of feedback are used, as detailed in this chapter's case study. Monthly customer satisfaction questionnaires are a primary measure and usually generate a 20 percent response. Data is collected and analyzed by the corporate quality unit, with critical information or trends being highlighted for the customer loyalty and retention team. Satisfaction levels, complaints, and defections are three examples. Data is also incorporated into monthly, quarterly, and annual customer performance and service reports for the board and around fifty business or team leaders.

Where appropriate, as in the case of complaints, reporting is followed through by action. For example, 10 percent of complaints from one early survey in 1991 related to low interest on obsolete accounts. At a cost of £13 million over a two-year period, 660,000 deposits were upgraded, removing a significant source of customer dissatisfaction. This enhanced the customers' trust in the society and helped brand building because it was first to market with this type of initiative.

The customer survey process is a continuous "listening and learning loop" of four stages, measurement, internal communication, action, and feedback, which has significantly reduced complaints. In 1992, 4,532 complaints were received from their 860,000 customers, versus the 1995 figures of 1,883 complaints out of 1,012,000 customers. Every complaint is pursued until resolved.

One customer measurement initiative that The Forum Corporation conducted with an Australian chemical organization resulted in accurately defining customer expectations as primary drivers of repurchasing and retention results. This was a top-level strategic objective for the business. To help implement customer-driven measurements, the Forum project included executive and employee customer focus assessments, six customer focus groups with buyers of chemical products, seven structured interviews among distributors, and a telephone survey of 60 percent of the account base. The focus groups used nominal group techniques[11] to reveal customer expectations, which helped build a customer expectations map and were also used to structure the telephone survey.

Based on this multisourced feedback, the organization identified priorities for process improvement and, especially, complaint handling. It discovered that customers were 127 percent more likely to repurchase if a problem occurred and was satisfactorily resolved than if no problem had occurred in the first place. Also, findings indicated that meeting customer expectations would increase revenues by 14 percent.

These examples indicate important considerations for examining customer feedback. First, you must never assume an arrival point, as for this form of measure to be effective, it must be a continuous improvement process. Second, you must be innovative in approaches. Third, customer measurement should ideally be a self-repeating loop, with effort and outcomes aligned to corporate priorities and business strategy.

Measurement Trends and Limitations

Although research indicates that a toolkit approach to measuring customer satisfaction is widespread, it also highlights shortcomings in application, a fact which is confirmed by experienced advisers. For example, the report *Managing the Management Tools* was based on surveying a 3,000-member sample for insights into corporate toolkits, their applications, and executive preferences.[12] The methodology's portfolio of twenty-five tools included two dedicated to customer measurement-satisfaction surveys and customer retention initiatives.

Surveys were the second most popular tool among U.K. managers for three quarters of respondents, after, intriguingly, mission and vision statements, and customer retention ranked eighth in importance. Approximately half the respondents reported they used this method, but without citing specific approaches.

Cross-cultural contrasts are also revealing from the report's top ten listing. Customer satisfaction scored tenth for North American executives and first among Europeans, did not appear in the list for Asians. Retention initiatives were eighth in North America and lower than tenth in both Europe and Asia.

Too many companies ask a couple of simple questions on whether their customers are, or are not, satisfied and ask for a performance rating on a scale of one to five. This does not provide any meaningful information whatsoever. Advances in measurement technology mean that it is now possible to ask very specific, scientific questions that can accurately measure satisfaction levels and predict the likelihood of loyal behavior.

A similar misgiving was one conclusion in *Managing the Measure*, from the Cranfield Service Operations Club at the University of Cranfield in the United Kingdom. This report established what primary measures of business success over 50 U.K. companies in financial services, retailing, leisure, utilities and telecommunications were using.[13] In order of importance, the "most mentioned" measures were the following:

- Financial, 78 mentions (profit and general financial were the main two)
- Customer satisfaction/service, 51 mentions including customer satisfaction, performance against published standards, retention levels, mystery customer schemes, customer feedback, complaints, and external reviews or recognition
- Productivity, efficiency, and effectiveness, 14 mentions
- Quality, 10 mentions

The report made three observations distilled from the findings. First, though customer satisfaction measures were included in a repertoire of key performance indicators (KPIs), first and foremost organizations tended to measure those activities that were easy to measure. Second, there was an overlap between customer-focused and quality measures, principally because of a lack of clarity in definition. Third, fourteen respondents experienced conflicts in KPI achievement, four of which related to customers:

- Cost against customer service or quality
- Profit versus customer service
- Customer service and productivity
- Conflicting interests of shareholders, customers, and employees

Of note is that four triggers, customer research (69 percent), the business planning cycle (64 percent), crisis (14 percent) and industry standards (8 percent), drove revisions to defined levels of customer service, such as KPIs and targets, as a result of feedback. Also, the survey found that customer complaints acted as a corporate barometer, or early warning system, or to provide general feedback on improvement opportunities.

Customer satisfaction surveys are, in effect, performance report cards for measuring or studying trends, spotting improvement gaps, and "taking a customer's temperature," usually against self-selected or predetermined criteria. This is a limitation, as customer surveys are useful for continuously monitoring performance but, unfortunately, too often become a crutch to show that a organization is "doing fine" instead of being a real analysis tool.

If users develop this type of survey, criteria must be included that are meaningful to customers, not just those an organization has grown accustomed to looking at. It is also important to first offer significant questions and then analyze data carefully to avoid obscuring any real meanings.

British Telecom: Evolution of Customer Measurement

British Telecom (BT) has taken the customer measurement evolution route, but only decided to do so in the early 1990s, despite having a long history of using performance measurement. This used to be internally focused, reflecting its own capabilities rather than customer requirements, and was duplicated nationwide, as confirmed by its own research. From once being structured around twenty-nine geographic districts according to local priorities, each catering to similar customer needs, BT is now organized into three redefined, national, customer-oriented divisions: global companies, national business, and residential.

Customer service is BT's competitive differentiator. Telecommunications have become mission-critical because service disruption can have potentially devastating consequences; thus, customer confidence is essential. The National Business Communications Unit serves all sizes of U.K. business and has around 1.5 million customers with considerably varying needs, all of which must be understood to deliver service and engender confidence. Building customer relationships and measuring their performance from a customer's point of view have become essential tools for long-term survival.

Although new measures were introduced to pinpoint critical and noncritical repairs and record completion speeds, the overriding customer requirement is for a resilient, "no-break" service. Customers want reliability, so if the basics of resilience are not right, you are not in the game. These are hard needs, which can be exceeded by focusing on softer service issues to engender customer loyalty. Newer measures of reliability now emphasize understanding customer requirements at the service design stage, which was never a priority in the past. To facilitate this, the unit now coordinates an ongoing program of qualitative and quantitative customer surveys, targeted at specific customer segments. Performance measures for each customer are therefore different and individually tailored.

One tool being used to understand the different performance dimensions of customer requirements is the Lochridge 5 technique. This model was originally devised as a framework of so-called SERVQUAL attributes by Parasuraman[14] and features five service qualities that must be met to satisfy customer needs:

- Assurance
- Responsiveness
- Tangibles
- Empathy
- Reliability[15]

In practice, a BT account manager discusses which of these dimensions is significant to a customer and then creates performance indicators for each relevant dimension. For instance, some companies ask that service engineers always report to security, involving the empathy dimension, whereas others seek a no-break service under the reliability dimension. Specific sets of measures are then listed in dimension priority order. These requirements are analyzed by a BT team to produce an action plan and specific targets for customer approval. Independent market research and account managers monitor performance against this plan through qualitative surveys. The latter also review performance and priorities every quarter with internal service providers. However, with over 1 million volume customers, face-to-face interviews or tailored service development plans cannot be applied to all, so monthly random surveys sample more general levels of satisfaction.

Event-driven surveys are also used monthly for over 1,100 customers across the U.K. who have had a recent service provision or repair. Conducted independently of British Telecom, this measure takes customers through questions to test satisfaction levels at different stages, from initial contact to work completion. It ensures that appropriate performance indicators are still being used, but could also result in significant process, technology, or service redesigns if shortcomings are revealed.

Because of the resulting volume of data, links can be traced between customer satisfaction and specific aspects of any service. This allows BT to present first-line managers with customer satisfaction ratings and direct feedback on what customers think of their team's service.

EVALUATING CUSTOMER VALUE
AND PROFITABILITY: THE VALUE
AND PROFITABILITY ISSUES

The underpinning theme of this chapter so far is that customer satisfaction drives desired customer buying behaviors, retention, and loyalty, which, in turn, contributes to business health and greater profits by as much as 25–85 percent. Conversely, customer defection can hit the bottom line, as demonstrated by the office services organization example earlier in this chapter, where 20 percent of customers did not repurchase because of delivery misperceptions.[16] Furthermore, quality of customer or market share, multisourced feedback, and response to complaints are crucial considerations. The focus should be on some interpretation of customer value as a foundation for enhanced profits or business growth.

For example, Birmingham Midshires Building Society has different interpretations of value. As noted previously, by upgrading interest on obsolete accounts, customer dissatisfaction was removed, trust improved, and market leadership was secured. Appreciably, nine out of ten "highly satisfied" customers said they would recommend the society to family, friends, or colleagues.

Loyalty levels are of great significance. The society has computed that, if the performance measure for "exceeding expectations" were improved by 1 percent, it could expect £50 of increased lifetime revenue per customer. Aggregated over a seven-year period for its current base of 1 million customers, an additional £50 million worth of business would result.[17] Such a wide range in customer value is not unusual. The best customer segments often are more than ten times as profitable as the worst parts. Moreover, 20–25 percent of customers account for 60–80 percent of industry revenues.

European research highlights similar potential. According to a report in *European Quality*, the Swedish Customer Satisfaction Barometer, an annual macroeconomic index which measures the experiences of 35,000 consumers, has also been applied to the micro level of organizations appearing in the top levels of the published index.[18] It is worth recalling that the 1996 EFQM customer loyalty research project concluded that customer retention could increase profits by up to four times more in some sectors over a five-year period. Also, loyal customers, as in the case of Birmingham Midshires, generate new business.

The extent to which fifty-two service-led U.K. companies evaluated customer value, profitability, and servicing costs was tested by research for the *Managing the Measures* report mentioned previously.[19] Its findings are significant:

- Less than half (44 percent) measure the value of a particular customer, with most calculating this on an annual basis as profit, spending, or value per year, five measuring lifetime value and some measuring only the value of major accounts.
- Less than one third (29 percent) measure the value of lost customers, some said they link order cancelation to new business ratios, others evaluate lost revenue or measure repurchasing intentions.
- Only 35 percent measure the cost of servicing a particular customer, especially in the banking sector; calculations generally take the form of a mean average of time spent on particular types of customer.
- Only 21 percent of respondents said they could demonstrate a link between customer satisfaction and profitability, a further 28 percent were identifying how this might be done, whereas the remaining 51 percent had not identified such a link.

Overall, these findings suggest that measurement systems lack wide-scale sophistication when it comes to understanding the value and costs of customers. Only a small proportion of respondents have the ability to understand the costs of a particular customer, what the customer is worth, and what that worth will amount to throughout the relationship. On the whole, companies appear unable to determine the value of customer loyalty.

For most organizations, the best customers are often many times more valuable than the average, yet most managers make strategic and tactical decisions based on a mythical, average customer. Very few organizations are willing to spend time on conducting accurate, in-depth customer valuation. This results in a multitude of sins. Organizations:

- Overinvest in customers of low value
- Underinvest in customers of high value
- Squander precious resources
- Unknowingly pass up significant opportunities for future growth and profits

The bottom line is simple. If you do not know how much your customers are worth, you cannot make rational decisions about how to serve them.

Rank Xerox: Building Customer Value

Evaluating and building customer value underpins Rank Xerox's twin drive to grow its customer base through retention and loyalty strategies, in addition to acquiring new customers. A key customer requirement is value for money, so the organization has to deliver better value at lower cost in order to improve the value of a customer to itself. Traditionally, Rank Xerox had measured its capacity to do so by both satisfaction and loyalty performance metrics.

Rank Xerox estimated that increasing customer loyalty by 50 percent improved its own net customer value by 30 percent. The organization now delivers value through nine actions under the Customer and Market Focus element of the Xerox Management Model:

- Customer first
- Customer requirements
- Customer database
- Market segments
- Customer communications
- Customer query management
- Customer satisfaction and loyalty
- Customer relationship management
- Customer commitment

An offshoot of the model is the Xerox Business Architecture of six core processes, two of which drive customer value, market to collection and customer service. These are further divided into subprocesses. For example, customer service has thirty-two subprocesses, each with desired state, inputs, outputs, linkages, in-process metrics, and so on. All are fully documented.

One subprocess is the Perfect Call, a closed loop process of its own covering any customer request for service that links two elements, the Voice of the Customer principle and in-process performance by Rank Xerox engineers or support, to align the customer satisfaction process.

Among many, typical metrics in the Perfect Call process are the percentage of customers very satisfied with remote call assistance and diagnostics, time per call, and the percentage of calls interrupted due to missing spare parts. All measure in-process effectiveness, are monitored monthly, and are then benchmarked across the entire organization.

To facilitate optimum customer performance, the customer service department has been reengineered, creating a customer service network of sixteen virtual units linked to business divisions and Xerox's Worldwide Customer Services Board. The network is a major facilitator in achieving Xerox's customer and business results.

Loyalty was strengthened by the launch of a Europe-wide Customer First: Xerox Loyalty Framework to emphasize the value, experience, and recognition that can be offered to customers. Facilitators are dedicated Xerox Loyalty (XL) teams, which have to go through an internal accreditation process before assuming their new responsibilities. These focus on having each team improve its collective value to customers, which strengthens the measures for quantifying customer loyalty.

Though 77 percent of "very satisfied" customers repurchase, nearly one quarter may still defect, so satisfaction questionnaires now specifically quiz respondents on future buying behaviors. Rank Xerox has learned that this reveals the drivers of customer loyalty. Financial measurements are also being rethought to align with customer loyalty and reflect both short-term revenue and longer-term value from the organization's customer base.

Customer Value Measurement Models

There are four basic elements to customer value:

- Acquisition cost
- Revenues generated
- Costs involved in servicing customers
- Length of relationship

More broadly, there are three steps in calculating lifetime customer value:

- Defining the relevant customer universe, including potential customers
- Collecting data from different sources on the behavioral and economic aspects of lifetime value such as revenues, retention, and costs
- Integrating these elements into annual measures of customer value, average purchase, gross margin, cost to serve, net margin, purchases per year, annual net margin, relationship duration, and acquisition costs, which result in either annual or lifetime values per customer

The real power of customer valuation is in translating different values into discrete market segments so that marketing and sales strategies can be tailored to the needs and behaviors of the customers that will create the greatest lifetime value. This maximizes revenue and profit growth, while helping the firm's leaders to craft strategies to acquire and retain the most profitable customers or to manage the cost of serving the least profitable ones.

The importance of measuring customer profitability, behaviors and lifetime value, and, as a first metric, customer satisfaction should incorporate three sets of business indicators:

- Organizational: covering manager and employee performance in serving customers, for example
- Communications: the contact methods and logistics used to acquire customer feedback
- Information: the relevance and accuracy of customer data and systems

This type of focus for measuring customer satisfaction drives sales and marketing professionals to better standards through definable, numerical objectives. Moreover, by setting goals for each customer in behaviors and profit potential, strategies can be evaluated and resources efficiently deployed for the best results. Articulating this in practice has led to the design of two sets of metrics for a customer marketing business model. First are customer pyramids of behaviors and revenues in a minimum of four categories; at the top are the most active revenue-creating customers, usually about 1 percent, and at the bottom, the 80 percent or so least active.

Monitored over time, migration upward or downward is usually evident, along with new entrants and defections. *Move them up, get them in, and keep them in* is the best description of working and amending the pyramid in practice.

Second, the customer marketing methodology is used for managing customer performance and focus by measuring three factors:

- Value through customer-based accounting techniques
- Behavior by using a migration matrix
- Satisfaction through customer marketing monitors, which have four elements: value satisfaction, value estimates, value propositions, and effectiveness estimates

In effect, if customers are satisfied and the marketing model rigorously applied, the ultimate goal for any organization is to achieve preferred supplier status with as many customers as possible. This is the critical success factor in measuring customer value.

OVERVIEW

The end result of the measurement process should be added to other critical success factors for customer measurement and boiled down to a crucial issue, the challenge of implementation and its impact on systems. After sharpening the strategic customer focus, all the rest is implementation. The big issue here is not collecting data but deciding how it is used to best effect. Organizational leaders never seem to think this through, yet transforming data into organizational action is the most critical step of all.

A data usage infrastructure integrated with management systems is key here, assuming that issues such as capture, storage, retrieval, analysis, and dissemination have been resolved first. The infrastructure will have many tools or tactics for using and deploying customer measures, including:

- Focusing processes
- Management reviews
- Work-out sessions
- Future search conferences
- Business process reengineering for customer value
- Balanced business scorecards
- Quality function deployment
- Visual management
- Continuous communication
- Training and education

An effective customer-driven measurement system must observe a first principle, that the system attend to, not only how data is collected, but also how it is used. To minimize waste and maximize payoffs, data from customer feedback must be driven through the organization and used to change employee behaviors or improve processes.

The key is to successfully analyzing the potential of customer value. An example is the airlines, which now use data warehousing to access past records. These are then *mined* for patterns in order to determine future projections in customer behaviors. The result is that information technology and marketing skills become integrated to predict customer life cycles. There are some very sophisticated techniques available that allow a vast number of variables to be taken into consideration so that strong customer profiles can be identified.

Utility organizations in particular are hooked on collecting customer data but fail to use it as information to boost profitability. Few utilities use data strategically to improve performance. The data collected through customer-facing systems contains vital information on customer profitability, buying patterns, feedback from marketing activities, new service offerings, and so on. These details are not instantly apparent because sophisticated analysis tools are required to uncover them. A data warehouse is the only viable technological solution for effectively analyzing large amounts of data. However, very few utilities are using or considering this for its analytical rather than storage capacities, despite having a huge commercial resource in their customer databases.

Information is critical to develop a clear customer focus. This has implications for the information systems department, which has a key role to fulfil in four areas:

- Analyzing customer profitability, which, the report observes, few businesses do
- Segmenting the customer base
- Contributing to customer relationships by assembling more reliable information about customer operations to help understand these relationships
- Customizing products and services because information is required to control customer processes

Successfully using systems to directly support customer measurement critically depends on information flows about customers, analytical tools, and the skills to exploit both. Information systems must support the arrival of the customer age, which heralds a sea change in the business environment. Far too many organizations implement technology for its own sake, without taking a strategic view. The most important best practice is a willingness to listen to the voice of the customer.

BIRMINGHAM MIDSHIRES BUILDING SOCIETY

Context

After a period of explosive growth and diversification, Birmingham Midshires Building Society was, on its own admission, suffering from management indigestion and a distracted strategy in the late 1980s. It was bloated and unfocused, with recession biting and profits falling. One city stockbroker put the society last out of a list of twenty U.K. building societies in terms of profitability in 1991. Intense competition and poor customer service did not help, and as credit losses and arrears mounted, another analyst suggested that the business was on a danger list.

By 1990, the society itself had reached the same conclusion and recognized it had to change rapidly and radically lest it be acquired or forced to merge. Step one was the appointment of both a new chairman and chief executive in 1990, followed by a critical review of infrastructure and barriers to change, and a new five-year corporate plan.

High-cost businesses were divested, staffing was reduced by 40 percent, and senior management was cut by one third. Reengineering began in 1991, driven by a "Rocket Plan," a renewal initiative to align the entire organization around the following five goals:

- Customer satisfaction
- People
- Risk management
- Business performance
- Profitable growth

In an important move, Birmingham Midshires developed its first customer vision. It said: "We will be 'first choice' for customers, business partners and each other, growing profitably and sustaining value for our members." Driven by a new style of leadership, this was demonstrated in practice by seven service values at the customer-facing front end of the business, as shown in Table 6.1. The vision and values

TABLE 6.1 The Seven Service Values

1 I will always act extraordinarily helpful and friendly by:	• Using my name and my customer's names • Smiling and being pleasant and polite • Volunteering to help • Remembering my customers • Never forgetting that we are all ladies and gentlemen assisting other ladies and gentlemen
2 I will provide an efficient and prompt service and always keep my customers informed by:	• Ensuring that all the information I give is on time and error free • Contacting my customers within twenty-four hours about their query or complaint and sending a full written reply within five days • Letting my customers know what is going on and keeping my promises • Acknowledging my customers if I have to keep them waiting • Following up to make sure I have fulfilled my obligation

3 I will be responsive to individual customer needs by:	• Finding out exactly what my customers need through
	  • Listening
	  • Understanding
	  • Asking questions
	• Providing confidentiality when it is required
	• Remembering that all my customers are different

TABLE 6.1 continued

4 I will always behave and act professionally by:	• Knowing the rules and the boundaries and asking for help and guidance if in any doubt
5 I will always earn my customers' trust by:	• Being there when I say I will be • Being skillful in my role • Being honest and open • Fixing customers' problems immediately • Admitting when I am wrong and apologizing when appropriate

6 I will take ownership when I deal with my customers by:	• Saying
	  • "I will make sure that . . ."
	  • "I will get back to you."
	  • "I will follow this up for you."
	  • "Let me know if there are any problems."
	• Not blaming
	  • People
	  • Processes
	  • Policies
	• When things go wrong
	  • Working with my team to "make it happen for the customer"

7 I will demonstrate pride in our business, my surroundings, and my personal appearance by:	• Doing a quality job • Looking and working smart • Projecting Birmingham Midshires as the best

send strong signals through the organization. They help ensure that all staff appreciate the importance of customer relationships, loyalty, and retention.

Business Results

The values, however, constitute more than an executive wish list. In a sector where product differentiation is paper thin, the society has outstanding results to show for its radical change. From regular, independent surveys in 1996, 97 percent of customers cited positive experiences when dealing with staff and almost 75 percent felt their expectations were exceeded or highly satisfied, versus 54 percent for the sector as a whole. Nine in ten said they would recommend Birmingham Midshires to family, friends, or colleagues and 60 percent said it delivered better service than competitors.

The business has directly benefited, too, reaching seventh in the top twenty societies for business performance. Moreover, its profits rose from £26.7 million in 1993 to £44.0 million in 1995. Assets of £3 billion in 1991 grew to over £7 billion by 1995. Account arrears were one third below sector averages, and return on capital for 1995 was close to the 18.75 percent board target. This figure represented best practice for most financial institutions. However, customer service, prioritizing retention, building loyalty, and getting customer feedback at every available opportunity is not a numbers game. Apart from demonstrating advanced practices, and winning the Management Today/Unisys Service Excellence Awards in 1996, the society's work is very personalized from the top down.

Once a vision is embedded, service excellence becomes a people issue, which is brought sharply into focus by the behavior of people at all levels of the organization. Top leadership has taken people with them throughout this decade. Consider, then, that chief executive Mike Jackson's home telephone number is on every customer survey questionnaire that goes out in case someone wishes to go right to the top with a complaint—and about 1.5 million forms have been issued since 1991. This was extended in the 1995 Annual General Report, where the home telephone numbers of all the society's directors were published. Lower down the organization, "thank you," "sorry," and "greetings" cards or letters, flowers, a check from the Service Recovery Budget, and even, on one noted occasion, a bottle of brandy, have been given by staff to help rectify the rare service shortcoming. In fact, during 1995, the society received 6,199 formal compliments from customers.

Twin Teams for Customer Focus

Although Birmingham Midshires is keen to emphasize that all 2,200 employees have some kind of customer role, Bob Gill and John Hughes have among the most significant strategic roles for focusing the society on the right issues to serve 850,000 depositors and 160,000 borrowers in the 114-branch network.

Gill described each branch as "a customer gateway," adding that all the work done by his eight-member team relates to the creation, delivery, and updating of its customer loyalty strategy and initiatives.

The critical priority is to save defecting customers, principally using profiling, methods which, by segmenting the customer base, identify those customers most at risk of defection and help the organization disengage from non–value-adding activities. This focus is crucial for two reasons: they cannot be all things to all people, given so many diverse products in the sector, and it costs £40 per £1,000 of business to replace a customer. Put another way, if the "exceeded expectations" score improved by 1 percent, they could expect £50 in increased lifetime revenue per customer. Aggregated over a seven-year period with its current 1 million customers, this figure equates to an additional £50 million of earnings for Birmingham Midshires. Defections are now one quarter of the levels of four years ago.

For Gill and colleagues, the society's Total Customer Management process and the Customer Value Matrix currently being piloted are strategic weapons and competitive differentiators. Hughes, in Corporate Quality, explained that the loyalty team is his internal customer as his team provides monthly, quarterly, and annual customer performance and service data, in addition to analyses for board members, business leaders in product groups, and their specialist business teams: 52 copies of the monthly report are disseminated at these three levels. Over time, they compile customer statistics from several sources that contribute to the loyalty team's work and their own mission to develop service values and improve capability for delighting customers.

There are eight sources of feedback for customer expectations and needs:

- The society's own questionnaires
- The customer loyalty and retention team
- Independent market research using telephone surveys and mystery shopping programs
- Customer focus groups
- Competitor analysis and benchmarking
- Media analysis
- Customer complaints or compliments
- Employee feedback

If the firm discovers that customer expectations are not being met, the policy is to fix current issues rapidly and correct failures, say sorry or thank you, and develop new products and services. As an example of this process of acting on feedback, 10 percent of complaints in 1991 were from customers concerned that their savings in "obsolete" accounts could be earning a better return. In response, and at a cost of £13 million over a two-year period, the society upgraded 660,000 deposit accounts to alternatives with higher interest rates.

Other feedback-related innovations include raising the cash withdrawal limit from £250 to £500 and establishing an exclusive customer telephone rate line at the cost of a local call. Additionally, check clearance has been reduced from ten to four working days. Feedback highlights improvement opportunities enabling better performance in the race for retaining customers. As such, then, corporate quality is the driving force behind the society's customer vision, and there is a coordinating unit for agreeing on targets with business leaders, meeting or exceeding customer expectations, reviewing performance every year, and prompting improvement action plans.

These improvement action plans are usually based on "stretch," but achievable, targets with SMART objectives. Further responsibilities for the unit concern training, or more correctly, behavioral development, through Birmingham Midshires's Continuous Personal Improvement (CPI) program and rewards and recognition initiatives.

Aligning the Organization

As Figure 6.1 shows, the culture and direction of the whole organization was originally focused on a vision of customer delight through the "first choice" values (friendly, informed, responsive, service oriented, and trustworthy), goals related to the corporate plan, customer-driven strategies, and a continuous performance improvement process.

On relaunching its new corporate plan in late 1996, the society's catchphrase was changed to "Recognized for Excellence," to signify striving to be the best in service and quality, combined with low cost and fast delivery. However, the original values and vision remain.

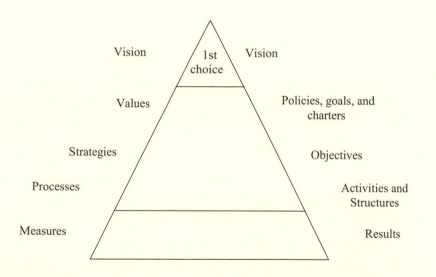

Figure 6.1 Visions to Measures

The ultimate goal is excellent business performance, as achieved by four corporate priorities:

- Priority one: service, always exceeding customer expectations by more than all competitors, as measured by the methods noted here
- Priority two: being recognized as an exemplary employer (the people dimension), with annual staff attitude surveys, monthly climate audits, staff retention rates, and levels of applications being used as performance measures
- Priority three: expert risk management, outperforming competitors in arrears and provision levels and gaining competitive advantage with measures including repossession, averages for outstanding mortgages and preprovision charges
- Priority four: growth in profits toward top three performance among the United Kingdom's thirteen leading building societies, as measured by comparisons for profits and cost or income and by expense-to-asset ratios

Each priority has one success factor, between one and six critical objectives, and several secondary objectives. These are weighted in importance as top, high, medium, or low for each year in the current corporate plan. As an example, for the service priority relating to the customer:

- The success factor is to work toward maximum exceeded expectations in the life of the corporate plan.
- Critical objectives concern specific programs such as a voice and data initiative is one example.
- Examples of secondary objectives include customer performance standards, point of sales systems and introducing service-level agreements where appropriate.

The hierarchy of performance measures is related to business priorities and the corporate strategy, which are tracked for monthly reports. They never deviate from the corporate goals, which are disseminated to every business unit and team, or from employee objectives. In this way, the entire organization is aligned to the "Recognized for Excellence" catchphrase.

From the main board of directors and throughout the organization, the CPI process enables this alignment as, for every individual, it spells out role, purpose, key accountabilities, and objectives, which are set in a measurable way around the five corporate goals. Each employee has a personal development plan, which includes SMART objectives and links to appraisal and review. In turn, outcomes from this plan determine individual pay awards and performance bonuses.

The CPI appraisal process enables the firm to identify, set, and agree on objectives with team leaders in line with the published corporate goals and objectives. Development plans then document new training and learning experiences to be gained in the coming year. The latter concentrate on values, behaviors and service attributes, rather than technical skills, with one of the most important courses being leadership training. Currently, of the annual total of 8,500 training days in fifty different types of courses, 75 percent focus on values and attributes and 25 percent, on work skills. And, over the last five years, the training of all branch staff and financial consultants in professional selling skills has been emphasized. Themed contact programs to enhance service standards are also used, including open quality days at which speakers include the society's customer champions and representatives of demonstrated best-practice organizations. The result has been substantially increased income and major improvements in customer satisfaction levels. All training is completely linked to the corporate plan goals, which evolve from the vision statement.

Communication and Recognition

Communication, without doubt, is the most significant contributor to alignment and the goal of exceeding customer expectations, but not in a linear or hierarchical fashion. It is perceived as multidirectional, multisourced, and open, a perception facilitated and driven by an internal communications team.

Business and support team leaders spend most of their time communicating and motivating people to achieve the vision and behaviors required for upholding the organization's values. First names are used throughout the society departments, internal job titles and offices have all been eliminated in favor of teamwork and an open-plan, nonstatus environment. No one, including the chief executive officer, has a walled office.[20]

Leaders meet regularly in a series of formal and ad hoc meetings, and top team members frequently visit branches to talk face-to-face with employees. The objective is to listen and then learn of any issues or roadblocks that impede the delivery of customer service. Around 200 actionable items occur each year from this program, in addition to 1,200 ideas a year from the society's suggestion scheme, 30 percent of which are implemented and which stimulated, for example, over 9,200 ideas for improvement in 1995.

Team leaders receive the monthly corporate quality unit report on customer satisfaction and use team talk meetings to discuss the results and plan their unit's responses. According to a Market & Opinion Research International (MORI) survey, their internal communication scores are among the highest in U.K. industry. Eight in ten people believe what they say in their communications, and 76 percent state they are fully informed of society activity.

Recognition is perceived as a key driver of service quality and, as an example, anyone in the society can nominate a colleague for a monthly Magic Moment award. This scheme recognizes and awards £100 to any who has "delighted and dazzled customers to exceed expectations." Holiday prizes to the value of £2,000 are given to Magic Moment winners of the year, and customer compliments are included in an individual's performance review.

The Corporate Center at Pendeford, United Kingdom, shows the photographs and testaments of these awards, and monthly presentations are made in the atrium area with audiences of 900 people. Business leaders make regular £100 cash awards for exceptional service, and a "thank you for doing a great job" scheme is used for instant recognition.

The annual people attitude survey by MORI shows the outcomes of this open, personalized approach. People satisfaction in 1995, for example, was 63 percent compared with the U.K. financial services industry average of 57 percent. The MORI results confirm that this is a creditable score given the significant changes in the society and the uncertainty in the industry as a whole.

Customer Loyalty and Retention

It is worth emphasizing the point of organizational alignment and effort toward exceeding expectations: that customer loyalty, and therefore retention (over a lifetime if possible), are more important than attracting new customers. The potential £50 million worth of earnings over a seven-year period from the existing customer base is worth recalling. The emphasis used to be on getting new business, but everyone now recognizes that it costs money to lose a customer. The society's loyalty and retention team of eight specialists has five key accountabilities:

- Establish retention targets across all business areas
- Develop measurement systems to enable accurate performance reporting
- Identify and analyze reasons for customer defection
- Initiate, develop, and influence strategies to promote customer loyalty
- Communicate and train in best demonstrated practices

In essence, the key is to identify which customers might potentially defect and should therefore be targeted, as in the 1991 accounts upgrade scenario, for example, and feed this in to the Society's Total Customer Management process. The obsolete accounts initiative took away a major area of dissatisfaction but also provided two spinoffs.

As the first society to address this issue, it achieved a significant market advantage in brand building, in addition to persuading many customers to trust it. It was a move that sustains business in the long run. Naturally, they encourage multiple and repeat purchases from the existing customer base, and to reward loyalty, these customers get a better deal. It might be a custom-made investment account or a competitive mortgage arrangement, but as buyers of financial products are far more active and astute than they used to be (which is no bad thing), they are more prepared to enter negotiation and discuss customer needs. They can offer most customers something.

Loyalty is also deliberately reinforced through building the customer relationship based on examining each interaction rather than simply preventing defection. In this, the society's team has identified four steps in the relationship:

- Formation: first impressions
- Development: building a partnership
- Decline: rescue process
- Termination: recovery strategy

For the latter two steps, brainstorming, research, and benchmarking have identified critical trends in order to design the new loyalty strategy currently being introduced. This aims to get service levels absolutely right with relation to the concept of a lifetime cycle relationship with any customer. Demonstrably linking retention to service quality is the critical issue, with retention levels being a key performance indicator.

The team's loyalty strategy and the Total Customer Management process should create a differentiator with competitors toward the ultimate goal of sector leadership. As such, customer loyalty is a strategic issue. The market moves all the time. Financial products have a unique characteristic in that they can easily and quickly replicated and, if based on prices, can have a short life in terms of appeal. Price is not necessarily the cutting edge it used to be, but service excellence can create a platform that lasts several years. As a result, the society sees service and occasional product innovations as inextricably linked. However, not all markets, products, or existing customers are necessarily desirable or profitable or add value, so Birmingham Midshires has a clear focus on targets for all three factors:

- Distribution channels concentrating on the direct and indirect retail, business, and professional markets.

- Servicing other organizations' needs or growing by acquisition and merger in their markets.
- Staying away from or exiting customers where the society cannot be their profitable "first choice," for example, chartered surveying, commercial insurance, property services, master check, cash and coin management, and commercial loans

The society must balance the cost of retaining a customer against the cost of replacement, so the ultimate issue is the value of a customer to it. For those it seeks to retain, it is devising an agreed-on, objective basis on which to determine what front-line staff should have available in their customer interactions.

Customer Value and Defection

The formula is a complex Customer Value Matrix, which was piloted in mid-1996 and was implemented organizationwide in 1997. It is software based and serves as a decision-making tool that values target customers objectively for all product groups and branches. Based on daily statistics, it records customer activity and identifies critical patterns or trends; repurchases, redemption statements, deeds requests, and references are examples. It is important that this matrix will also reveal trends in potential defection; if a customer requests a credit reference, for instance, this might indicate an intention to switch to another provider. Switching is endemic to financial services when the market is stagnant.

According to the society's own research, customers defect on mortgages, as an example, for three reasons, a better deal, enhanced rates, or a cash-back offer. Broadly speaking, 80 percent of Birmingham Midshires customers who have switched cite one of these product factors as the cause. However, for the other 20 percent, service is the crucial issue. According to the same research, a second significant factor in defections is that 60 percent of lost customers do not contact the society before switching their business, which is a major source of lost opportunity. By the time the defection is discovered, it is too late. Thus, it is vital to watch for signs or triggers, such as an inquiry about interest rates, and act accordingly by suggesting a better offer. Communicating more effectively will also prevent defection.

That said, Birmingham Midshires' performance in customer retention is good. According to Building Society Association and Bank of England statistics and internal extrapolations, it has, as one example, the lowest annualized redemption rates of the U.K.'s top eight financial societies. As to being proactive where a potential defection is indicated or to prevent a trigger in the first place, better communication comes naturally from stronger customer relationships, though three additional methods will also be more effectively used. These are monthly statements as a medium for messages, introducing related products at the launch of a new one, and the society's biannual customer magazine, which is mailed to around 350,000 customers.

In addition to service excellence and greater external communication, customer segmentation also enhances retention because it reveals the types of customers at risk of defection. Also, by examining the customer database and testing or matching different approaches or product packages to different categories of customer, more tailored responses or product options can be provided. However, in terms of loyalty, customers who are personally recommended by family or friends usually turn out to be the most loyal in the long run, hence the use of reward schemes to introduce new customers from existing ones in return for gift vouchers. Other initiatives are always under consideration within the loyalty team, providing they occur naturally from a strong customer relationship rather than being introduced blatantly as bribes.

Customer Feedback as a Driver

In creating a differentiator of retaining valuable customers, customer feedback is of appreciable strategic importance to the business. Apart from executive reports, feedback is used to inform teams and front-line staff every month, revealing issues and trends, performance against service values, improvement opportunities, and suggestions or ideas.

The principal tool is the society's own monthly service satisfaction questionnaire, with around 1.5 million of these having been sent out since 1991. Typically, they generate a response rate of 20 percent, and each is responded to with a telephone follow-up. Not surprisingly, the survey indicates that 90 percent of customers think the society is easy to do business with. The survey is further reinforced by telephone surveys and mystery shopping programs.

The process is a continuous "listening and learning" loop of four stages, measurement, communication, action, and feedback, underpinned by the principle of continuous improvement. The entire customer-focused improvement process is shown in Figure 6.2.

Responses and comments from the survey are collated and analyzed by the corporate quality team in order to reveal drivers of customer satisfaction and then used as a basis for the society's monthly review of figures. Appropriate figures and observations are then distributed to business unit and team leaders, with the measurement process giving rise to change or improvement projects. For example, customers at one time expressed dissatisfaction over the management of the tax relief for

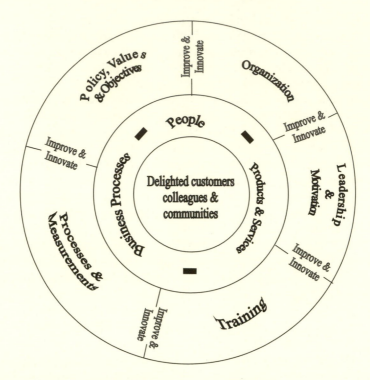

Figure 6.2 Customer-Focused Improvement Processes

mortgages scheme, so a team was set up to specifically deal with this problem in order to improve customer satisfaction.

To illustrate how negative customer feedback results in a solution or action within Birmingham Midshires to reduce complaints and, ultimately, enhance customer satisfaction, six broad issues mentioned by customers in the survey have been tracked over time. Using 1992–1995 comparisons for figures and including the solution or action adopted in each case, the issues were:

- More information on better interest rates for obsolete accounts: 1,481 mentions in 1992 decreased to 422 in 1995 after affected customers were moved to the special BEST account
- Receipt of junk mail: 71 to 37, in the same period because of improved targeting
- Refused loan: 62 to 37, after rethinking credit policies
- Wanting a wider range of products: 585 to 393, after introducing equity-linked products and unsecured loans

- Improved locations for opening hours, access, and privacy: 1,384 mentions, decreased to 667 following branch refurbishment, home visits, and longer opening hours
- Competitive interest rates: 949 in 1992 versus 327 in 1995 after improving competitiveness.

The totals of issues raised against survey populations is significant. In 1992, there were 4,532 specific complaints mentioned in these areas from a customer base of 860,000, whereas in 1995, the figures were 1,883 complaints from 1,012,000 customers, respectively.

The absolute imperative in the case of any complaint or issue is to fix it for the customer. Action always results from this ebb and flow of customer feedback data, or internal narratives after analysis. Any individual is empowered to resolve a problem or recover a customer. Allocating the Service Recovery Budget is an example of this empowerment in practice. Any member of staff can use money from this fund to "fix it for the customer" and justify the expenditure later. A further research-driven innovation at the society which is also unique for the sector and has been used as a crucial tool for determining training and personal development needs in relation to customer interactions, is as follows. Certain questions in the customer surveys identify which staff, location, or service factors result in either a positive or negative experience from the customer's point of view under two categories, enhancing or hygiene factors.

For 97 percent of customers in a sample of 523 who reported positive experiences, enhancing factors totalled 83 percent, split 37 percent for being helpful and 46 percent for being friendly, versus 17 percent who cited hygiene factors. Service was mentioned by 14 percent and product related factors, 3 percent. For comparison, the 3 percent indicating negative experiences said 94 percent of these were because of hygiene factors, about the same scores for service, product-related factors, and access, and the remaining 6 percent were attributed to enhancing factors.

The significance of the project is that it was extended to a fuller analysis of 8,500 questionnaires, which revealed over 500 different adjectives to positively or negatively describe a customer's service experience. By correlating positive adjectives with factors that contribute to exceeding customer expectations, the society compiled a list of ideal staff behaviors into a service value card that each employee carries; the behaviors are also reinforced by training.

In this case, customer feedback helps to improve individual behavior, which links the firm's listening and feedback process with the customer vision, service values, performance, training, and action-oriented, continuous improvement in service quality. Potentially, this allows the firm to go beyond pleasing the customer.

Critical Success

In taking an overview of Birmingham Midshires' customer focus, the loyalty and retention team cites as outcomes the improving satisfaction and business figures and the fact that behaviorally biased training is beginning to pay off. The deliberate strategy to disengage where value, or future added value, is not being created. The firm worked hard originally to determine the customer groups it wished to serve, which meant a discontinuation of business areas or product lines that could not be delivered against their vision and goals. Moreover, after customer profiling and segmentation, some customers were let go. The end result is an increasingly single customer interface and a desirable product portfolio, versus the multiple interfaces and distressed purchase products of old. Resources are more efficiently deployed, too, and through the emerging Customer Value Matrix, subjectivity is being taken out of customer transactions or negotiations.

The society has discovered that the more products are intertwined, the less likely a customer is to defect, but a critical point involves recognizing that a defection trigger may be displayed. Awareness of these triggers at the grass roots is vital in every service encounter; defections, after all, are a competitor's easy access to new business. This explains the importance of training by Hughes and colleagues, which emphasizes twenty-five core competencies and development in customer first values, interpersonal skills, decision making, and, in the reengineered, open-plan headquarters, working across boundaries. However, leadership is a crucial point, from the chief executive down. Since 1990 the current CEO has led the regenerated society on the basis of personal belief, style, and presence.

In whatever form, corporate change will never happen unless it is led from the top. The society's process began with a vision of customer delight and has moved through exacting performance standards and society-wide continuous improvement to business results. Along the way, it has learned from their experiences and celebrated success. It likes to think it does more than others think is possible.

NOTES

1. Deloitte & Touche L.L.P., *Survey of American Business Leaders* (Bridgeport, CT: Author, 1995).

2. W. Whiteley and D. Hessan, *Customer-Centerd Growth* (London: Century Books, 1996).

3. Coopers and Lybrand, *IDEAS—Innovative Approaches to Deliver Excellence through Improved Customer Practice and Total Quality Service* (Toronto: Author, 1995).

4. F. F. Reichheld and W. E. Sasser, Zero Defections: Quality Comes to Services, *Harvard Business Review*, 68(5), pp. 105–113.

5. European Foundation for Quality Management, *Customer Loyalty: A Key to Business Grouwth and Profitability* (Brussels: Author, 1996).

6. J. L. Heskett, T. O. Jones, G. W. Loveman, W. E. Sasser, and L. A. Schlesinger, Putting the Service Profit Chain to Work, *Harvard Business Review*, 72(2) (1994).

7. S. Kahn, *Setting the Standards and Measuring Results for Customer Service, Proceedings of the 17th Annual Spring Conference* (Cincinnati: Association for Quality and Participation, 1995).

8. B. A. Murray, *Maximizing Customer Value: The Step Beyond Satisfying Expectations, Proceedings of the 17th Annual Spring Conference*, (Cincinnati: Association for Quality and Participation, 1995).

9. The danger with using such tools on an annual basis is that an organization can lose a customer in a very short period. Thus, whether there is a real value in holding annual reviews is a serious question for management of any organization to consider.

10. Similarly, as in Note 9 above, can an organization realistically deal with feedback received that may be too late in retaining customers who may become dissatisfied with the organization's performance?

11. In nominal group techniques (NGT) participants write down their initial ideas or a topic, the moderator of the focus group asks each participant in turn to announce their answers, and then group discussion commences.

12. Institute of Management/Bain & Company, *Managing the Management Tools* (London: Author, 1996).

13. G. Clark, A. Kirby, and P. Stanley, *Managing the Measures* (Cranfield Service Operations Research Club, 1995).

14. A. Parasuraman, V. A. Zeithami, and L. L. Berry, A Conceptual Model of Service Quality and Its Implications for Future Research, *Journal of Marketing*, 49 (1985): 41–50.

15. Ibid.

16. W. Whiteley and D. Hessan, *Customer-Centred Growth* (London: Century Books, 1996).

17. In the United States, McDougall, Wyner, and Vazdauskas cite Banc One of Columbus, Ohio, as a constrast in financial services. Having studies its customer base, the bank discovered that the top 20 percent of customers provided all its profits, whereas the remaining 80 percent actually cost money, D. McDougall, G. Wyner, and D. Vazdauskas, Customer Valuation as a Foundation for Growth, *Managing Service Quality*, 7(1) p. 5.

7

Strategic Quality Measurement Frameworks and Approaches

STRATEGIC QUALITY MEASUREMENT

Key Questions and Issues

Over the past 15 years, there has been a heated debate on the question of whether total quality management (TQM) and quality, along with their parallel systems and measures, pay off through improved business performance.

At SGS-THOMSON Microelectronics, a French semiconductor manufacturer, the rerunning of four years of complex ratios and results from the period 1991–1995 enabled it to estimate the minimum direct impact of TQM to have been worth 4 percent of sales annually. Over this period, around 60 percent of performance improvements were proven to be linked to TQM practices, whereas the other 40 percent would have occurred regardless of whether TQM had been introduced. It stands to reason that, in less than four years, at least $300 million from TQM implementation has gone straight to the bottom line. TQM principles guide all decisions and activities, from strategies, policies, operations, self-assessment, and corporate behaviors to daily business management.

The SGS-THOMSON case study in this chapter shows how the review, auditing, and measurement of quality against breakthrough or continuous improvement goals and targets is of strategic significance. Quality has also achieved strategic significance for electronics multinational Motorola, arguably TQM's international role model, which launched its Six Sigma goal in 1987. In short, this meant a tenfold improvement in quality across the product range, to achieve a maximum defect rate of 3.4 parts per million, which was a critical contributor to competitive differentiation in telecommunications markets. Quality measures and reviews are of fundamental importance to ensuring that Six Sigma is on track.

U.S. retailer L.L.Bean is a byword in customer response and total quality, winning Maine state's prestigious Margaret Chase Smith Quality Award in 1994. However, when faced with oversupply in the retailing sector and pressure on overheads, a 1995 internal survey measured the cost of quality at $230 million a year, or over 20 percent of net sales.

The cost of quality is a relatively common measure, which is usually achieved through audits of product returns, scrap, and rejects. In recent years, however, it has been widened into more systemic or structural reviews. Therefore, L.L.Bean's discovery led to a strategic review and a rethinking of its previous high growth strategy to complement changing business conditions.

Driven by the Total Quality and Human Resources (TQHR) department (an amalgam of quality and HR process experts), a three-year program of cost reduction, process improvement, and better productivity would add $30 million to the bottom line. First, however, came the cost of the quality audit to reveal the problem. That same $30 million is about half of Ottawa-based filing cabinet manufacturer KI Pembroke's entire annual turnover, albeit achieved from a zero start in 1992. The organization won a Canadian Award for Excellence in 1996 on the basis of its unique, embedded quality culture.

"The customer is always first; measurement, teamwork and partnership are key priorities; and mission, vision and values are living words," said the Canadian judging panel's citation, thus listing the very attributes of any exemplary TQM organization. In contrast to L.L.Bean, KI Pembroke's cost of quality is 0.72 percent of sales. Measurement features performance against its market-driven quality (MDQ) philosophy, under which an array of customer satisfaction measures are reviewed weekly, monthly, and biannually. This is in addition to the integration of ISO 9001 audits, process, and leadtime measures, plus financial and other measures like value added per payroll dollar.

Quality is measured and controlled from person to person and team to team, throughout the organization, at each stage of the customer satisfaction process. Success rests on the firm's collective ability to document the changing customer base and service new markets, hence the MDQ strategy. A central message is clear from these highlights. In any quality-focused organization, business imperatives, for example market leadership, customer satisfaction, competitiveness, rapid product development, or service excellence, will rarely be successfully addressed without TQM or another related activity being aligned with strategy.

SGS-THOMSON determined a decade ago that it would achieve top ten supplier status in a global league table of 200 companies through TQM. It has done so and, in the sector's 1996 downturn, was a top worldwide performer. Performance indicators or internal and external data highlight where improvement is most needed. This continually extends capability against four sets of corporate standards, manufacturing, quality, service, and human resources. Underpinning these examples are other key points:

- If quality indicators, consisting of measurable targets related to goals, are to be monitored at strategic levels, they should come from strategic objectives. Motorola converts Six Sigma into specific, time-lined targets, which are tracked by high-level Quality System Reviews.
- Effective quality measurement can cause a rethinking of strategy, as shown by L.L.Bean's new, slower growth, cost-focused strategy.
- Measuring TQM performance should include its wider dimensions, that is, employee satisfaction, participation levels, customer retention and so on, all of which clearly link to the bottom line. As reported later, Ritz-Carlton Hotel Company reaps a $5 to $10 reward for every dollar invested in service quality improvement.
- Inevitably, new performance measures in quality will emerge over time and existing ones will be discarded or adapted as business conditions or strategic priorities change. Examples are Ford's Total Quality Excellence and QS-9000 initiatives, also detailed later in this chapter.

Clearly, as these case notes indicate, rather than being merely a functional toolkit of metrics related to pure quality performance, quality measurement must serve business direction and needs through an integrated, holistic measurement portfolio.

Research Indicators

A late 1996 European Foundation for Quality Management (EFQM) survey of 230 business leaders in the United Kingdom, France, and Germany found that 56 percent of respondents, on average, did not commit enough time to quality management.[1] Among U.K. directors, that figure reached almost 70 percent. Other significant findings include:

- 67 percent said that quality management was more important than it had been 12 months previously; only 2 percent argued otherwise.

- 60 percent of U.K. respondents planned to increase spending in this area, versus 50 percent for French executives and 44 percent for Germans.
- 25 percent of U.K. participants strongly disagreed with the following statement: "Quality is a strategic issue for the most senior executives in the organization", 0 responses and 5 percent were the figures given by their German and French counterparts, respectively.
- Almost 75 percent had implemented a quality program, with ISO 9000 being the predominant approach for 58 percent of those.

It is significant, however, that after citing the two drawbacks of quality management as bureaucracy and staff attitudes, business leaders were asked about the extent to which the effects of quality management were measured. In reply, 25 percent stated they already did so or "see it as very possible" and 52 percent said it was "possible, but not very easy." Notably, 9 percent of U.K. executives regarded this form of measurement as "almost impossible." What is not clear is whether people at the very top give enough attention to these programs for them to deliver maximum potential. The message is that chief executive officers must get more involved.

A shortcoming in relating quality and other nonfinancial measures to strategy. The more common measures according to the 1996 survey were:

- Customer satisfaction, 60 percent
- Market share, 55 percent
- Quality, 51 percent
- Employee satisfaction, 39 percent
- Workforce skills, 35 percent
- Customer acquisition and loyalty, 30 percent
- Cycle time, 20 percent.[2]

Despite their reasonably high level of use, nonfinancial measurements and associated targets are frequently treated in isolation from strategic objectives. They are not reviewed regularly, nor are they linked to short-term or action plans. Nonetheless, TQM as a key management tool is widely applied. Total quality management was ranked, compared to twenty-five other tools as follows:

- Third in importance for U.K. executives, being used by 68 percent of respondents
- Eighth for American managers, 72 percent
- Third in European organizations, 70 percent
- First for Asian executives, 78 percent.[3]

However, in terms of satisfaction with its use, TQM was rated sixth in the United Kingdom and Europe but did not appear in top ten ratings at all for North America and Asian executives. Research from the United States in 1993 by Delta Consulting Group for the Business Roundtable's National Quality Conference provides a worthwhile contrast.[4] Over 180 chief executive officers and quality officers in 106 companies were surveyed on their TQM efforts and drivers. A key question for business leaders was the likelihood that TQM would be a top organizationwide initiative by the year 2000, thereby asking for a forecast seven years on. Of the respondents, 45 percent said definitely, 41 percent suggested it was probable, 7 percent were unsure and a further 7 percent said probably not.

Comments from quality officers were revealing. "Quality will be indistinguishable from business objectives, both strategically and tactically," reported one. Another said: "It won't be necessary to differentiate quality from the way we do business." The study made important conclusions or, at least, raised points for any senior team agenda, as follows:

- TQM is "clearly alive and well," having a positive impact on performance with the organizations that are seeing the greatest benefits also perceiving a sense of urgency around its implementation.
- The key levers for implementing TQM are training, management behavior, communications, measurement, and information; the chief executive officer's role in these levers involves championing the integration of TQM with business processes.
- Quality implementation problems, at least according to experience in the United States, tend to result in long learning curves, have an impact on existing skills and knowledge, and lead to misconceptions over costs and benefits.
- Chief executive officers themselves agree that leadership, behavioral, and cultural issues are the most critical and problematic in implementation, and all of these take time to resolve.

After the first wave of pioneering efforts, TQM is moving into the mainstream, evolving from a movement to a set of management processes and practices that will remain a priority for years to come.

Ritz-Carlton Hotel Company: Mainstream Quality and Measurement

Since being founded in 1983, total quality has been mainstream policy at the Ritz-Carlton Hotel Company. Service standards in its thirty-one luxury hotels are built on the credo of "a memorable visit" for all of its guests, 97 percent of whom leave with that impression, as measured in hard and emotional attributes by external ratings, reaction surveys, incident reports, focus groups, and employee feedback. Service quality planning, which is integrated with business planning, begins at the top. The executive leadership team doubles as Ritz-Carlton's senior quality committee and draws up goals in response to multisourced feedback. In practice, top managers are expected to spend 25 percent of their time examining quality issues.

Aggregated in real time, daily quality reports provide data for analysis from 720 separate work areas in the hotel system. The prevention of negative guest experiences is critical, so reports serve as early warnings for identifying problems that might impede the organization's ability to meet quality and customer satisfaction goals. Data feeds into the hotel's guest and travel planner satisfaction measurement process, the end results of which are improvement project completions and quarterly reviews by the steering committee.

Improving quality, reducing cost, and increasing speed are essential to Ritz-Carlton's competitiveness and profitability, so improvement projects come from many sources in addition to the quality reports, for example business planning, customer surveys, sales input, and employees from all levels of the organization's workforce. Cross-functional teams run most improvement projects, which are typically completed in six to twelve months as part of a formal, nine-step quality improvement process (QIP), featuring fact-based management and decision making. Within a matrix of core, support and employee processes, QIP is one of six quality and cost reduction subprocesses. The other five are: inspection, cost of quality, benchmarking, problem solving, and error proofing.

Given that cost of quality is interpreted as being more than an accounting technique, its three dimensions are worth detailing:

- Costs of conformance, including prevention costs, that is, money allocated for training, communications and appropriate capital investment made with the sole purpose of ensuring that any job is well done. Appraisal costs, such as hotel time taken for inspections, quality tests, and audits, are also taken into account.
- Costs of nonconformance, including internal and external failures or excess costs, such as unnecessary extras or overelaborate presentations.
- The cost of lost opportunities, represented by unearned potential profits due to customer defections or because of decreasing business with existing customers. Customer satisfaction, loyalty and retention are key here.

All the hotel's plans focus on effectively directing resources, time, money, and people to the wishes and needs of the guests and travel planners in order to provide continuous price and value improvements. It aims to be the number one hospitality organization with 100 percent customer retention.

The Ritz-Carlton measures itself against the best in its sector, or any industry for that matter. Independent, external ratings come, for example, from the American Automobile Association, the Mobil Travel Guide, and the prestigious Zagat Survey. In the United States, Zagat named the hotel group as the U.S. benchmark over the last several years because it was the only one to receive the highest possible rating for all service attributes. The Zagat criteria cover those areas most wanted by any discerning customer: reliability, timely delivery, personalized service, genuinely caring staff, exceptional food and drink, and value for money. All told, the survey includes over one hundred specific measurements.

The hotel's motto, "Ladies and gentlemen serving ladies and gentlemen," is a cultural belief created by executives, practiced among employees, and experienced by customers. Much responsibility for ensuring that their published gold standards are practiced rests with employees. They are surveyed annually to ascertain their own levels of satisfaction, their perceptions, and the degree to which each understands that service excellence is a top priority. In short, Ritz-Carlton is the best, with a 10 percent market lead over its nearest competitor, itself the leader eight years ago. Over 120 quality or "best hotel" awards have been received since 1991, plus a Malcolm Baldrige National Quality Award in 1992. I is significant that since then, the organization has not had to run a single advertising campaign based on reputation. It calculated that,for every dollar invested in quality improvement, the return is between $5 and $10.

BEST CORPORATE PRACTICES: MEASUREMENT EVOLUTION

Clearly, over time, performance measurement related to quality has evolved, and continues to do so. Once focused purely on conformance to specification, defects, for example, more holistic interpretations have emerged, which still include the conformance dimension but also incorporate other important areas.

Often through TQM, the emphasis is now on customer satisfaction, integration within management systems, and measuring process performance rather than pure outputs, as in process control, and predictive or action-related measurement. In fact, a key question raised is whether performance measures should relate to quality focus on processes, the outputs of processes, or both. There are no neat answers to this question, as each organization will have its own wisdom and the results to show for it. One thing is certain, however: the more global an organization, with all that implies, the greater the internal and external expectations. This scenario has led some world-stage players to design their own quality measurement philosophies, which incorporate the shifts in emphasis, shifts noted previously and, in many cases, are used in measuring supplier quality performance. Overall, intense competition, market share, and positive moments of truth with customers, have driven developments. Thus, they have strategic dimensions.

The global IT organization Hewlett-Packard is an example. Its methodology is the Quality Maturity System, which employs the principles of leadership and participation, quality direction, employee contributions, management, and training and has four integrated elements:

- Strategic focus, with high-level measures involving the customer interface, satisfaction surveys, feedback processes, and competitive benchmarking
- Planning process, including strategic business plans, Hoshin or breakthrough planning, and planning reviews
- Process management: identification, documentation, management, monitoring, and process improvement
- Project improvement cycle based on "plan, do, check, act applications"

In effect, there are four levels of measures associated with the quality methodology. These are single performance measures such as defects and response times; key process measures related to business fundamentals, including order generation, customers, and people development; planning reviews; and customer results. These are reviewed monthly on a selective basis, with a full review every quarter to allow for trend analysis over time.

Philips Electronics: The PQA-90 Process

Philips Electronics BV successively introduced four tiers of quality frameworks throughout the 1990s, originally triggered by its Centurion restructuring and revitalization process. The stages of this evolution were:

- Product conformance, driven by quality assurance (QA) systems to meet 150 of the 9001 standards, introduced in 1990 for the multinational's quality professionals

- Operational excellence, introduced in 1991, with the driver being continuous improvement to achieve standards equivalent to the Ford Total Quality Excellence program (a global benchmark detailed later, which, in this firm's case, concerned engineers)
- Service satisfaction, introduced in 1994, driven by supplier partnerships, and measured by management using the organization's PQA-90 assessment process
- More recently, stakeholder delight is the business emphasis, with customers, suppliers, and employees related to the internal Philips Business Excellence Award.

PQA-90 was perceived as a stepping stone toward an internal equivalent of the European Quality Award with application restrictions. The standard was deliberately established below European Quality Award criteria to allow its application at all sites instead of just the organization as a whole.

The PQA-90 structure has six categories, role of management, quality improvement process and activities, quality system and procedures, relationships with customers, supplier relationships, and results. Moreover, as detailed in a reported titled *Philips Quality*,[5] it has three consecutive, high level examinations to assess quality improvement and progress against internal change processes:

- Self-evaluation: a business unit applies the PQA-90 criteria to its own activities, identifies improvement opportunities, and measures progress
- Peer audit: in addition, a team of colleagues conducts a thorough unit investigation, providing a broader perspective and creating learning across divisional and functional boundaries
- Management assessment: senior managers assess the unit to make sure organization standards are maintained and give feedback on adherence and deviation from them

The guidelines to these examinations point out that all elements of Philips Quality come together in the PQA-90 process. It is the mechanism for closing the improvement cycle for the process itself. Audits assess results and processes against diverse criteria and use deviations from the norm as opportunities to learn.

Philips business units accredited for PQA-90 are encouraged to work toward externally validated awards. If this is not appropriate, they may enter the Philips Business Excellence (PBE) Award competition as an alternative means of recognition and are assessed using European Quality Award criteria. PQA-90 meets approximately 60 percent of the requirements of the European Quality Award. PBE must be fulfilled, and accreditation to this standard is believed to equate to an approximate 45–50 percent EQA score. Moving from PQA-90 to business excellence typically takes at least two years, depending on factors such as size, how well quality issues have been addressed, and the effort devoted to improvement.

Ford Motor Company: Quality Excellence Frameworks

Improvement is the central purpose of two measurement frameworks at the Ford Motor Company. The first is its Total Quality Excellence (TQE) self-evaluation program, which was launched in 1987 for external suppliers and applied to internal suppliers three years later. Second, the QS-9000 global automotive standard, jointly devised with General Motors and Chrysler, was introduced in the United States in 1994 and in Europe by mid-1995.

TQE sets out requirements of suppliers in four areas:

- Quality: twenty criteria grouped around planning, statistical methods, measurement and auditing, customers, and support processes
- Engineering: design, product development, testing, manufacturing engineering, processing, and support, with over forty criteria are used in this section;
- Delivery: seven criteria
- Commercial: cost competitiveness, capability, and responsiveness to business needs, with twelve criteria in this section

The program is Ford's highest form of supplier recognition and sets new performance thresholds and establishes consistent quality standards worldwide. To achieve a TQE rating, suppliers have to score a minimum of 90 percent for each section, currently, 30 external and 16 internal suppliers have been recognized out of a total of 2,040 global suppliers.

According to a quality executive at Ford, any supplier can use the self-evaluation process and qualify for a TQE award, though it is not a requirement for doing business with the organization. It really impacts on all Ford's suppliers if they want to take part, but the decision to do so lies with them. However, companies with a TQE award are clearly in a better strategic position than those without, by virtue of the effort invested in ensuring that processes and systems are world class and constantly improving. Ford views TQE-rated suppliers as long-term strategic partners.

By contrast, the QS-9000 quality system defines the fundamental expectations of the big three automotive makers for internal and external suppliers and harmonizes global automotive requirements. The essential idea is to promote better quality with reduced costs and avoid or replace the multiple on-site assessments and different reporting formats formerly used.

The standard uses ISO 9000 as a core with additional customer-specific requirements: advanced quality planning, statistical product control (SPC), business planning, failure mode and effect analysis, and new parts approval are five examples. Expectations include 100 percent hit rates for just-in-time supply and less than 25 parts per million rejects.

Awarded a Canadian Certificate of Merit for Excellence in 1996, Polywheels Manufacturing was the first Canadian organization to achieve QS-9000 registration with Ford. Polywheels makes compression-molded vehicle parts and realized that the new standard was a prerequisite for doing business with any of the three major automotive manufacturers.

Though it had adopted Ford's Q-101 system in 1991 (the forerunner of QS-9000), executives recognized that quality assurance is but one aspect of total quality. Over the last eleven years, quality principles and measures have been integrated into the improvement planning process and business goals have been disseminated right down to the production line. Polywheels uses methods such as Advanced Product Quality Planning to ensure that Ford's and other customers' needs are rapidly converted into parts design and production.

In terms of business results, since deploying QS-9000, scrap rates have dropped significantly, productivity and process efficiency have increased, and Polywheels is now rated as a tier one supplier within the automotive industry, all the more notable since it is an SME with just 150 employees. As a U.K. contrast, Coventry-based Dunlop-Topy Wheels was the first supplier of General Motors Europe to become QS-9000 registered. This was achieved in around eight months, between May and December 1995. Dunlop-Troy seized on the standard because of its unique focus on business planning and quality improvement. It provided an ideal yardstick for measuring the firm's progress. With ISO 9000 as a base, it had a significant advantage in securing accreditation, but QS-9000 is focused more on business performance. This is how they interpret total quality in any case.

Federal Express: Service Excellence

Total quality and business performance apply equally as much to the service organization, exemplified over many years by Federal Express. They apply because of the firm's logistical needs. Every day, worldwide, over 5 million packages are moved, 500,000 calls taken, and 50 million electronic messages transmitted. Operational excellence is its imperative, guided by TQM and driven through the People, Service, Profit (PSP) business philosophy.

Human resources manager Steve Rutherford explained that the PSP cycle starts with the strategic business plan and disseminates down to every operational level. In effect, it is a process of management by objectives. Executive management produces written statements outlining their part in achieving corporate goals, which then are distributed to each level of the hierarchy. Every individual is aligned to an objective with his or her immediate manager.

Performance is assessed against twelve service quality indicators (SQIs), related to areas such as deliveries, pickups, lost packages, and customer complaints. SQIs are the bedrock of business performance measurement and are each given weighting to reflect the attributes that customers consider to be essential, thus creating a direct link to customer requirements and satisfaction. As a result, customer service (or, for Federal Express, service excellence) is measured precisely every day. Individual and station scores are aggregated into a total corporation rating every week using its SuperTracker electronics system. The results are communicated to all employees through Federal Express's internal television network, other media, and local managers. The specifics of SQIs are considered within the overall business plan and according to strategic goals. Thus, if they want to offer a more reliable service, operational teams look at the practicalities of what they are being asked to achieve and what their performance is like every week.

An example is courier performance, which is measured against corporate standards on a daily basis and links back to the business's SQIs and service quality. Indicators for the couriers include pickup and delivery deadlines, along with package volumes per mile, per hour, and per route. Appearance codes and standards for personal style are also important. However, the firm does not want employees simply to be motivated to hit their target by delivering packages. They have to do it in the right way by working smarter, not harder. A courier throwing a parcel at customers because he or she is in such a hurry to get the next drop completed will not impress the customer.

Couriers receive a performance review twice a year, over half of which is focused on objectives for on-road performance, pickups, and deliveries. Jointly with managers, they establish standard guidelines and goals for what they both consider to be best practice in this line of work. Rewards are also tied to the process. If courier goals are exceeded, they receive a bonus as part of performance-related compensation, and further lump sums are given for special individual commitment or the overall success of an operational team in which the courier works.

Strategically, individual performance, rewards and satisfaction are integrally linked through customers to business success. If you take care of your people, they will provide the type of service customers want, which in turn results in profits. It is a cycle that works, measurably.

The Point of Integration

Without doubt, a central message of the previous case reports is that any form of total quality–related measurement should be integrated within business management systems or processes if it is to contribute to improvement, better results, or shaping of an organization's capability. Follow-through action is also essential if measurement is to be more than a metrics exercise.

Integration has a second dimension in linking with other models or methodologies. For example, Philips PQA-90 aligns with the European Foundation for Quality Management's model and its own Philips Business Excellence scheme, whereas Ford's QS-9000 extends from ISO 9001 into business planning, which will take any user a step nearer business excellence and self-assessment.

Additionally, a third dimension of integrating quality measurement concerns people and the sometimes difficult area of behavioral standards, reward, and recognition. As Federal Express experienced it, if employee contributions to daily and weekly workstation or organization SQIs can be demonstrated in practice, then performance, and therefore the business, improves accordingly.

RETHINKING QUALITY MEASUREMENT

The People Dimension

The Federal Express example raises a considerable point about total quality and its strategic measurement, namely that line of sight between individual effort, quality approaches, outcomes, and reward is crucial. Grouped in stations and teams across over two hundred countries, Federal Express couriers are an excellent example of this cycle in practice. The people issue is equally as important in manufacturing environments. Control-systems multinational Honeywell, for instance, had used most standard quality metrics as basic measures until it introduced TQM as the lead business process in the late 1980s.

There are three primary measures of the TQM process:

- Levels of staff participation, including education
- Staff perceptions or expectations of the TQM benefits to Honeywell revealed by opinion surveys
- Customer satisfaction

More broadly, the organization uses an internal measure for all business units worldwide, called the Honeywell Quality Value (HQV). Through self-assessment against national quality award schemes, head office executives monitor performance annually and those units that match predetermined world-class benchmark levels are awarded the HQV, based on employee and customer measures and results.

As these examples illustrate, rethinking quality measurement must include people dimensions, values, ownership, involvement, education, and reinforcement through rewards and recognition. This may be a concern as executives embrace total quality, thinking to deliver business performance for all stakeholders. In effect, this integrates TQM into business thinking. Understanding and communication are crucial issues. First, one must clearly define priorities. Then one must communicate what these are and make clear what is expected at each level of the organization in a catch-all process. This is an iterative approach for deploying plans, business objectives, and improvement goals by sharing intentions, and soliciting input, from others before any implementation action is taken. Users typically claim that catch-all encourages commitment, involvement, and ownership; in some organizations, all contributors are named in project documentation.

It is worth noting a comment on people and total quality performance from the Delta Consulting report.[6] The survey of 106 companies revealed that TQM had a "positive" or "very positive" impact on employee satisfaction for 86 percent of respondents. As one chief executive officer said: "We have come to learn more about the soft side of quality. It produces good results but also good human resource management."

Confirming this point, eight in ten respondents regarded intensive and systematic communication as important, and nearly as many valued the development of measurement and information to support problem solving, quality planning, and identifying of improvement opportunities. The importance of employee training in the concepts and tools of TQM was cited by 84 percent of the survey's chief executive officers.

The crucial point of incorporating people issues into TQM and measurement is confirmed by SGS-THOMSON (case study in this chapter), now a leading example in the Western world of total quality in the semiconductor industry. In addition to the three TQM principles of customer focus, continuous improvement, and fact-based decision making two more relate the organization's total quality ethic to people. Along with practical activities, these are:

- Management commitment and leadership: direction, deployment, support, review, communication, and recognition
- Employee empowerment: training, suggestion schemes, teamwork, measurement, and recognition

It is worth highlighting an additional employee dimension, which helps pull together individual involvement, quality achievement, communication, and understanding. Gradual, continuous improvement through the Kaizen approach, using quality assurance, cost management, and delivery systems, in contrast to two or three more dramatic breakthrough efforts every year, is endemic to the organization's activities.

Actions may come from any individual or team, and progress is reviewed monthly, quarterly or periodically, as appropriate, at group, division, business unit and operations levels. On average, through Kaizen, productivity has grown by 15 percent a year since 1990. Kaizen provides a unifying, focusing framework for countless improvement initiatives which have become akin to the corporate wallpaper. Kaizen improvements can be so prevalent that it is often difficult to keep track of them all. Softer measurement also relates to SGS-THOMSON's total quality principles and corporate standards. For example, the annual climate or employee opinion survey has over sixty points covering:

- The organization
- Its image
- Work
- Skills
- Tools
- Training
- Communication
- Teamwork
- Relationships
- Problems and issues

It is important that employee responses to TQM and continuous improvement are solicited while the climate survey also gauges their feelings about the management commitment principle referred to previously. This is formally reinforced by the organization's TQM role model questionnaire. The survey is a behavioral performance tool of 23 questions currently being used by 80 of the top 250 managers, which they complete themselves to self-assess their own performance against TQM standards. Subordinates also complete the survey to provide a bottom-up view on the quality of TQM leadership.

Critical Areas to Address

This level of participation brings greater business success for SGS-THOMSON. In addition to an insistence that people involvement as a distributed responsibility is essential when implementing TQM-based performance measurement systems, there are six other critical areas that need to be addressed:

- Having a customer focus
- Clearly understanding the process
- Auditing performance measurement
- Planning performance measurement
- Implementing systems
- Establishing review mechanisms

There are thirteen steps to total quality performance measurement, with six for planning and seven for implementation. The former include:

- Measurement purpose
- Blending individual and group measures
- Establishing indicators
- Incorporating internal and external customer needs
- Careful selection of measures against performance standards
- Allowing time for adaptation to new measures and learning[7]

In summary, critical points for implementing TQM measures include identifying the highest leverage points through cost-benefit analysis, spreading measurement as widely as possible throughout business operations, and incorporating enough flexibility to reflect changes in strategic intentions. For this reason, measurement systems have to be continually reviewed to support accurate decision-making processes.

Quality Reviews

In fact, underpinning the previous points is the critical linkage that reviewing quality measurement and its results acts as a higher-level scan to confirm that business strategy is on track or assess capability in the light of any changes of strategic intention.

As outlined next, Motorola uses one key review to assess performance against its Six Sigma process; Armstrong World Industries Business Products Operations (BPO) has a multifaceted framework of quality reviews conducted by members of its Quality Leadership Team; and Toshiba UK's use of a Quality Review Program is fully customer facing. All have strategic outcomes.

Given its TQM leadership and Six Sigma process, Motorola uses a quarterly management review process, formally called the Quality System Review (QSR). This is a self-developed internal audit model guided by a manual and ten subsystems:

- Quality management system
- New product and technology

- Supplier control
- Process operation and control
- Quality data program
- Problem-solving techniques
- Control of the measurement equipment and systems
- Human resource involvement
- Customer satisfaction assessment
- Software quality assurance

The quarterly management review points out that each department and division undergoes a mandatory QSR every two years conducted by a seven- or eight-member team drawn from a pool of internal assessors. Units receive a numerical rating in each subsystem, which is used to identify strengths and weaknesses. Many also use the methodology for unofficial reviews as part of their continuous improvement process.

Armstrong World Industries Building Products Operations (BPO), a 1995 Malcolm Baldrige award winner, is a self-confessed quality fanatic,[8] a point made because the division's parent actually won the Crosby Quality Fanatic Award in 1987. They have spent the seventeen years improving the improvement process and benchmarking how they reach the top. Quality reviews were introduced in 1990 when self-assessment against Baldrige criteria began and were then strengthened when the division launched its 80-in-5 stretch goal initiative, designed after examining Motorola's Six Sigma. For BPO, this meant an 80 percent reduction in nonconformance in five years or less.

Every year during the initiative, BPO managers learned more about the true drivers of business excellence and the cause-and-effect relationship between process change and business results. Unprecedented improvement was achieved. The ten-member Quality Leadership Team (QLT), which includes BPO's president, meets twice monthly to review, evaluate, and manage performance against the strategic plan. The standard agenda includes business performance, quality excellence, strategic changes and operational issues. QLT members also review their function's performance against its own action plan once a quarter, in addition to the following:

- Six-monthly quality and service review meetings at each plant
- Annual meetings with quality improvement teams at BPO's seven facilities to review their quality improvement process (QIP)
- Annual Quality Council Meetings which review the organization-wide QIP
- Business excellence process annual reviews
- Individual employee performance reviews, including their commitment to the QIP

In overview, quality measurement, which is one of fourteen published BPO actions for quality improvement, has four purposes: to know if customer requirements are being met, to understand and communicate current performance, to identify nonconformance costs, and to speed up improvement rates by increasing organizational learning and knowledge.

TOSHIBA UK: QUALITY REVIEW PROGRAM

Consumer electronics manufacturer TOSHIBA UK, which links the principles of total productivity, quality, and direct customer feedback, uses a different form of quality review. This is because a crucial determinant of business success and a competitive differentiator is high-quality supplier-customer relationships. A key to ensuring these relationships flourish is the organization's adoption of the Quality Review Program (QRP), a licensed framework from P-E International in the United Kingdom, which measures customer assessments of product and service quality.

QRP was first used in 1994 as a tool to confirm a rethinking of strategy for its core consumer goods business. Then, Toshiba decided to exit microwave markets in favor of vision products and air-conditioning systems and was keen to assess customer, or specialty retailer, reactions. The firm realized that statistical information from the process could provide leading indicators. Through QRP, Toshiba surveyed 15 of its largest customers, interviewing 75 influential decision makers, including managing directors, to acquire both qualitative and quantitative information. Questionnaire and interview responses were analyzed by P-E International to produce a profile of how the organization stood in customers' eyes, along with a list of potential action points. Toshiba was rated against four indices:

- An overall rating of sixteen performance criteria, including product quality, value for money, technical effectiveness, and delivery
- Conformance with customer expectations
- Improvement in performance since the last survey
- Comparative ratings against competitors

The resulting data is used at a number of levels to trigger departmental action or for organizationwide reviews. In practice, the first survey had an effect on the advertising and promotions strategy, product design, and product availability. Of note, reviewing the importance of QRP findings took over a year and, given the potential revealed, led to an increase in QRP use.

For example, some findings had a direct impact on production with the manufacturing emphasis switching from reducing lead times or stockholdings to thinking how supply against customer requirements could be more focused. Production staff were given a new brief to exceed customer expectations on product availability without increasing cost. This was a different approach, which meant looking at supply in very customer-defined terms, thus moving from a focus on internal measures to others set by customers.

The emphasis in manufacturing is on continuous improvement through the concept of total productivity. This features cross-functional group work and deploys a portfolio of seven analytical techniques, for example, affinity and matrix diagrams and process decision charts. Continuing to use QRP has wider implications for business management. It has been introduced to account management and to IT, and Toshiba's distributors are being encouraged to apply the program to their own customers. Moreover, Toshiba is now working on integrating QRP with the higher-level business measures of market share and gross margins.

Another radical departure from traditional thinking is QRP's use as a basis for incentive schemes in the customer finance department. Instead of relating these to business volumes, the focus is now on QRP indexes and the number of quality-related interviews undertaken with customers during any quarterly review period. At first, customer finance felt the system was an easy way of guaranteeing bonuses. Realistically, however, only a certain number of interviews can be carried out within the time frame if they are to be completed to the highest standard. Therefore, the initial integration of QRP targets into incentive schemes was slow. However, QRP has had a direct effect on business, and as building relationships with customers is of paramount importance, the targets have stimulated behavioral change.

OVERVIEW

By its nature, measurement represents a search for perfection, at times compulsive and metrics obsessed. In the course of research for this book, for instance, many examples of quality charts and matrices came to light, superbly constructed and completed, duly signed and filed. With some, little appeared to change as a result, perhaps meaning perfection had been achieved! There are two important points here. It is still a widespread belief that perfect performance measures exist and, once deployed, that they will improve performance. Both assumptions are mistaken. Moreover, as this chapter finds, quality measurement, at whatever level it might be perceived, has become an integral part of three business elements in leading companies, strategy, management, and operations. This is confirmed by a substantial study from the European Commission's Directorate-General III Industry.[9] Comprising case studies on how thirty-five private and public sector organizations use quality management, the work drew seven conclusions about being best in class:

- Quality management is defined as the quality of management.
- A customer focus is key to an organization's continued existence.
- Organizations must be employee-oriented in recognizing that people make organizations work.
- Each organization is unique and develops its own approaches.
- While change is difficult to accomplish, it is not impossible
- Learning principles must be converted into practice.
- Organizations must be results focused.

A central point of the study concerns the first conclusion, namely, that the organizations described have successfully searched for sound ways of management in order to improve the quality of goods and services they deliver. Foundations for this include management by fact, a process focus, variability analysis, developing organizational competencies, balanced stakeholder management, and the alignment of structures, systems, and procedures to quality approaches. The report also spelled out that quality professionals working with top management have a special role to play in making quality a first priority, in which approaches like ISO 9000, benchmarking, and quality circles are nothing more than useful elements. This is an important observation from best-in-class companies, considering that all three are widely regarded as primary quality measures or, in the case of circles, major contributors to them.

For organizations rethinking this area of measurement, it is important to reflect on why quality measurement systems are ineffective. It is through failure to:

- Define operational performance
- Expose poor performance
- Identify performance priorities
- Relate performance to processes
- Define process boundaries
- Understand measures
- Distinguish between control and improvement issues
- Measure the right things
- Use information effectively
- Appreciate that autonomy must not be threatened[10]

Defining priorities, allocating resources, understanding, and communicating are essential. Metrics are also essential to measure and review progress, but appreciate that you will always get what you inspect. You must spend time developing measures and, once deployed and established, review them in detail if performance is not tracking to goals. It is a case of plan, do, check, and act. Quality improvement and measurement cannot be made for quality's sake without regard for overall strategic objectives. There is no point in either unless there is an impact on business performance and profitability.

CASE STUDY: SGS-THOMSON MICROELECTRONICS, FRANCE

Time to market for new architectures in the semiconductor industry is now measured in months rather than years. Within the next decade or so, the lines etched into microchips will be less than one tenth of a micron, bringing the industry to the threshold of quantum theory technology.

The price of microchips, on average, drops between 20 and 30 percent each time cumulative volume doubles, which can occur in as short a time scale as one year. These ever more powerful and cheaper microchips are helping to create new, sometimes unanticipated markets, resulting in outstanding growth in the 1990s for semiconductor companies. In 1995, worldwide sales leapt by 44 percent, to $155 billion and the industry is expected to build 140 fabrication plants in the next three years at a minimum cost of $1.5 billion each.

SGS-THOMSON Microelectronics is an active player in this market, now tenth in world league tables out of more than 200 suppliers and first among Europeans. Achieving top ten status was its vision when the organization was created through the merger of two European semiconductor suppliers, SGS (Italy) and THOMSON Semiconductor (France). The merger took place in 1987, and the organization made a U.K. acquisition two years later.

The original goal of top ten status was realized through continuously improving strategic capabilities and ramping up performance, year on year, in technological competency, operations, and supply and demand. The results are demonstrated in profitability, productivity, growth, service, quality, people, performance, and customer satisfaction, and SGS-THOMSON was a top industry performer in 1996. Constant change is the status quo. Although the firm has achieved much, self-satisfaction is not an option, as trying to reach perfection is a constant struggle.

Articulating Strategic Capability

Giving more has become the SGS-THOMSON way. In the last twenty years, product defects have improved by one order of magnitude every four years to below 10 parts per million, and 3 parts per million beckons. On-chip critical dimensions have decreased by a factor of six and chip complexity has increased by a factor of three. SGS-THOMSON's product portfolio now totals 15,000 devices in twenty families, and the organization is a leader in intelligent power and nonvolatile memory. Currently, SGS-THOMSON has three high-level objectives:

- Become the number one semiconductor supplier in terms of customer satisfaction
- Sustain world-class manufacturing capability
- Become a TQM leader in the Western business world

Underpinning these objectives is a range of specific policies or business requirements, which may change annually. Four examples are: maintaining the growth levels noted previously, profitability, cycle times, and accountability in environmental performance. It is management's primary responsibility as part of the strategic planning process to achieve current year results and improve capability for getting better results in the future. Consequently, developing capabilities becomes the "how" and producing results becomes the "what" of business performance measurement. In principle, the objectives, when articulated as either long-, medium-, or short-term policies and so-called urgencies, reflect the need to improve strategic capability. They do so in practice through sequential sets of goals focused on operational capabilities and performance, for which there are four different horizons on which to focus organization efforts:

- Long-term: improving strategic capabilities through human resources, technological breakthroughs, multiprocessing, design know-how, time to market, and so on
- Medium-term: improving operational capabilities through concurrent engineering, total productive maintenance, logistics planning, scheduling, self-managed teams, shop-floor control, and so on
- Short-term: improving operational performance through just in time manufacturing, cycle time, inventory turns, defects, yield, and productivity
- Urgencies: improvement through problem solving, as with quality problems, process breakdowns, customer complaints, or, by contrast, new opportunities

This is the framework, shown in Figure 7.1, for establishing or improving capability. Key words are speed, focus, balance, consistency, and lean operations. In practice, the framework drives continuous improvement, from the CEO's office to the shop floor, and is crucially linked with established corporate values and a TQM ethic. The latter is embedded into the organization on the basis of five principles. Along with practical initiatives or TQM applications, these are outlined as follows:

- Management commitment and leadership: direction, deployment, support, review, communication, and recognition
- Employee empowerment: training, suggestion schemes, teamworking, measurement, and recognition
- Fact-based decision making: SPC, experimentation, Failure Mode and Effect Analysis, statistical tools, and team-oriented problem solving
- Continuous improvement: systematic measurement, focus on nonconformance costs, cross-functional process management, and teamwork
- Customer focus, internally and externally: supplier partnerships, service relationships, and customer-driven standards

The TQM principles guide all decisions and activities. The decisions and activities, in turn, are applied to strategies, policies, operations, self-assessment, and corporate behaviors and were defined by a top management–led, iterative process using brainstorming techniques and focus groups. TQM is the way the firm manages rather than an add-on to operations.

How Capability Is Improved

If, then, for example, SGS-THOMSON can reduce chip dimensions by a factor of six over a few years, boost productivity annually by up to 15 percent, or achieve rapid growth in its available markets, where does this level of improvement come from and how is it achieved? How are the areas of improvement, that is, the *what* and the *how*, driven? Which performance indicators or data highlight where improvement is most needed?

First of all, there are the indicators, of which there are two sets, external and internal. External data includes market requirements or trends and customer feedback, for example perception surveys, report cards and dissatisfaction reports, and benchmarking. Among other sources, internal data comes from:

- Prior year or period results relative to business plans or goals

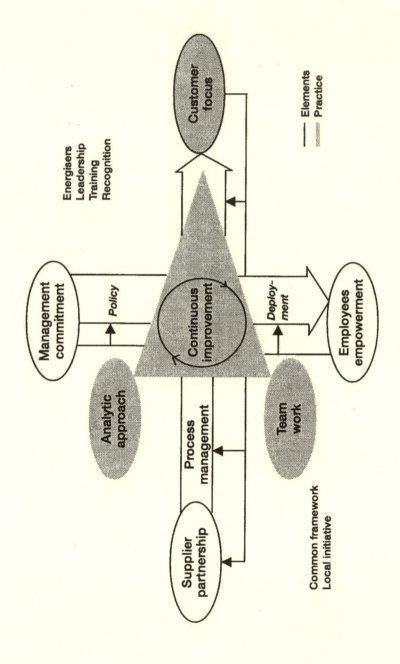

Figure 7.1 The Framework for Improving Capability

- Performance against four sets of corporate standards, in manufacturing, quality, service, and human resources
- Internal feedback from self-assessment, climate surveys, and the chief executive officer's TQM audits

An improvement area can be any process, activity, or result, for which the firm needs to enhance performance or capability. Indicators are measurable targets contributing to goals that show that progress is being made, or conversely, that a problem or urgency needs to be addressed. SGS-THOMSON's policy deployment process is the primary method for TQM implementation, thereby improving performance or increasing operational capability. In practice, it is used to convert goals and improvement plans into daily actions on the shop floor.

The process schematic is shown in Figure 7.2. It is driven by thirty-five TQM or policy deployment steering committees, supported by subcommittees at operating levels and individual or team "goal owners." They deploy policy into local actions and continually review progress. Managers or process owners thus use policy deployment as a methodology or operating guide to identify, plan, and achieve improvements at two levels.

The first level involves gradual, evolutionary continuous improvement through the Kaizen approach, which is now endemic to the organization's activities. Actions may come from individuals or teams, and progress is reviewed monthly or periodically, as appropriate. Kaizen provides a unifying, focusing framework for countless improvement initiatives that are now so prevalent that it is often difficult to keep track of them all. Furthermore, it is through Kaizen that productivity has grown successively by an average of 15 percent a year since 1990. The book *Kaizen*,[11] by M. Imai, has become SGS-THOMSON's "TQM bible." It has been condensed and published in three languages for use at SGS-THOMSON.

The second level or breakthrough improvement occurs when quantum progress in short time frames or significant step changes are required. These are determined as corporate improvement priorities which are visually tracked and reviewed on a daily or weekly basis. Breakthrough priorities are generally limited to no more than three a year for any operating unit. While these may concern dramatically reducing product costs, scrap or lead times, as examples, one organization breakthrough cut shipping times from twenty-nine days to six for 95 percent of deliveries. Then, through Kaizen, this was further reduced to four days. As such, breakthroughs are exceptional achievements tied to stretch goals, which require and receive continuous attention.

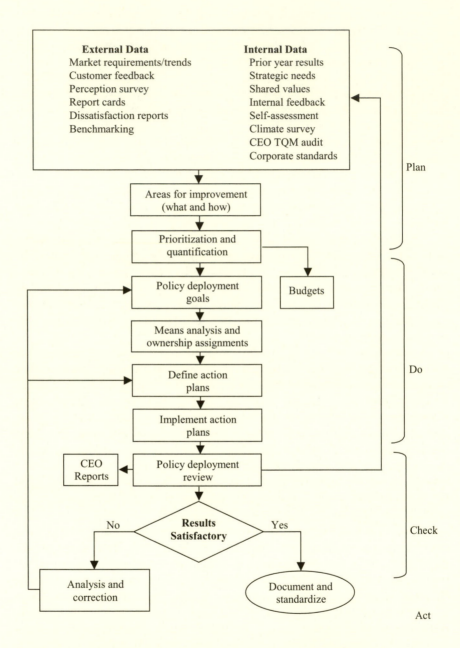

Figure 7.2 The Policy Deployment Process

Improvement targets and more generic requirements, as in, say, reducing cycle times or improving productivity, are classified according to the five TQM principles and then deployed, typically using the "plan, do, check, act" model. Of note, teams are of fundamental importance to greater capability and performance improvement, with around fifty teams per one thousand employees typically active at any given time. The teams operate at four levels:

- Continuous improvement teams following the Juran concept of excellence teams and applying Kaizen principles to common cause problems or opportunities
- Problem-solving teams, which examine special cause issues or problems by focusing on root causes
- Process improvement teams, which are trained in process methodologies and follow the "plan, do, check, act," or Deming, cycle
- Self-managing production teams

Issues in Improving Capability

However, the crucial issue in effective policy deployment, and therefore performance improvement, is ownership, from group to division, departmental, and production team levels. If policy, objectives, and goals are dictated from the top down, as can occur in large organizations, the process becomes unworkable. After all, an organization can have a great policy that does not work in practice.

SGS-THOMSON avoids this, partly through identifying and naming goal owners, who could be an individual, team, department, or one of the TQM sub-committees. Ownership is documented for any activity and spells out the policy, related objectives, and means of achievement, along with agreed on and named contributors to an improvement activity.

As an example of this documentation in practice for environmental performance, the policy goal of eliminating ozone-depleting substances, led to the objective of 100 percent compliance with the Montreal Protocol and, as the means, the drafting of an action plan by an appropriate subcommittee, as the owner, to meet those demands. Ownership is also ensured by adopting the Japanese concept of catch-all. This is an iterative process for developing plans and objectives, soliciting input, and sharing intentions with others to encourage involvement and commitment, before any plan or objective is finalized.

Another critical aspect of policy deployment concerns its implementation. Though the process is now fully integrated with strategic planning and provides line of sight between individual effort and business objectives or corporate priorities, it has taken some years to evolve, and continues to do so. Originally introduced and goal driven in 1993, the process then operated as separate elements, for example, quality or operating system goals were not related to corporate standards or budgets and there was little standardization or follow-through. These problems were offset to a significant degree by devising and publishing a policy deployment manual during 1994–1995. It is mportant that, for the first time, this also distinguished whether improvement should be achieved incrementally by Kaizen, or changed through breakthroughs. The final phase of evolution, in the late 1990s, was for policy deployment to become fully integrated. This integration was to become the SGS-THOMSON way of managing the business and the backbone of its TQM process.

In strategic terms, business performance measurement at SGS-THOMSON is driven by higher-level, or shareholder, goals. Because they are too consolidated to be achieved, they have to be decomposed through as many levels of value contribution as necessary to permit ownership and improvement.

All the improvements aggregate through the organization's value-tree drivers to meet the higher level goal. For return on net assets at the director or shareholder level, it begins with profit after tax and asset returns. Each is repeatedly broken down into very specific measures at the shop floor, such as units per hour or machine mean production times. Due to the multiple branches of the value-tree drivers as they are disseminated throughout the organization, there are hundreds of measurements, replicated at numerous sites or operations. Therefore, improvement has to take place at the detail, and not strategic, level.

There are many performance elements that are defined, measured, and improved to realize business performance excellence. They relate both to the results and to the developing capability. Broadly, they can be categorized as hard and soft audits or measures.

Audits and Reviews

Auditing is an example of a hard measure, covering:

- Financial aspects of the business
- Quality, policies and procedures, which are internally audited by quality assurance in line with ISO 9000 and QS 9000 requirements to ensure conformance with standard operating procedures
- Environmental performance tracked against ISO 14000 and the SGS-THOMSON Eco-Management and Audit Scheme requirements
- Certified standards such as the ISO series, for which external audits are periodically conducted

In addition, the chief executive officer conducts TQM audits to review progress relative to the five TQM principles and the extent to which they are practiced. He audits about ten sites or operations a year and reviews all major activities every two years. These audits are not inquisitions, but more a give-and-take discussion by which the chief executive officer can get feedback on TQM deployment in operating units. In addition, the CEO receives very condensed status reports as evidence of performance against the TQM principles and goals at six-monthly intervals. These audits are a useful medium to assess progress, recognize individual achievement, receive feedback to help focus the chief executive officer's attention, and demonstrate a commitment in practice to TQM across the organization.

Naturally, Kaizen and breakthroughs are primary activities for progress reviews. For the former level, day-to-day improvement, it should be recalled that a multilevel auditing process applies. Supporting the chief executive officer audits are monthly or quarterly steering committee reviews at the group, division, business unit, and operations levels. Local TQM champions compile reports, which are then consolidated into group status reports. These reviews always receive follow-through. Managers meet goal and action owners to review improvement area targets and action plans for positive or negative deviations.

All deviations are handled with equal zeal in the review process. Although management makes every effort to identify causes for negative results to instigate corrective actions, the pleasant surprises derived from positive deviations are also used as learning points for future operations. Breakthrough measurement differs significantly from Kaizen in one respect: there is far greater urgency because the focus is on rapid improvement. Progress reviews for breakthroughs cannot wait for monthly meetings. A near real-time review process is required.

Sophisticated techniques are used for monitoring breakthroughs. First is SGS-THOMSON's Visual Management for Breakthrough system (VMB), a set of tools for monitoring an improvement plan in near real time, which effectively gives continuous measurement. The system rapidly identifies bottlenecks for corrective action. Sub-VMBs can be used for Kaizen activities if required.

VMB tools include cause-effect diagrams with the addition of charts, which aid visual management and measurement, and the X-matrix system to correctly decompose important targets and clarify ownership. Also contributing to continuous improvement are customer measurements, which are primary sources of data for determining improvement areas. Annual customer perception surveys rank organization performance in fifteen areas on a 1–10 scale, which has revealed over time that the top customer issues are on-time delivery, quality, reliability, response, warning in case of delays, and lead times.

These measures are continually tracked internally and reported to management weekly. Customer scorecards have been adopted as a formal system involving direct feedback and comparison with other suppliers among SGS-THOMSON's top thirty or forty customers worldwide. Data from these is analyzed and reviewed by management every quarter.

Soft Measure

The two principal areas for "softer" measurement again relate to corporate standards through the human resources element of the organization scorecard and to the TQM principles of management commitment and employee empowerment. The first is SGS-THOMSON's annual climate survey, or employee opinion, survey conducted by corporate HR as one of its own performance standards. Anonymously completed, over sixty statements are graded on a 1–5 agree-disagree scale covering the organization, its image, work, skills, tools, training, communication, teamwork, relationships, problems, issues, and so on. It is important that employee response to TQM and continuous improvement is also sought. The employee survey is a reliable source of upward feedback, which helps gauge response to the management commitment principle. Ten agree-disagree statements relate to the effectiveness of an immediate supervisor, and there are others for management style, performance, and decisions.

This aspect of the climate survey is formally reinforced by the organization's TQM role model questionnaire, a behavioral performance tool of 23 questions currently being used by the top managers which they themselves complete to self-assess their own performance. Their subordinates also complete the questionnaire to provide a bottom-up view on the quality of their TQM leadership.

The technique has being deployed throughout the top SGS-THOMSON management population and covers all managers. Apart from its obvious impacts on role modeling TQM in the organization, the tool illustrates two important principles of broader performance measurement. As business units or product groups themselves decide on their own forms of measurement, self-determination is the first principle, followed by self-assessment. Since 1992, the latter has also become a catalyst and refocusing tool for continuous improvement.

Self-assessment. The year 1992 was a threshold in strategic business measurement for SGS-THOMSON, in that the organization adopted the EFQM Business Excellence Model of nine criteria, which are facilitators for leadership, people management, policy and strategy, resources, and process, matched to results in business, people, customers, and impact on society. That same year also saw the introduction of the chief executive officer audit cycle and formal benchmarking against global leaders for areas such as revenue per unit, defect densities, cycle times, and yields.

However, the EFQM model was adopted in preference over others of the time. First, even considering the Deming model and Baldrige, the firm felt it was the best one available because it has allowed us to conduct meaningful self-assessment for several critical business dimensions. Second, it is easy in an organization like SGS-THOMSON for engineers to concentrate on engineering matters and not consider issues such as leadership and people management. The model helps broaden the horizons of mid- to senior-level managers.

The first organizationwide self-assessment was undertaken by twenty-three specially appointed teams over a three-month period in late 1992 but, as with the shortcomings of early policy deployment cited previously, guidelines for the teams were too generalized and follow-up actions, the main reason for self-assessment, were not clearly defined or implemented. Between 1993 and 1995, important changes in self-assessment were devised and deployed. The teams were extended to twenty-seven, criterion owners and subteam assessors were trained and appointed, self-assessment kits were produced, and follow-up was standardized. These initiatives have since led to computerized self-assessment and a detailed scoring matrix, which are relatively advanced extensions of the EFQM model.

This evolution of self-assessment is of considerable significance for strategic business measurement because it is a source of input to policy deployment. To date, there have been three parallel developments, which, it should be emphasized, are not cause-and-effect related:

- 1992: first generation self-assessment was introduced to identify performance gaps and improvement opportunities, connected to policy deployment in 1993.
- 1993 onward: self-assessment began to create the foundations for more refined policy deployment during 1994–1995.
- 1996 onward: a further evolution of self-assessment set the climate and culture for policy deployment during 1996–1997 and beyond.

In overview, adopting the EFQM Business Excellence Model aligns with business management, as it develops from the four sets of corporate standards:

- Quality: covering product and process quality and mainly relating to customer satisfaction

- Manufacturing: productivity, efficiency, and effectiveness, which principally affects profit and loss, and therefore shareholder satisfaction
- Service: the key contributor to customer satisfaction
- Human resources: meeting employee needs, which is related to employee satisfaction

In addition, SGS-THOMSON's Environmental Decalogue, a set of ten goals related to environmental performance and improvement tracked by impact measures, eco-audits, and stakeholder surveys, is analogous to corporate standards and contributes to the EFQM's criteria for impact on society.

SGS-THOMSON cover all the four results criteria of the model, with clear goals and measures both for current performance and improvement. All the other things they do, whether policy deployment, self-assessment, customer perception surveys, employee climate surveys, process improvements, or team activities, are either mechanisms of, or inputs to, the EFQM facilitator criteria.

The TQM Results. Since 1997, the loop connecting TQM principles, corporate standards, policy deployment, self-assessment, business performance measurement, and continuous performance improvement has been closed. The process is embedded and has become the way of managing the business. However, there is an end point, as performance improvement is perceived as a continuous journey, not least because of the industry drivers referred to in the previous context.

As noted earlier, "Inspired, creative dissatisfaction will give maximum thrust" is their response to the observation that the world—customers, industry standards, and, by implication, competitors—demand more. Despite this, there is satisfaction at SGS-THOMSON, primarily because top management can demonstrate improved bottom line results from TQM.

In 1995, a "what if" calculation was computed on performance data since 1991 and how certain elements of performance affect profitability, cash flow, and returns on investment. Examples are the costs of nonquality or nonconformance, yields, expenses to sales, and inventory turns. A key question for the scenario was what would have happened in terms of business costs and revenues if the organization had not introduced TQM.

By running all the business's financial ratios and actual results, the minimum or conservative impact of TQM between 1991 and 1995 was estimated at 4 percent of sales annually. In short, revenues, profits, and cash flows would have been 4 percentage points, or nearly 30 percent, lower if TQM had not been rigorously, and systematically, implemented.

About 60 percent of the improvements experienced are demonstrably linked to TQM, whereas the other 40 percent would have been achieved without it. However, it stands the test of reason based on the fact that, in less than four years, at least $300 million has gone straight to the bottom line. At the risk of repetition, it cannot be overemphasized that the ongoing purpose of TQM is to continuously the firm's capabilities to provide even better results in the future.

NOTES

1. European Foundation for Quality Management/NOP, *Quality Management and European Business Leaders* (Brussels: Author, 1996). The results do not make it clear if EFQM or the respondents say that the time commitment was not sufficient.

2. Renaissance Solutions Ltd., *Translating Strategy into Action* (London: Author, 1996).

3. Institute of Management/Bain & Company, *Managing Management Tools* (London: Author, 1996).

4. Delta Consulting, *Ten Years After: Learning about Total Quality Management* (New York: Author, 1993).

5. Philips Electronics BV, *Philips Quality: Let's Make Things Better* (Eindhoven, The Netherlands: 1995).

6. Delta Consulting, *Ten Years After*.

7. M. Zairi, *Measuring Performance for Business Results* (London: Chapman and Hall, 1994).

8. The danger with becoming a fanatic in this area is to fall into the trap of overmeasurement. Devoting too much time, people, and other resources has a negative impact on productivity, profitability, and so on. It also begs the question of how they know they are measuring the right things in the appropriate ways or whether they simply measure everything for the sake of producing statistics.

9. T. W. Hardjono, S. Ten Have, and W. D. Ten Have, *The European Way to Excellence* (Brussels: Directorate-General III, European Commission, 1996).

10. M. Zairi, *TQM-Based Performance Measurement: Practical Guidelines* (London: Technical Communications, 1992).

11. M. Imai, *Kaizen* (New York: McGraw-Hill, 1986). For an updated version, see M. Imai, *Gemba Kaizen: A Commonsense, Low-Cost Approach to Management* (New York: McGraw-Hill, 1997).

8

Employee Measurement

EMPLOYEE MEASURES AND BUSINESS STRATEGY

Key Questions and Issues

Dealing as it does with human nature and the outputs of its endeavors, employee measurement can be a difficult prospect or process. On the one hand, it is tempting to run a quick opinion survey to "take the organization's temperature" on one or more issues. A purpose is served, but the results may be biased or invalidated; employee expectations will also be raised, as will such valid and commonly experienced employee questions such as the following:

- Why is the survey being used?
- Can I state what I really feel?
- What happens to the data?
- Will anything change as a result?
- What comes next?

On the other hand, institutionalizing employee measures involves similar considerations or potentially wider impacts, for example on culture, communication, performance issues, logistics, and working relationships. By its very nature, employee measurement is as much reflective of an organization's communication processes as it is of behavioral or performance issues. If a survey is used for the first time, there can be suspicion or skepticism if the ground for the survey is not prepared, as there may be if any established practice does not deliver to expectations.

Clearly, surveys and broader employee measurement are more than merely paper or data exercises. As this chapter finds, the best practices coherently align with HR strategy and business objectives. They address business issues, individual performance, employee turnover or retention, satisfaction or well-being, absenteeism, and HR costs, for example. Whichever approaches or means are used to secure the end of business results, key words and a truism lie behind them. Improving organizational capability is key, and once structures, processes, or functions have been physically refined as far as is realistically possible, employee capability remains.

Without recourse to research, a truism also holds good: motivated, satisfied, and challenged individuals usually produce better results. How these qualities are measured is the first business issue, illustrated by Texas Instruments (TI) Europe. By most standards for employee satisfaction and motivation, this company is world class and is often the benchmark for others. Remarkably, it has been soliciting opinions through attitude surveys for more than thirty-five years and its internal survey now covers eleven categories of satisfaction.

In 1991, an additional survey to test employee understanding of total quality principles and deployment was introduced, which was completely redesigned in 1994 in the form of the Partnership Report and then piloted and adopted in 1995. Quality Steering Teams review survey results and assign improvement projects to tackle specific issues. Progress is then measured at the next attitude survey, thus completing the critical feedback and action loop of any good corporate communication process.

TI Europe also uses benchmark studies to compare internal practices and assess its standing over employee satisfaction. For example, in 1993, the organization joined a best-in-class consortium created by the HR benchmarking consultancy International Survey Research. In the same year, quarterly *dialogues for excellence* were set up as informal exchanges between employees and senior managers, adding to the organization's established, open round-table meetings at department levels. Face-to-face reviews between individuals and supervisors are common.

At the health care multinational SmithKline Beecham, a fundamental principle of business performance measurement is that any activity is institutionalized through the annual planning process. All measures are distilled into so-called "vital signs" for executive meetings: these "signs" are critical success indicators and therefore become business issues. Four of these issues concern employee measures. They are:

- Absenteeism: In the longer term, a reduction in absenteeism indicates a higher level of staff morale.
- Presentation time: This measures the number of hours management devotes to communicating with the organization's employees.
- Safety: This is a key issue, so measures show the number of accidents and their prevention through training.
- Staff turnover rate or retention: This measure is a reflection on how motivated employees are, along with their development prospects.

The first three were in advance of targets, whereas a shortfall in retention rates is being examined more thoroughly through in-depth exit interviews, a growing technique for employee feedback when reasons for leaving an employer are revealed.

An action orientation is also key at Royal Mail, which first introduced employee opinion surveys in 1993. Currently, they are conducted twice a year for all employees, in addition to face-to-face interviews with a 1 percent sample to focus on specific issues. Typically, after the results are published, corrective action plans ensue. Conducting the poll is only half the picture. Acting on the results is the other half and is the justification for the survey in the first place. In the past, new practices resulting from surveys have included long-service awards, tailored line-manager training, and improved employee communication.

However, in the United States, AT&T represents the macro view of employee measurement with the key word being value. In 1993, the telecommunications giant introduced three corporation-wide value-added performance measures for the customer, for the firm's economic or financial aspects, and for people dimensions of its business. For the latter, people value added (PVA) is a measure of the degree to which associates' perceptions of leadership, job satisfaction, and diversity issues, among others, meet or exceed stated goals and objectives. PVA is used for all requirements under AT&T's human performance system model of four HR processes:

- Competencies
- People planning
- Performance management
- Organizational culture and design

With data from the annual PVA index, HR process teams use structured root-cause analysis and improvement methodologies to continually upgrade their practices. Also, performance data are correlated with indicator variations so that countermeasures can be established to improve individual or corporate performance. The model and PVA measures prove that personal targets for employee satisfaction are being achieved by managers and also help role-model behavioral standards throughout the organization.

The previous case notes highlight contrasting dimensions of employee measurement.

- First is the need to develop an action-focused portfolio: at TI Europe, this includes climate and TQM, or business practice, measures, face-to-face dialogues, and benchmarking in a complete feedback and action loop.
- Specific business issues can be measured vis-à-vis employees: at SmithKline Beecham, for example, levels of absenteeism, safety performance, and staff turnover are key indicators.
- Integrated methods or specific integrated tools are more effective than single measures, as in a one-off or once a year opinion survey. For example, Royal Mail runs parallel face-to-face focus groups with an employee sample.

Underpinning all approaches at AT&T is the notion of added value, or PVA. In effect, here (for other organizations, too) lies a central question: how can greater value be achieved from human endeavor to benefit the organization as a result of employee measurement?

In considering the strategic implications of employee measurement, there are three points that need to be seriously considered. First, intensely, competitive market pressures impact on the organization and, therefore, its people dimensions, morale, job satisfaction, absenteeism, likeliness to stay with the employer, and so on. All these dimensions have to be measured. Second, any employee measures must align with business objectives and eventually result in proven outcomes. Two examples include certifying knowledge and skills and examining attitudes to work. Both are critical indicators of an organization's readiness to perform in competitive climates, and therefore represent a strategic issue. Third, staff turnover is another factor, which, if accurately measured, supports the business issue of more realistic succession planning. The number of people able to do a key job must be two or three deep because strong retention and employee satisfaction rates will correlate with repeat business.

Measuring employee activities should be driven by three attributes, which also relate to organizational values and business performance. With appropriate measures and their related business effects, the attributes are:

- Service: satisfaction levels, morale, and climate surveys lead to higher retention prospects and repeat business.

- Quality: time to fill vacancies, benefits claims, human error records, hiring performance skills levels, improved business performance and results for delivery times, reworks, warranty costs, and scrap levels
- Productivity: costs per hire, costs per trainee and numbers trained, which should be shown directly on unit costs, production times, and order fulfillment

External benchmarking can be a powerful form of employee measurement. The U.S.-based Saratoga Institute's own database of HR effectiveness measures is an example. Compiled in 1986 and updated every six months, this database covers many aspects of human performance. Participants have access to over sixty preprogrammed categories of employee-related factors gleaned from twenty industries, including over 600 U.S. companies and another 500 firms worldwide. These are used as benchmarks, and as the basis of the institute's regular *Human Resource Financial Report*, which contains performance data covering 6 million employees. Both constitute the most comprehensive human performance measurement tools available and allow users to compare and monitor performance for monthly, quarterly, or annual cycles. Gone are the days of being introspective about employee surveys; today organizations need to know whom to emulate in the landscape of employee opinion. When properly conducted, they develop the link between business processes and human capital and help set realistic parameters for improvement.

Recent trends in employee survey measurement show that results are being integrated with strategy in exemplar organizations, especially those following business excellence models that include criteria for people management and satisfaction. If organizations incorporate *people as assets* statements in their corporate missions and values, they should prove this in practice. This incorporation requires the same attention to measurement and action as any other aspects of these models.

A further trend away from using employee surveys for monitoring morale "among the troops" (often to avoid industrial relations problems) involves asking significant questions of employees:

- What is the extent of their involvement in decision making policies and program formulation?
- How does management perform, and in which areas?
- How satisfied do employees feel customers are with various aspects of the business?

Surveys are much broader and far-reaching than in the past. Foremost practitioners like Texas Instruments and Rank Xerox have advanced HR policies with key indicators and measures, and they are committed to working with survey results. Regular audits also ensure that business benefits are derived.

The cutting edge of employee measurement is ever more sophisticated, as represented by three broad stages:

- Traditional: basic satisfaction surveys covering pay, benefits, etc
- Transitional: examining areas such as the quality of work relationships, or management style, etc
- Impact oriented: linking directly to business issues, outcomes, and results

Whereas most corporate practice is at transitional levels, the best practices feature impact measures. Typically, these are forward-looking and are used as predictors of customer retention and loyalty. The key question, and therefore the measurement issue, is: *How does employee behavior positively or negatively affect customer buying behaviors and patterns?* As an example of an adopted impact-oriented employee measurement, over time, a car manufacturer compiled an employee behavioral index that supervisors use to score individual performance in relation to the effects that internal behaviors have on customer relations and satisfaction. Should shortcomings be evident, a 100-page best practices handbook is used to improve behaviors. The leading edge, therefore, is to think through the drivers of employee behaviors to identify the satisfiers and dissatisfiers. You must build a framework for them, with measures focused on how organizational capability is strengthened by improving employee capability.

The strategic or business issues of employee measurement require managers to:

- Consider the effects of low ratings for absenteeism, staff turnover, skills shortages, morale, and satisfaction: if improved, how might the business gain?
- Determine how staff surveys or wider employee measurement integrate with strategy: what, then, will this mean for policies or practices?
- Appreciate that employee measurement is a transitional process, which should, in practice, have an increasingly significant impact on business issues and results.

If these points figure highly on an executive or board agenda, they will certainly be virtual preoccupations for HR units and practitioners and contributors to new forms of HR role and strategies. The following research provides indicators on trends and practices.

Research Indicators

In the United States, a survey of 151 HR professionals in Fortune 500 organizations found that, typically, HR used traditional measures such as assessing employee satisfaction with benefits (93 percent), employee relations (91 percent), and compensation, (89 percent).[1] Of note, almost six in ten respondents said they were improving measurement and assessment tools, citing benchmarking as the primary means of doing so.

Another U.S. survey, this time of 516 professionals, sought to establish the extent of HR best practices and measurement.[2] It found:

- Number to regularly develop forecasts for the number and types of employees needed for each job category related to recruitment strategies, 23 percent
- Number to use information systems to track employee skills, and abilities, training, performance appraisals, benefits, and compensation (tied to HR skills, capabilities, and reward strategies), 38 percent
- Number to track and analyze absenteeism and turnover, including the reasons why employees resign retention strategies, 60 percent

Despite strong indicators in measurement practice for some of these organizations, it is worth emphasizing the low responses for the first two points in the list: after all, 77 percent and 62 percent of respondents, respectively, did not use these strategic measures. This is markedly contrasted in a study of sixteen Baldrige award winners by the International Human Resource Group. Respondents tended to use many employee feedback methods, including annual climate surveys, cross-functional team communications, and round-table discussions with management.[3]

Whereas these organizations systematically benchmarked HR best practices, they collectively led in different areas:

- They value accomplishments, link compensation to specific performance measures, and widely celebrate or reward achievement.
- HR frequently designs programs with input from employees, line managers, and other functions and teams.
- Annual employee climate surveys are common and typically comprise 25 to over 100 questions.

The survey also found that Baldrige winners continually update employees on business results and performance indicators, thus connecting individual effort and corporate objectives.

Lutheran Hospital, LaCrosse, Wisconsin:
Employee Measurement and Strategic HR Response

The Lutheran Hospital in LaCrosse, Wisconsin, with over four hundred beds, is the second largest employer in its region. The hospital's founding philosophy is to treat patients with dignity, respect, and compassion. However, employee retention in high-demand positions has become a corporate priority because Lutheran wants to be an employer of choice in the area in order to attract the best people possible. That said, turnover rates had reached a high of 18.5 percent in the early 1990s, versus corporate targets of 12 percent.

As a result, HR more rigorously examined turnover and analyzed the rates for each position. It found that specialized areas such as physical therapy, occupational therapy, pharmacy, and nursing had the highest levels of turnover, but this was only partially due to high marketplace demand. The inference for Lutheran executives was clear: some groups were less than happy with work and conditions at the hospital. These findings led HR to redesign hiring and retention strategies and the measurement of their effects. The department now reviews data annually for each position and, if a specific position is experiencing high turnover, it is studied more closely to address position-specific issues.

Turnover levels are now down to 12.3 percent, compared with the U.S. health sector mean of 15.7 percent. A key factor in this turnaround has been the revised HR strategies, which, through emphasizing employee development, concern, and choice, have improved both productivity and satisfaction. The hospital provides many services for staff to sustain these outcomes, including:

- Competitive compensation and benefits packages
- Extensive wellness programs
- Promotion systems
- Educational opportunities
- Flexitime/part-time work options
- Leadership development
- Peer review
- Redesigned disciplinary processes

Lutheran uses a cross-functional employee group, the Human Resources Advisory Committee, to evaluate how these programs are used, review their design, and trigger improvements where required. It also balances hard data against individual needs by surveying employees' opinions on the hospital as well as their perceptions of wider issues, such as health care costs and the use of hospital facilities.

An important contributory initiative to lower retention levels and enhance employee prospects has been an extension of the hospital's leadership development program for managers, supervisors, and other professional-level employees. Under this initiative, participants devise personal plans with short- and long-term goals. To measure performance, progress is monitored by peer reviews, written and verbal tests, and measurement against predefined leadership standards. Ten measures are used for the latter, after managers and supervisors themselves considered a list of fifty leadership qualities.

To help participants apply the ten measures, performance criteria have been developed for each measure. For example, interpersonal sensitivity is one criterion, and its measure is "treating people with respect." The hospital says that one way to succeed here is to respect confidentiality in the exchange of information. Peer reviews are another innovation to help improve feedback and productivity for nursing and managerial staff. Each unit devises its own system, which is run by an employee-management committee. The scheme is being extended to other disciplines.

Every two years or so, the hospital conducts an employee opinion survey to obtain wider feedback on HR programs. Recently, almost 90 percent of employees responded positively when asked about the quality of benefits, compensation, wellness programs, promotion, educational opportunities, work options, leadership development, peer review, and the disciplinary process. Of note, since Lutheran surveys employees leaving the organization were commenced, the prime reason now for departure has been relocation of a spouse or a better job offer rather than internal problems or the hospital itself. These findings vindicate the emphasis on retention strategies.

EMPLOYEE MEASUREMENT IN PRACTICE

As performance underpins employee measurement and can have many interpretations, for the purposes of this chapter, four dimensions are highlighted by case examples:

- Motivation as a performance enhancer
- Perceptions about performance targets
- Applying competency models to business results
- The ubiquitous performance review

Case Study One: ISS

The Danish group ISS is one of the world's largest facilities management companies. Core activities are cleaning, maintenance, related products, catering, and energy services, so business success comes from employees worldwide delivering customer satisfaction. A substantial contributor to this is employee satisfaction.

A group of internal experts originally developed the ISS employee satisfaction measurement model, based on examining approaches to motivation and running five pilot projects. Ten questions are used, representing three fundamental conditions for any employee to be satisfied: management, collaboration and the job. Three additional questions also solicit feedback on job security, working conditions, and training. The primary issues concern:

- Management, or the immediate superior's professional skills, ability to manage and allocate tasks, treatment of the individual and colleagues, information about the job and feedback
- Collaboration, with nearest colleagues and other departments, broader social relationships
- The job in terms of independence and variation

Employees grade the importance of all these elements relative to their job and then indicate how satisfied they are with each. By comparing levels of importance with ratings for satisfaction, ISS management determines any factors requiring improvement, whether in working practices or business and HR strategies.

The point of ISS's employee survey is the link between quality of working conditions and practices, motivation, satisfaction, and individual performance. This significant issue had to be addressed by the San Francisco Region Wage and Hour Division at the U.S. Department of Labor in the late 1980s when introducing TQM and more participative approaches to management. The division enforces the Fair Labor Standards Act, which establishes national minimum standards for hours of work, child labor, wages, and employment conditions. Traditionally, enforcement and investigation used to be its modus operandi, with the 140 employees being measured on tightly defined case resolution and production targets. A report by the Federal Quality Institute concluded that this form of performance measurement was counterproductive.[4] It measured the wrong things (production at the expense of quality) and used measures for the wrong purposes in coercing or disciplining individuals if targets were not met rather than using them as a tool for improvement.

This emphasis on production indicators generated perverse incentives. Frequently, investigators would seek out cases that could be quickly resolved or pursue easily targeted violations. The emphasis was on generating quick, personal results with no regard for the organizational payoff. Accordingly, through total quality, the division changed its focus from enforcement to compliance, under which employees were no longer judged against their former targets.

The division continues to collect and report enforcement data, but only where it does not judge individual performance. Employees establish their own priorities for anew range of expedited investigations and local employer audits. As a result, organizational achievement is higher, individual productivity is up, customer complaints have been halved, and job satisfaction is far greater than it used to be.

Case Study Two: Holiday Inn Worldwide

Also wanting to improve business effectiveness and individual performance, Holiday Inn Worldwide designed and disseminated a competency model of core competencies and position-related knowledge, skills, and abilities (KSAs) throughout all the employees in the organization between 1991 and 1993. This directed work behaviors to business results by linking three strategies, business, HR and remuneration, and established a new, companywide vocabulary for employee performance measurement. In practice, feedback from employee focus groups was important in adjusting the design, along with its acceptance. Holiday Inn intended to change behaviors and expected higher performance, so front-end acceptance and ongoing feedback were critical.

Performance management is a key issue. Specific KSAs are agreed between managers, supervisors, and function staff at the beginning of each year. Employee appraisals are conducted twice annually, an optional one at mid-year and a mandatory one at year-end. Managers also obtain input from an employee's peers, customers or, if applicable, subordinates to ensure accuracy in their performance review.

After training in review processes and methods, employees also rate themselves on a 1–7 scale used by superiors and list special accomplishments. In order to achieve a fair, accurate, and balanced performance measurement tool, key words for the process are:

- Openness
- Discussion
- Negotiation
- Task clarification
- Minimizing subjectivity

As Holiday Inn Worldwide perceived the competency model to be a foundation for its performance-based pay philosophy, agreed ratings determine an employee's annual base pay increase, which is one element of a remuneration package. Higher increases and additional incentives are awarded for superior performance.

Case Study Three: Magee Women's Hospital, Pittsburgh

For some years, Magee Women's Hospital in the United States has aligned individual performance and its measurement to an established TQM context and has wanted to strengthen performance reviews. After considering several approaches, the hospital developed its own. Its method is the performance coaching review, which comprises a traditional review based on job descriptions but also extends to include team activities and performance against departmental service goals. To start a review period, managers and employees jointly decide on individual performance measures, personal objectives, improvement activities, and team participation activities and then weight each of these dimensions. For example, performance against job description, basic tasks, and standards may count for 20 percent of an employee's overall rating, with the remaining 80 percent being divided between team and continuous improvement activities.

As the year progresses, both parties keep performance data, and for review, employees complete their own self-assessment, in addition to the manager's coaching review. Other levels of management are consulted to avoid any obvious subjectivity or misperceptions before a final review meeting. This grades performance and sets new career and personal goals.

Research Indicators

The competency models and reviews in the last two examples are just two means of measuring employee performance. This can only be achieved once a clear view has been formed of what performance means to the organization and individuals along with indicators and measures. Also important are outcomes, that is, what is expected to result from performance measurement and the effectiveness of measures used, including annual appraisal? One U.K. survey, which indicated trends in corporate practice, sought to establish the types and extent of employee appraisal mechanism used, along with their effectiveness as motivators.[5] Responses came from almost 200 HR practitioners in a range of U.K. companies. Seven types of performance measures were used:

- Manager appraisal: 74 percent of organizations
- Line appraisals: 70 percent of organizations
- Self-appraisal: 31 percent of organizations
- Customer appraisal: 15 percent of organizations
- Upward feedback: 12 percent of organizations
- Peer appraisal: 9 percent of organizations
- Team-based methods: 5 percent of organizations

As a performance motivator, rankings for *totally* or *highly effective* were:

- Upward appraisal: 67 percent of organizations
- Customer appraisal: 59 percent of organizations
- Self-appraisal: 55 percent of organizations
- Peer appraisal: 45 percent of organizations
- Line manager appraisal: 42 percent of organizations
- Manager appraisal: 35 percent of organizations
- Team-based appraisal: 25 percent of organizations

According to respondents, the four least effective methods were appraisal by:

- Managers: 18 percent of organizations
- Teams: 17 percent of organizations
- Peers: 15 percent of organizations
- Line managers: 12 percent of organizations

Though relatively rare, upward appraisal was effective in two thirds of cases and scored the lowest of all seven for ineffectiveness. However, comments by respondents reveal organizational concerns over this form of employee performance measurement, including:

- A lack of training for appraisers
- Information being used for other purposes
- Difficulty ensuring that appraisals are actually completed (postponements are, apparently, relatively common)
- Inadequacies in assessing employee potential
- Varying standards among appraisers
- The effectiveness of appraisal itself

All represent significant issues to be considered when reviewing performance management and measurement. Further findings on corporate practices come from a survey among 1,028 personnel and HR practitioners.[6] First, it concluded, performance management is pervasive, with two-thirds of respondents saying that the great majority of employees were covered, from 70 percent for manufacturing and the voluntary sector to over 90 percent for financial services. Specific findings for performance appraisals and reviews included:

- Performance management aims: the top four objectives of appraisal were setting targets (75 percent), identifying training needs

(72 percent), performance feedback (69 percent), and improving job performance (35 percent)

- Appraisal elements: line managers conducted appraisals in 97 percent of cases, though other forms used included self-appraisal (71 percent), upward feedback (11 percent), and team appraisal (4 percent)
- Performance review frequency: 45 percent reviewed annually, 26 percent binannually, 15 percent quarterly, and 1 percent monthly
- Performance indicators: the main discussion points at appraisal were individual objectives (40 percent), individual performance standards (35 percent), key results areas (15 percent), personal targets (8 percent), and competencies (8 percent)
- Appraisal completions: over two-thirds were completed in 73 percent of organizations, between one third and two thirds in 13 percent, and under one third in 3 percent
- Appraisal linked to pay: 48 percent of organizations link appraisal results with an individual's pay, usually in determining the amount of any increase

Survey respondents cited the principal organizational benefits of performance management and measurement as, first, helping training plans (65 percent), followed by better motivation (59 percent), and employee involvement, (37 percent). Of note, only two in ten listed quality or customer service outcomes, whereas possible benefits in upward communication, employee relations, financial performance, and succession planning were cited by 15 percent or fewer of respondents.

If multiple benefits can be demonstrated in performance measurement, as the previously mentioned research and case reports indicate, more widespread employee measurement practice has its shortcomings. Management intentions, analysis paralysis, metrics obsession, and a lack of focus are four deficiencies, according to personal or consultancy experience. All these shortcomings, along with others, may represent significant executive dilemmas.

Negative mindsets and shortsightedness among managers inhibits the effectiveness of employee surveys. Many managers are nervous about putting their ears to the ground lest their heads get trampled in the process. This type of manager displays resistance at any mention of employee surveys, even for those supposedly enlightened managers brought up on a "steady diet" of teamwork and TQM. Such shortsightedness is likely to prove disastrous if managers do not base their decisions and actions on an accurate understanding of what employees feel. Doing so can prove invaluable in flushing out anxieties, getting to the root of emotion-based problems, and maintaining morale. A starting point is to use initial interviews to generate ideas, which can then be tested in a main survey and refined through focus groups before and after a major corporate intervention.

Before conducting a quantitatiave survey, it is important to have a clear idea of issues to be raised before embarking on survey measurement by using qualitative methods, focus groups. Agenda items will emerge here that will often be contentious issues. Management personnel should ask themselves at this point whether they want to proceed with what might be a Pandora's box. Once an employee survey starts, the organization is committed to a long haul. I admit to being skeptical over current trends toward quickly completed short indices based on ten to fifteen items, which leave a lot to chance. Organizations sometimes learn the hard way, in practice. Some go over the top, requesting analysis to the nth degree, by group, subgroup, and so on. Apart from leading to problems of confidentiality, the more people see data, the greater is the danger of paralysis by analysis. It might be fine to spend all day examining interesting response patterns, but surveys must drive action. However, of significance to this latter point, it is crucial to restrict those actions so that outcomes are meaningful, to take on only a few and do them well. One client organization, for instance, limits itself to three immediate actions and three for the medium or long term.

Take the manager who, after an employee survey, proudly showed me a document listing over ninety actions for him to take, which was an impossible situation to be in. Another way of looking at a similar aspect of this problem is in terms of what organizations do wrong in employee measurement. It can be taken too far if people become obsessed with metrics. Organizations also waste time and money because they lack a clear focus. They allow themselves to be pulled off track, grabbing the next train that comes along as pressures of the moment change the destination, if they even know where this should be in the first place. That said, there are several recommended destinations in employee measurement, which can ultimately have a beneficial impact on customer satisfaction, the cost of pay and benefits, labor turnover, absenteeism, skills levels, and the cost and quality of hiring, all of which are contributors to big issues such as retention.

Certainly it is important to measure all these performance areas, but if you cannot retain employees, it will cost the organization a lot of money in the long run. Along with performance, motivation, and satisfaction, retention is a key issue to be resolved before "doing" or practicing employee measurement. Other issues include:

- First principles: why is the organization intending to measure? For what will the data be used?

- Alignment: in what ways will data analysis relate to business strategy?
- Action: how will measurement lead to action or the resolution of a problem?

These points are real management dilemmas. The most difficult to resolve is what happens once data is available, as most organizations are not clear on intended outcomes or goals for this. In effect, they must ask, where is the value in employee measurement?

To recap, there are four executive issues that require attention when employee measurement is being reviewed or extended:

- Are management mindsets, from board to HR and the line, attuned with the fundamental principles of employee measurement emerging in this chapter?
- Is management clear on the business issues to be addressed and the potential outcomes after measurement?
- Is there a danger of metrics obsession, involving concentrating on the minutiae of measurement at the expense of the all-important macro business focus?
- Can alignment between employee measurement and business objectives be demonstrated?

Harris Corporation: Performance Measurement Tools

A division of Harris Corporation faced these issues and developed an integrated portfolio of performance measurement tools that is considered leading edge in North America and a source of best practices or benchmarking inquires. As is common in heavyweight bureaucratic organizations with long-standing practice, in the early 1990s, the 1,200-employee Government Communication Systems Division (GCSD) of Harris Corporation in Palm Bay, Florida, realized it had an embedded entitlement culture among employees. In practice, there was little finite performance measurement and a negative correlation between performance and pay, plus labor costs were rising at 4 percent per annum.

Throughout a two-year change process between 1991 and 1993, the HR department of GCSD was given the critical task of devising from scratch an integrated portfolio of performance measures and salary planning tools, rather than addressing these areas as separate issues (as is still common practice). The portfolio's aim was to create mechanisms for both managers and employees to understand performance and see how it related to business and compensation strategies. The portfolio comprises:

- Performance profiles, worksheets, indicators, and assessment tools
- Redesigned reward systems
- A system of compensation aligned with individual performance and business outcomes

Deployment of the new performance measures and remuneration incentives has dramatically raised the bar of performance. Competitiveness is strong, bed pay rates are in control, they attract top-notch people, and they retain the best on the basis of pay, prospects, and job satisfaction. Although there were several contributory factors to the portfolio's effectiveness, some represent significant good practice. For example, desired performance, and therefore the basis for devising appropriate, business-focused measures, was originally articulated by tracking low and high performers in GCSD for success criteria, inhibitors, and role characteristics.

This was an incredibly powerful means of determining performance expectations. Managers and supervisors, plus the employees themselves, use the performance worksheets to rate individuals on a five-point scale relative to expectations for the position or grade. They do so in three weighted sections, which eventually total a 100 percent, salary-related performance score:

- Key results indicators, worth 50 percent for performance against customer expectations, assignment challenge, and the business impact of an assignment
- Outcomes or the results achieved against fourteen job dimensions for behaviors, skills and knowledge, worth 30 percent
- An overall assessment of an individual's value or contribution to the organization, worth 20 percent.

The latter weighting comes from two sources, skills definitions, such as *critical* or *replaceable,* and an individual's potential for skills acquisition to meet future business needs. This score principally applies to fast-track employees.

For comparative purposes, the fourteen job dimensions, which use a five-point scale for performance from "highly effective" to "requiring a development need," are worth detailing:

- Functional expert knowledge
- Customer focus
- Quality commitment
- Work standards
- Initiative and sense of urgency

- Judgment and decisiveness
- Oral communication
- Written communication
- Planning and organizing
- Innovation
- Adaptability
- Problem solving
- Critical thinking
- Teamwork and cooperation

Once performance weighting and scores are complete, three salary planning tools are added to the process: computerized, graphic scatterplots, which show employees how they rate against colleagues for pay versus performance; spreadsheets to help business managers make decisions on local compensation levels; and a salary matrix to give guidelines on actual allocations.

Though the two-year process was not easy and the system is continually updated, it has had useful outcomes. The previous entitlement culture is changing, staff understand how it works, managers make better salary decisions, and performance is tied to business needs. Employees regularly ask to see where they are on the scatterplot, usually following up with the question all HR professionals love to hear: *What do I have to do to shift my dot up the scale?*

DIFFERENT APPROACHES
TO EMPLOYEE MEASUREMENT

Leader and Manager Measurement

A recurring theme of this chapter is "the management issue" in relation to successful employee measurement, mindset, commitment, decision making, and so on. It also involves a significant trend for employee measurement in terms of testing the quality of leadership and management from an employee's point of view. After all, managers are employees themselves! Federal Express and Skipton Building Society illustrate two corporate approaches in this area.

Apart from having many forms of employee measurement, such as appraisals, face-to-face discussions, job knowledge tests, performance reviews, and so on, Federal Express (FedEx) is uniquely known for its Survey, Feedback, Action (SFA) process. This measures employee satisfaction but also evaluates the quality of management or leader performance, as this chapter's case study explains. The survey part of the process refers to the voluntary associate questionnaire every spring, which is used to establish the climate in the company. It covers how employees feel about FedEx, including the job, pay, benefits and other issues, but also takes their ratings of corporate or operating unit leadership in terms of style, communication, fairness, and praise.

For the first element of SFA, effectively an appraisal of the work unit once survey data is processed, each manager or work group leader receives a scoresheet of results, which is analyzed and discussed at formal feedback meetings with staff. This ensures that the group as a whole reviews unit performance and its immediate management. A documented improvement action plan is then agreed on and drawn up, itemizing unit shortcomings, corrective actions, and time scales. This forms the basis of objectives for the coming year for both the group and the manager.

Leadership evaluation is the second element of the employee satisfaction survey, through rating a manager's abilities according to a number of statements. Each manager receives a personal performance score after analysis. This results in a Leadership Index, which is compared with a corporate goal for the index, which is set every year. This measurement is relevant to the balanced view of associate and leader performance the firm is trying to achieve throughout. It accords with the open door policy, which actively encourages employees to respond about the quality of executive leadership, decision making, and management style. The SFA process at FedEx is, strictly speaking, upward feedback rather than 360-degree or multisource assessment. The corporation has discounted the latter for practical and logistical reasons: for instance, couriers being on the road means that peer appraisal is impracticable.

By way of contrast on manager or leader performance measurement, the U.K. Skipton Building Society is a good example. The society chose 360-degree appraisal as an important contributor to personal development programs (POPs) for senior managers three years ago and, given its success, this form of appraisal is being extended to middle managers and supervisors. The approach is one of six integrated elements for POPs:

- Attendance at a development center
- Development report feedback from HR
- Personal development action plan, agreed with HR and a supporting mentor
- Quarterly follow-up meetings
- Review group meetings for six to sixteen program participants
- 360 degree feedback after two years

According to the society, at least three anonymous reports are required to make 360-degree feedback useful, though more reports are usually preferred. Subjects are graded from 1 to 6 on their effectiveness in forty-eight different fields covering personal, supportive, and motivational skills. The results, if given candidly and genuinely to the employee, are seen as a potentially powerful complement to self-appraisal and standard appraisal processes. They give participants an in-depth report on their strengths and highlight further development areas to keep the POP process going. However, the process is more than a measurement mechanism or campaign with a finite life. What they are doing is part of the new culture of the society: they show people the POP cycle, which thus will become self-perpetuating.

These forms of assessment are increasingly being used for senior management, as research next indicates and, where proven for effectiveness, they are being extended further into organizations (as far as line management in some cases). However, research touches on the extremes of 360-degree appraisal or feedback and multisource assessment.

Research Indicators for Alternate Approaches

A survey of 1,500 executives in 1,000 U.K. organizations on the issues behind the form of assessment just discussed. It indicates that its practice is well received as the following points indicate:

- Three-quarters of companies using 360-degree feedback rate it as successful
- Proportion of firms planning to expand it, 78 percent
- Proportion using the measure in personal development programs for middle and senior managers, 69 percent
- Proportion viewing it as an assessment tool to help make decisions on promotion and pay, 29 percent
- Proportion of managers who have experienced the process and say they found it helpful, 92 percent[7]

Despite having mostly positive experiences of 360-degree feedback, however, more than half of the managerial respondents say it has disadvantages: half feel it is time-consuming and expensive, and almost four in ten say being on the receiving end of feedback is threatening. Also, nearly half of respondents believe peers providing this feedback find it difficult to be openly critical about their colleagues.

A U.S. contrast comes from a survey of 201 organizations.[8] It reveals significant trends and practices in multisource assessment (MSA), also known as 360-degree feedback or multirater assessment. MSA was used by 29 percent of respondents, and another 11 percent planned implementation within twelve months. Almost half had not considered the technique, 9 percent rejected it, and 2 percent tried the measure but

discontinued it. Moreover, 55 percent of users deployed MSA throughout the organization, whereas the remaining 45 percent limited its
application to a division or function. In practice, the following findings
are based on 79 organizations that either had adopted this form of
assessment or planed to do so:

- Managers (89 percent) and top executives (82 percent) typically
  receive this form of feedback, but other target employee groups
  include technical or professional staff (47 percent) and sales representatives (24 percent)
- The main reasons for using MSA are individual development (86
  percent), performance appraisal (52 percent), and succession planning (14 percent)
- Half of employees providing ratings are trained to do so; it is
  mandatory for 32 percent, and voluntary in 18 percent of organizations
- Seven in ten respondents coach appraisees on how to use MSA
  evaluations
- MSA measures mainly derive internally from corporate values
  being translated into desired behaviors, 36 percent, or custom-
  developed competency models, 33 percent; 15 percent of organizations use a standard instrument adapted to their needs, whereas 8
  percent use external or off-the-shelf models
- Only 43 percent had not validated MSA questionnaires, though
  where firms practiced validation, more than one method is used
  (including validation interviews with groups or individuals, vendor validation, and statistical methods)

As to effectiveness, just 19 percent of respondents claim they are
"very confident" that MSA questionnaires truly predict high job performance, and 49 percent are "somewhat confident"; 25 perent are not
sure; and 7 percent have "no confidence" in their assessments. What is
not clear from the survey is whether these findings relate to the multisource process itself or the tools that were used. For the fifty-seven
organizations deploying MSA, only 12 percent said they could measure
the impacts on business results. However, 41 percent could measure for
the effects on employee behaviors; 40 percent could do so for performance management; 37 percent could do so for employee opinions; and
36 percent could do so for employee development.

Given that this wider form of employee measurement has rather more
extensive cultural and interpersonal implications than traditional man-
ager-subordinate or senior manager–middle manager appraisal, several executive considerations emerge when the process is considered.
For once, although 360-degree feedback can be a powerful catalyst for
change, it is equally capable of creating conflict and confusion. Failing

to grapple with the positioning of 360-degree feedback is a major reason for its failure.

Moreover, given the sensitive and valuable nature of feedback data, senior managers can quarrel about who should get access to the information. Mixed messages can be sent to the rest of the organization, resulting in employees becoming distrustful and defensive. It is significant that managers often interpret 360-degree feedback as an organizational process rather than a mechanical tool, hence the cultural and interpersonal implications already mentioned. It is more than some form of questionnaire sent to disparate groups of employees.

In addressing extended performance appraisal, a distinction between upward appraisal and 360-degree feedback as detailed in the FedEx and Skipton Building Society examples above is needed. Both should be established elements of any performance management system. Upward appraisal is mainly designed to achieve action for change in boss-subordinate relationships and performance, according to respondent companies. By contrast, 360-degree feedback is more about increasing people's own awareness of how they are generally perceived.

It is recognized that executives often behave differently according to whether they are interacting with their bosses, peers, or subordinates. Of the respondents to the survey, 40 percent had introduced 360-degree appraisal to meet two broad contexts. These are:

- Changing organizational culture: developing leadership skills and building confidence and trust at the most senior levels
- Quantifying, managing, and closing perception gaps through feedback to achieve personal development and effectiveness[9]

Although there are benefits from 360-degree appraisal, such as increased awareness of strengths and weaknesses, improved management style and behavior, and better communication and relationship building, there is also a potential downside. If you are planning to introduce 360-degree feedback for the first time, do not expect everyone to feel comfortable about the initiative. It is part of a process of change, and change is uncomfortable. To have one's self-perceptions of behavior and performance challenged with a new set of views is unpleasant, but, as with all learning, the initial discomfort enables constructive development to take place.

The problem with single-source, typically top-down assessment occurs when performance appraisals are related to salary and employee development. Goals cast managers or supervisors as judge, jury, coach, and counselor, but combining these conflicting, incompatible roles serves no one's interests. It is recommended instead that 360-degree data gathered collectively and anonymously from six to ten sources, managers, supervisors, peers, and subordinates. In this form, it is more powerful, less open to dispute and misperception, able to provide meaningful comparisons, and developmental rather than judgmental.

For example, at a 5,000-employee health care group in Dallas, a 360-degree feedback pilot program was first introduced for a group of 12 team leaders as the forerunner of wider organizational transformation and cultural change. Once completed, the trial was extended to an additional 150 team leaders over a six-month period and will, ultimately, flow through the organization. For each team leader, thirty-six leadership traits were rated by colleagues on an anonymously completed feedback form. Assessors were first coached on how the process worked and the terminology used. But, to use a TQM analogy, there are two typical groups of multisource assessment users, the pioneers and the early adopters. Both typically experience problems because they try to add on yet another measure or dimension to performance appraisal. It does not work that way. Who would think of fixing a Mercedes emblem onto an old Ford car?

Case Study Four: Philips BV—Biannual Employee Surveys

As another case study to this chapter, Philips BV meets all the criteria for success highlighted by the examples in this book. Moreover, in a logistics sense, finding out what a quarter of a million people think is a mammoth undertaking. However, to the consumer electronics giant, it was so important that 265,000 staff worldwide were surveyed in 1994, 1996, and 1998. These companywide surveys, originally introduced in 1994 as the multinational's Centurion corporate change process, moved from an organizational focus, (costs, productivity, asset utilization) to one centered on quality, customers, and the "softer" people issues of business performance. The catchphrase "On Our Way" (to the Philips "Way" of five corporate values) was used to mobilize the organization.

Centurion was introduced in 1990 to first restructure and then revitalize the ailing company. Performance against a range of goals and targets is now measured through self-assessment against Baldrige and EFQM criteria, along with Philips's own quality standard, PQA-90 (detailed in Chapter 7). Measurement is regarded as vital to satisfy shareholders, customers, and employees and the importance of gathering opinions and feedback from the latter is underlined. People satisfaction in Philips is not just an outcome as in the EFQM model, but a facilitator designed to get results.

Philips worked closely with specialist survey designers International Survey Research (ISR), not least to benchmark against international norms. Nevertheless, for the first survey in 1994, deciding upon a survey of this scale was a high risk given the logistics and multiple cultural and linguistic differences of operating in almost sixty countries. In addition to core questions, survey designers contacted Philips managers worldwide to ask what measures of local or regional importance should be considered for local supplements to the main questionnaire and found, surprisingly, no significant variance between the core and local or regional questions.

The core survey was intended to gauge and validate progress in implementing company values under the Philips Way. The values are:

- Delight customers
- Value people as the firm's greatest resource
- Deliver quality and excellence
- Achieve premium returns on equity
- Encourage entrepreneurial behavior

Apart from setting up a network of survey coordinators, a balance had to be achieved between those activities organized in Holland at the Eindhoven headquarters of Philips and others at local levels. The former included:

- Questionnaire design
- Project management
- Coding structure
- Scheduling
- Progress control
- Devising management guidelines
- Quality checks
- Finance

The local emphasis was on trade union relations, translation, feedback for questionnaire drafts, administration, communication with employees and results analysis. For the 1994 survey of 220,000 employees (in 59 countries and speaking 42 languages), there was a response rate of 78 percent. The entire interactive process from initial contacts with ISR consultants to the availability of results, lasted from May 1993 to September 1994.

Among success factors were the involvement of the top one hundred managers at Philips, centralized coordination with decentralized implementation, and acceptance at the supervisor level. However, a critical objective of these companywide motivation surveys is to ensure follow-up. Philips interprets this as closing the loop in the cycle, with reporting at the lowest possible level. After the 1994 survey, for example, eight thousand reports were ordered by local managers. Follow-up is done through an eight-stage process that:

- Identifies strengths and weaknesses
- Communicates results
- Identifies priorities and integrates them with other actions
- Generates solutions
- Formulates and implements action plans
- Communicates actions
- Monitors actions
- Measures progress

It is important that the results of surveys feed current businesswide priorities, including quality initiatives, dedicated customer days, performance appraisal objectives, and continuous improvement. Apart from noting that employee motivation surveys help make the company less introspective and are instrumental in the change process, the first survey in 1994 created a high level of energy throughout the firm. Employees felt good about their involvement, and it created expectations among them all. However, this meant that those expectations had to be managed.

OVERVIEW

The Philips case report highlights a relatively advanced form of employee climate survey in a remarkable logistics context that, through expert coordination and collaborative management, flows throughout the organization and results in action. It demonstrates a form of internal employee measurement at its best. In short, countless other employee measures can be used, representing virtually every form of individual activity. To recall, the Saratoga Institute's database has over 60 benchmark categories and ISR's has 17, which raises the point that employee measurement has both internal and external dimensions.

Broadly, however, performance, motivation, satisfaction, absenteeism, and staff turnover are crucial areas for any organization to measure, with two provisos: that there is a proven link with business objectives, and that HR practices improve as a result of data analysis. As indicated in this chapter, there are many means of achieving these ends. One key is to examine employee trust in management, which is a significant predictor of company success. That said, this and the dimensions already mentioned are best measured through multiple forms. As with job selection, where one uses interviews, tests, and assessment centers, so it is with employee measurement. A combination of techniques always gives the most valid indicators and results.

There are a number of recommended guidelines when considering or extending this method:

- Survey during periods of stability, because a survey taken in the midst of radical change will not give a stable baseline.
- Survey a representative employee sample unless you are prepared for the major resource commitments of a full staff census, of which the Philips case is a practical example.
- Give respondents enough scope to express their views, avoiding a "superficial soundbite approach" or overly simple surveys that can be completed in a few minutes.
- Avoid analyzing the results in too much detail, thus risking "analysis paralysis."
- Prepare a structured follow-up.
- Identify responsible parties for all reports.
- Limit any actions taken.

As to the wider context of surveys, there are two essentials: you must integrate employee measures with other process or functional activities and business objectives, but you must also set realistic targets. Many organizations adopt too much measurement for measurement's sake, which indicates a critical weakness. It is essential to have an employee measurement strategy aligned to corporate strategy and business results. Alignment should demonstrate the degree to which employee performance delivers customer requirements and improves customer satisfaction. A business analysis should first reveal key issues.

Apart from considerations such as overly obsessive measurement and the absence of strategic links, there are a number of other recommendations:

- Use both internal and external measures, the latter through benchmarking, which allows for validated performance comparisons.
- When analyzing data, keep in mind that there has to be a fit with business strategy or objectives, and HR policies.
- Analysis may well lead to remodeling the measurement process or model itself to effect more substantial or faster business outcomes.

A note of caution: you should avoid becoming confused if employee measurement reveals too many messages, as it may well do. Focus clearly and target action for only those response patterns that are of most value to the organization. This is crucial to avoid wasting time and money. That value may be interpreted in two ways: first, by improving organizational capability through better employee performance, and second, in creating a collaborative win-win context for more participative working. Employees always feel better when the employer measures their feelings, work, and behaviors. It shows concern and a commitment to do something about the results.

FEDERAL EXPRESS AND EUROPE

Federal Express (FedEx) was founded in 1973 and is now one of the world's largest express transportation corporations. Every day it moves more than 5 million packages, serves over 220 countries and 350 airports, employs over 560 aircraft and 37,000 vehicles, takes over 500,000 calls, and transmits about 45 million electronic messages.

The secret of its success rests with the performance of over 127,000 employees worldwide and a business philosophy of "People, Service, Profit," articulated by founder, chairman, and chief executive officer Frederick W. Smith. Right through the corporation is a belief in "people first," as, Smith has long argued, superior employee performance and satisfaction will get FedEx as close as is possible to 100 percent customer satisfaction. Smith is also known for business wisdom. After winning the first service category Malcolm Baldrige award in 1990, he said: "Not to have competed would have relegated our quality focus to a secondary status." However, when asked if FedEx had thus achieved the ultimate level of quality, he noted: "The receipt of this award is simply our license to practice."

The founder has been instrumental in the notion that "If you can't measure it, you can't manage it," being deployed throughout the organization, where it is fully applied to employee performance and satisfaction. Managers, too, are graded annually by people in their section, which could affect bonuses or result in training if performance is below par. The organization is known for best employment practices, which ultimately, through employee satisfaction, it says, lead to business success.

Values and Employee Measurement

Federal Express (FedEx) relies on some of the most sophisticated electronics systems in business today to track its 5 million-plus packages and 37,000 couriers a day, with performance being measured against a dozen demanding service quality indicators (SQIs). However, the business drivers come from People, Service, Profit (PSP), which is woven into the corporation's heart, management, structure, and every distribution line across the world.

This corporate belief has given considerable impetus to a whole range of employee, or more correctly, associate, best practice measurements. Strategically, individual performance and satisfaction are integrally linked through customers to business success for Federal Express. If you take care of your people, they will provide the type of service customers want, which results in profits. It is a cycle that works, measurably. Federal Express is emphatic that PSP is not just a slogan but considerably more, representing the way the company defines and operates its business. For instance, Smith himself wrote a section on values and people for the company's *Managers' Guide,* and PSP is a concept understood and practiced by the workforce, from a one-person suburban office to those who run midnight shift at the central Memphis, Tennessee, hub.

Linking the need for business measurement in operational minutiae, whereby any client anywhere in the world can ask the status of a package and be given an instantaneous answer or receive back their transportation charges, to performance that is integrally aligned with service excellence, it follows that employee measurement and satisfaction are crucial to the people element of PSP.

Business measurement has become far more rigorously defined for FedEx during the 1990s, mainly because of pressures from changing business conditions, competition, and recessionary influences. Over the last 10 to 15 years, competition has become stiffer. FedEx has had to be more efficient because costs have been driven down while value to customers has risen. Measurement is therefore much more critical as the firm tries to balance the three elements of the corporate philosophy more finitely. As an example of seeking this balance, much thinking at executive and HR levels has focused on the evaluation of discretionary effort, or the difference between an employee working at a level sufficient to just maintain the position or on a higher plane, which ensures total commitment to the job. This includes the classic FedEx catchphrase, "May I help?" delivered genuinely when approached by a customer, despite whatever logistics pressures that office might be experiencing.

By meeting the needs of employees, FedEx has proved that it can increase the value of discretionary effort. Reward systems for effort have to fit with customer service, align with the PSP cycle, and also provide a strategic business link between employee performance and customer satisfaction. This link is crucial for any service industry. The firm is highly dependent on people, so it is important it represents what customers want at the front-line interface.

In meeting the needs of employees, FedEx has few equals. It has a no layoff philosophy and a Guaranteed Fair Treatment procedure for grievances, which, if unresolved through appeals and reviews, can go as high as the company's chief executive officer. Training is extensive, promotion is from within, and recognition programs are innovative, Golden Falcon (service excellence) winners receive company shares, for example, and pay is very good in relation to sector-best yardsticks. In addition, internal communication is advanced, including its own television station, FXTV, started in 1987, and extensive e-mail. However, it should be stressed that employee satisfaction is not to be confused with motivation, which can affect performance but not necessarily a customer's perception. The company does not want associates who are simply motivated by delivering packages to hit their targets. They have to do it in the right way by working smarter, not harder. The customers will not be impressed by a courier throwing a parcel because he or she is in a hurry to get the next drop completed.

Studies have been conducted within Federal Express to examine notions such as organizational commitment (for example, how staff identify with the company and whether they want to stay), along with levels of satisfaction regarding rewards. It is worth emphasizing that these areas are intrinsically linked because internal research has proved that the more positive perception an individual has over the correlation between effort and reward, the stronger his or her commitment to the company. Naturally, FedEx values the characteristics of its employees, with self-motivation, pride in appearance, and an outgoing personality regarded as essential.

Operationalizing PSP

The PSP cycle works at all levels throughout the corporation, starting with the strategic business plan and flowing down to every operational level, which is, in effect, a process of management by objectives. FedEx starts at the top with executive management, which develops written statements outlining their parts in achieving a whole range of corporate goals. These then flow to each level of the hierarchy, ending with every individual being aligned to an objective with his or her manager. For example, in stations where parcels are picked up for delivery, an operating plan is put in place that covers the essential business elements of actually doing the job, such as revenue, costs, time scales, and so on. It will also set goals for the functional attributes deemed necessary for customer satisfaction, such as reliability.

An essential aspect of business strategy is total quality and, for operations, the related SQIs. Total quality emphasizes service excellence through customer satisfaction, including the internal customer-continuous improvement, people, and productivity. Practical initiatives encourage problem solving as low down the organization as possible, and include the ongoing deployment of quality action teams.

There are twelve SQIs related to deliveries, pickups, lost packages, and customer complaints, for example. The SQIs form the bedrock of business performance measurement and are given weighting to reflect the attributes that customers consider to be essential. They therefore link to customer satisfaction. As a result, customer service is measured precisely and is reinforced by an aggregated SQI total every week which is communicated on FXTV and through other internal media. The specifics of SQIs are considered within the overall plan and according to strategic goals. Thus, if FedEx wants to offer a more reliable service, operational teams would look at the practicalities of what they are being asked to achieve and what their performance is like every week.

Measuring Courier Performance

Despite complex systems for control and measurement at Federal Express, business operations have a simple concept, as demonstrated by its U.S. operations. All 2 million packages a day out of the worldwide total are routed through four U.S. hubs by air, rerouted out, and cleared either overnight or the next day to 1,400 U.S. facilities. There, the simplicity ends. When hub staff leave around 6:00 A.M., the day begins for 37,000 couriers whose job is to deliver all priority items for the company's 8:00 A.M. service.

Picking-up has its pressures too, creating a crunch time in the afternoon when couriers have to balance how long to let customers delay in sending a package while knowing that a scheduled FedEx jet is near take-off for Memphis or another hub. Obviously, the company has standards and daily measures for courier performance. These include the near-immutable deadlines, along with package volumes picked up or delivered per mile, per hour, and per route. Appearance codes and standards for personal style are also important. Behind these measures is the SuperTracker system introduced in 1986, which uses scanners, bar codes, and satellite links for every package handled. It tracks the status of packages and transmits information by satellite to Memphis control for compiling the ubiquitous SQIs. More broadly, couriers receive a performance review twice a year, over half of which is focused on objectives for on-road performance, pick-ups, and deliveries. Jointly with managers, the couriers establish standard guidelines for what both consider to be best practice in this line of work.

Managers go on observation rides with couriers to observe performance and then consider how many stops or deliveries are reasonable within a set time scale. Between them, they set a goal, which might be, for example, fifteen stops in an hour, assuming normal conditions and following established FedEx procedures. This mutually agreed goal then becomes the objective and, if the courier exceeds that goal by delivering, say, seventeen packages according to procedures, he or she will be eligible for a bonus on their hourly pay rate as part of performance-related compensation. In addition, regularly exceeding goals can lead to further lump sum bonuses for special individual commitment or for the overall success of the operational team in which the courier works. If everyone in a group exceeds targets, a team bonus applies to encourage leadership and teamwork. The station bonus system also stresses quantitative skills because efficiency can be enhanced with good planning and logistical abilities.

Noncourier Appraisal

Staff groups with less quantifiable work objectives are evaluated through appraisals and discussions, alongside job knowledge testing for customer contact people. Employees with customer contact are regularly tested on their general knowledge of Federal Express and job knowledge. For example, they are questioned on what they know about features and services, how they use company resources and facilities, and other areas linked to customer care. Those not considered to have the right level of knowledge are given study time for training. Feedback occurs after each test so that employees understand weak or strong areas of performance. These tests ensure people stay current with what is going on in the company, and the job knowledge score has an effect on the overall results of their performance reviews. The rest of the review score comes from performance on administrative tasks, safety matters, attendance, punctuality, sales, general practices, and specific items: as an example for couriers, whether they maintain the company vehicle well.

Although FedEx has considered a 360-degree appraisal process, it did not work well in practice for the firm so the technique was not adopted. Performance reviews are still undertaken by one's boss, and FedEx provides for "skip" interviews, which allow staff to talk to a manager's superior. One reason why 360-degree appraisal does not work for FedEx is that it is very difficult for peers to assess the work of the couriers, who operate on their own most of the time. They are the backbone of the business, but their colleagues do not necessarily know how they are viewed by the customer. This is a critical element of performance. The main problem with staff appraisal by peers is getting agreement on how it should work. Therefore, the systems are constantly modified and updated to allow for the best evaluation of individual performance according to clearly defined criteria.

Survey, Feedback, Action

The primary FedEx process for measuring employee satisfaction and evaluating the quality of management or leader performance is the Survey, Feedback, Action (SFA) process, introduced in the late 1970s.

The first part refers to the annual associate survey every spring, feed-back to joint employee-management discussions on the findings, and action, in the form of future work unit and manager activities, which is the result. Survey completion is voluntary and forms are received from every group with a manager or supervisor in the corporation.

The survey is used to establish the climate of the company. It covers how employees feel and also takes in the achievements of the work groups, problem-solving teams that continuously look at quality im-provements and other areas such as corporate or operating unit leader-ship. The first ten questions of the survey ask for reactions to statements on performance about an employee's immediate manager, covering areas like management style, keeping people informed, fairness, treat-ing subordinates with respect, listening, and awarding praise. Other questions cover the job, pay and benefits, safety, and so on. FedEx uses the results to ascertain trends and understand associate reactions to the corporation. Once survey data is processed in the central office in Memphis, each manager or work group leader receives a scoresheet of results for his or her area, which is reviewed at formal feedback meet-ings with staff. This ensures the group as a whole reviews unit perfor-mance and its leadership.

A documented action improvement plan is drawn up itemizing short-comings, corrective actions, and time scales, which is the basis of the unit's and the manager's objectives for the coming year. Where re-quired, specialized team briefing techniques are used to guide the feedback process, though a key emphasis for managers is to elicit response to the unit's performance measures, directed by three ques-tions: Are targets being reached? Is performance improving? Are targets challenging enough? Any groups that fall into the lowest 5 percent of aggregated results for the corporation as a whole are designated "crit-ical concern" groups and are led into improvement actions by specially trained facilitators. In these cases, the survey is repeated after six months to monitor progress.

Leadership evaluation is a critical element of the employee satisfac-tion survey, which is achieved through rating the abilities of a manager according to a number of statements. For example, one statement is, "I feel free to tell my manager what I think," to which a survey respondent could anonymously choose *agree sometimes, agree, strongly agree, some-times disagree,* or *strongly disagree.* Once the results are tabulated, each manager receives a personal performance score for each of the first ten statements. These are combined to give a Leadership Index, which is compared with a corporate goal for the index set every year. The empha-sis is on executive visibility and performance vis-à-vis employees.

If the score is particularly low, then as policy, human resources managers will be asked to intervene to address potential problems, perhaps with training programs. The individual manager will also be resurveyed after six months to establish whether staff attitudes have changed. The Leadership Index affects promotions and rewards. It is relevant to the balanced view of performance the firm is trying to achieve throughout. For example, if FedEx is considering rewarding a member of the staff for successful selling, it will not do so if high sales have been achieved at the expense of leadership skills, as perceived by their subordinates. This accords with FedEx's open door policy, which actively encourages employees to respond to the quality of executive leadership, decision-making processes, and management style. The firm actively promotes the idea that staff can send memos to senior management to ask, for example, on what basis decisions were made and how they meet company objectives.

Extending Measurement to Europe

Becoming a U.S. exemplar in employee measurement is summed up as follows: FedEx believed from day one that people are critical to successful business, thus giving considerable impetus to models and practices for measuring associate performance and satisfaction. As one of the world's largest express transportation corporation, it is interesting to assess the extent to which, and how effectively, corporate imperatives and best practices in these areas are transferred and adopted in other, multinational, territories.

The European division has used the United States as its internal benchmark and follows a number of years behind in terms of experience. U.S. colleagues have been running Survey, Feedback, Action since the late 1970s, whereas FedEx Europe started a decade later. FedEx Euorpe is not far behind in terms of response, though there are subtle differences between the U.S. model and how it is implemented across Europe and the Middle East. The firm used to use exactly the same survey for all European division employees but found there were certain cultural problems to overcome, including linguistic and interpretation issues and logistics.

As a result, the annual survey had to be translated into many local languages so that it has greater national relevance and addresses cultural norms or preferences. There are a significant number of differing cultures within this division, which have to be considered individually. To illustrate the point, Middle Eastern countries currently use the English version of the survey, but this is likely to change in the future. Apart from being published in an acceptable cultural form, good communication throughout Europe has been essential to emphasize, for example, that survey completion was voluntary and not mandatory. Also, a task force representing different levels, countries, and functions meets regularly to review what can be done to improve the SFA process.

In addition to translating the survey into different languages, the European headquarters office has the added dimension of having to consider national laws. For example, there may be a requirement in Germany to discuss any review and feedback issues with the Works Council, which is mandatory in that country and became increasingly expected across Europe with the 1996 European Union (EU) directive on this matter. FedEx cannot just assume that action toward corporate requirements from the United States can be interpreted in exactly the same way as in Europe. Often it is necessary for them to use consultants in national areas to help FedEx adapt or amend corporate plans.

Federal Express in the United States also addresses very large employee populations, whereas Europe has approximately five thousand in total. This represents a smaller sample, which may produce significantly different numerical results. However, the philosophy of employee evaluation is the same; it is not about pure data or number crunching but is an attempt to get a true, broad picture of how people, nationally and worldwide, respond to business objectives and what makes individuals perform in certain ways.

To avoid too much emphasis on raw figures, the firm is keen to move away from pure results and to emphasize the importance of the feedback and action elements of the SFA cycle. Europeans tend to answer questions more literally than Americans. For example, the latter will give a high score if they broadly agree with a statement, but Europeans will consider their response more seriously, weighing up different aspects of any statement's point, which can lead to lower overall scores on a manager's performance for his or her division.

The amalgamation of the Middle Eastern section with Europe opened new areas of cultural issues. The open culture and management style of Federal Express is very Westernized, so the firm had to be careful how this comes across in different countries. For example, in the Middle East, it is very difficult for employees to accept that they can openly criticize the performance of their managers. The firm has to explain that it is not a personal criticism but is in the interests of improved business performance. Much of the human resources work now is involved with more subtle interpretations of culture and its related issues.

Conclusion

In conclusion, critical success factors for employee measurement at Federal Express follow founder Frederick W. Smith's original philosophy of management. In essence, it stands to reason that if performance is measured, it should be done so accurately and, through individual contribution, should link with both rewards and overall business success.

It is essential to define what is being measured so that the appropriate reward systems can be put in place. In reality, all compensation and assessment mechanisms need to be controllable and appropriate, for example, sales leads. The firm may need sales, but there is no point rewarding someone who brings in lists of names that are not useful. The firm has to require qualified sales leads, those that do result in business and ultimately profit for the organization, whose originators are then rewarded.

The principle of control also applies to how the associate survey is designed and the Leadership Index. Statements used have to relate to actions that are controllable by the particular individual who will be affected by a response. There is no point using the statement, "I like working for Federal Express" within the survey because it is not a direct leadership matter. The manager might not be able to do anything about an employee's overall corporate perception. However, he or she can do something about his or her ability or willingness to listen to a colleague's viewpoints.

Areas of particular importance for corporate success need to be given special weight in terms of rewards and measurement. Incentives have to be tied to employee measures, which are first applied to essential and specific areas of individual performance. For example, if the firms wants people to be good at delivering parcels, it does not want them to just look at the speed of delivery. Customer satisfaction demands that other aspects be considered, including courteous service, flexibility, attention to detail, and accuracy. Integrating employee measurement with business objectives has therefore become a natural process under the People, Service, Profit philosophy at Federal Express. Though the corporation is highly capital intensive (because it needs to invest large amounts in transport, including aircraft), its critical emphasis is on people.

To recap, Federal Express has set objectives aligned to a functional operating plan, with performance being modeled and measured according to, ultimately, minimum and maximum profits contributions. As it is also an employee-intensive organization, the main variable is workforce productivity. It is crucial that people and employee satisfaction be made part of the overall business plan. They are moving over 2.5 million packages a day and have to get the logistics right to ensure they are successful. If the paperwork for air dispatch is incorrect, it can be costly for the business. Avoiding mistakes like that comes from discretionary effort, which drives employees to work smarter, not harder, and "get it right" the first time at all levels of operation.

NOTES

1. Hewitt Associates, *HR's Strategic Role in Building Competitiveness* (London: Author, 1992).

2. Society for Human Resource Management, *Human Resource Management, 10th Annual Survey* (Alexandria, VA: CCH Inc., 1995).

3. S. Y. Wilson, Effectively Recognizing and Rewarding Employees: Lessons from Malcolm Baldrige National Quality Award Winners, *ACA Journal* (Summer 1995).

4. Federal Quality Institute, *High Performance Organizations in Federal Agencies* (Gaithersburg, MD: Author, 1994).

5. Personnel Today, *New Mechanisms for Pay, Appraisal and Career Development: A Study of Success Factors and Results* (London: Author, 1995).

6. Industrial Society, *Managing Best Practice*, Vol. 2 (London: Author, 1994).

7. *360° Feedback—Unguided Missile or Powerful Weapon* (Berkhamstead, U.K.: Ashridge Management College, 1996).

8. William M. Mercer Inc., *Trends in Multi-Source Assessment* (New York: Author, 1996). Those organizations surveyed consisted of service businesses (58 percent), manufacturing (39 percent), and government agencies (3 percent).

9. *360° Feedback—Unguided Missile or Powerful Weapon.*

Trends and Practices in Financial Measurement

A QUESTION OF VALUE

Key Questions and Issues

What is the Coca-Cola trademark worth? The 115-year-old brand grew by 6 percent in 1995, and the corporation estimated its worth at US$39 billion for that year, which is equivalent to about 42 percent of the organization's entire market value. Yet in accounting terms, it is worth precisely US$1. This point indicates two extremes of contemporary financial measurement. The first, for many businesses, is solely through traditional reporting systems, measuring after the fact performance, operating margins, cash flows, return on investments, dividends, and so on. For investors in public organizations, price/earnings ratios, dividend yield, and ratios of share price to sales or book value are key measures to determine whether a stock is worth buying. These factors link a share price to some aspect of financial performance.

The second, more emergent extreme, is analyzing value creation. This is primarily done by shareholders but also, in some cases, other stakeholder constituents, such as employees, suppliers, and customers. Traditional valuation methods include book value and enterprise value, that is, market capitalization plus debt, though an approach gaining credibility is economic value added (EVA). In short, EVA measures the extent to which business activities earn more than the cost of capital to create, or conversely, destroy, value.

Coca-Cola is an EVA exemplar, creating value in 1995 when its accounts reported that the average return on capital more than tripled the cost of that capital, building immense sums of value, as noted next. Devised and applied since the 1980s by New York consultants Stern Stewart & Co. (though originally propounded by economist Irving Fisher at the turn of the century), advocates claim that EVA drives added value to the point where it has become a framework for reengineering financial management and measurement systems in some organizations.

Coca-Cola integrates EVA with traditional measures. In 1995, good performance was evident: operating income up 10 percent, earnings per share up 20 percent, and economic profit 15 percent. Economic profit is an EVA ratio, calculated on the basis of net operating profit after taxes (NOPAT) less operating capital charges. Economic profit at the organization has grown at an average rate of 27 percent per annum since 1983.

The stock price improved by 44 percent in 1995, versus 34 percent for the benchmark Standard & Poors (S&P) 500 Index, while dividends rose for the thirty-fourth consecutive year. Around US$27 billion of value was created in 1995, according to EVA calculations, and a further US$39 billion was created between January and September 1996, thus raising the organization's total worth to US$132 billion.

"Saying it the way that matters most to you, $27 billion of additional wealth was created for our shareowners," said Roberto Goizneta, chairman and chief executive, in Coca-Cola's 1995 annual report. "We must further ingrain throughout our business system the practice of value-based management, a simple methodology that evaluates the economic value created or destroyed by every decision we consider." This leads us to observe that in traditional, hierarchical, and overbureaucratic firms, value-enhancing energies are suppressed. EVA releases them from this problem and, by incentivizing management, allows its energies to be released in the interests of shareholder value. This is experienced at the U.S. corporation Lucas Varity and its U.K. engine-manufacturing subsidiary, VarityPerkins, both of which adopted EVA in 1993. However, it is more than just a financial measure. Rather than concerning investment appraisal alone, EVA is a way of running the business. Of note, EVA at VarityPerkins links to total quality, continuous improvement, and corporate change.

In the end-of-chapter case study, which explains in full how EVA works and is applied, VarityPerkins's economic value added is, more appropriately, a strategic performance measurement framework, linking strategic and financial objectives. It therefore directs business growth and decisions, from strategic reviews, acquisitions and capital investment to the detail of continuous performance improvement. The firm has a measure that brings together all the elements of corporate performance so they make consistent decisions. EVA is more embracing than most other financial measures.

By contrast, U.S. telecommunications multinational AT&T uses EVA principles as one of three integrated business measurement frameworks, which also align with annual self-assessment against Baldrige criteria, individual objectives, and rewards. Introduced in 1993, the other two are:

- Customer value added (CVA), which measures the perceived overall value of products and services compared with competitors
- People value added (PVA), which analyzes employee perceptions in relation to leadership, job satisfaction and other issues, with executive compensation being tied to the results

As PVA impacts on pay and personal image, organizations have a unique way of setting desired organizational behaviors through role-modeling to create customer and economic value.

As a brief overview, a question of value for multiple stakeholders and the strategic integration of EVA into the organization underpins these examples. To create and eventually sustain this, as Coca-Cola has done since 1983, begs a reconsideration of traditional financial measurement systems and, possibly, the function itself in terms of two central questions. First, what are the limitations of traditional systems in terms of more advanced practices or requirements in corporate measurement? Second, how might they relate to, or more fully balance in principle, with nonfinancial performance measures?

The discernible trend is for more realistic strategic performance measures is in response to, or is exposing, the limitations of traditional accounting-based measures, which:

- Are too historical
- Lack predictive power
- Reward the wrong behavior
- Are focused on inputs, not outputs
- Do not capture key business changes until it is too late
- Reflect functions that are not cross-functional processes
- Give inadequate consideration to quantifying difficult or less tangible business activities such as intellectual capital

In developing a strategic measurement system, our case study organizations generally clarify their strategic goals and develop a relatively short list of key performance indicators to measure their success in achieving these goals.

A number of critical points in linking financial measures with strategy are:

- Strategic performance measures are intended to capture, not only the value of current assets, but also the ability of those assets to produce wealth in the future.
- Measurement of performance is only a means to an end, which, ultimately, is enhancement of performance.
- Key performance measures should augment, rather than replace, financial measures.
- Most important, they are measures that focus the organization on the elements that are critical to achieving its strategic goals.

Traditional financial measures are fine for taking the temperature of an organization but inadequate for providing a complete health check when this is required. In addition, they tend to be historical through focus on past performance, despite the growing need for measurement to be predictive. Also, financial measures are not integrative, for example, in the case of a manufacturer, where the production process and outputs might be thoroughly measured but not directly aligned with sales figures and financials. Traditionally, measurement monitors performance, checks progress, and identifies areas that need attention. Many organizations still measure in this way, though increasing numbers are realizing that the process should give a more rounded picture of how healthy the business is and whether it is managed effectively. Ultimately, the best performance measures should assess health, stimulate learning, improve communication, and influence behavior, so a critical first question for executives is to ask: Do we have a balanced mix of financial and nonfinancial measures?

The rest of this chapter reviews financial measurement, which serves the attributes cited by examples so far (predictive, integrated, value creating, balanced) and examines newer trends that are having certain business impacts. Among these are EVA and activity-based cost management, but first we must ask about the strategic drivers of rethinking financial measurement and how, in practice, integration is achieved.

Widening and Integrating Financial Measurement

Next we consider the issue of strategic drivers and strategic performance measurement among major global corporations. Among these are Dow Chemical, First Chicago Trust, Kellog's Australia, Kleinwort Benson Investment Management, Pitney Bowes, Polaroid, Skandia AFS, and Toyota. All have developed this form of measurement for three outcomes:

- Better management
- Enhancing future performance
- Building investor value

Taking an overview of their practices as learning points, these organizations are searching for ways to capture the value of strategic investments in physical and human capital, but also to communicate their potential for creating investor value to financial markets.

These intangibles provide leading indicators of an organization's potential for growth. Also, as true drivers of business success, they provide innovative measures to compensate executives, thus linking the differing interests of investors, managers, and boards of directors. These organizations are implementing ongoing, dynamic measurement systems, through which strategic performance measures are converted into recognizable financial outputs such as sales and profits.

Key performance measures contribute, first, to strategic achievement and, second, toward the higher level financial performance measures of sales and profits. Ten of the former performance measures are typically integrated into the following process in best-practice organizations:

- Quality of output
- Customer satisfaction and retention
- Employee turnover
- Employee training
- Research and development (R&D) investments
- R&D productivity
- New product development
- Market growth and success
- Environmental compliance
- Other measures, specific to each organization

The link between strategic performance measurement, investors and markets can be established by citing a *Fortune* survey that asked eleven thousand executives, directors, and financial analysts for input in compiling its list of America's Most Admired Organizations.[1] Participants rated them according to eight characteristics in order of importance:

- Quality of management
- Quality of products or services
- Ability to attract, develop, and keep talented people
- Value as a long-term investment
- Use of corporate assets
- Financial soundness

- Innovativeness
- Community and environmental responsibility

Of note, the eight ranking factors include, not only traditional financial measures, but also strategic and intangible nonfinancial performance measures. External observers therefore expect integrated practices and measures. Reputation entails much more than just minting money. As measured in the survey, half comes from intangibles such as the way an organization treats its employees, how much it spends on research and development, and the strength of its management team. These abstractions count more than you might think.

Case Studies on Integration

BP Chemicals interprets both reputation and intangibles in this way. BP Chemicals's main financial goal relates to a specific return on average capital employed or ROACE target, though there are others. BP is determined to align its activities and measurement systems toward this goal, having first identified key success levers such as volume, health and safety, reputation, and capital efficiency. In a devolved, empowered, and geographically diverse organization, you need a framework of common goals and value to keep the entire organization pointing in the same direction.

BP Chemicals has ROACE, return on sales and cash, all ranked against competitors, as its key financial goals toward which six so-called success areas provide leverage through two integrated performance measures (IPMs) each. These success areas and IPMs are:

- Value: as measured by margins and capital efficiency
- People: with external reputation and employee morale measures
- Technology: competitive gap and capability growth
- Productivity: fixed costs and tons produced per person
- Volume: reliability and utilization
- Health: safety and environment, emissions, and accidents

Every quarter, the organization's financial summary now includes a one-page report on the nonfinancial IPMs. Moreover, in disseminations the success areas and IPM process between 1994–1997, ROACE training and awareness and a major poster campaign were essential, along with coordination by an IPM steering committee and executive support, especially those in BP Chemicals's accounting and finance functions. The integrated performance measures framework links executive team targets through the line to ground level activities and measures. Conversely, most IPMs align employee activities up the line management structure to the shareholder. This is absolutely necessary because, ultimately, the end is business success, as usually determined by achieving financial goals.

A similar end result is sought by U.K. investment firm Kleinwort Benson Investment Management Holdings Ltd. Organizations choose varying numbers of strategic measures, ranging from a minimum of three up to twenty. Kleinwort Benson uses twenty integrated measures grouped into four major categories:

- Growth:
  - Operating profitability
  - Business volumes
  - Value of client assets

- Client satisfaction:
  - Retention
  - Satisfaction survey ratings
  - Satisfaction index
  - Service standards
  - Investment performance

- Marketing and sales:
  - Audience perception
  - Recognition of client needs and opportunities
  - Innovation index
  - Sales pipeline
  - Product movements

- Business management:
  - Staff retention
  - Staff satisfaction
  - Training process
  - Project process
  - Internal customer relations
  - Credit quality
  - Balance sheet

Broadly speaking, this portfolio of measures represents good corporate practice but also the significant trend toward "inclusiveness."

Evaluating Inclusiveness

The inclusive approach requires important criteria to be demonstrated in practice, including clear leadership, an emphasis on strong business relationships, communicating values, and applying some kind of success model with integrated business measures. Kleinwort Benson demonstrates these attributes, but the significance of inclusiveness becomes apparent when considering that the organization launched the U.K.'s first two investment funds in late 1996, based on portfolios of organizations that deliver and sustain returns or performance against its principles.

The Kleinwort Benson investment model demonstrates a strong correlation between inclusive-type organizations and better investor returns through three stages:

- Evaluating management
- Assessing business processes
- The interaction of the previous two factors to build shareholder value

It broadens the scope of the investment process and includes analysis of the behavioral aspects of organizations, as well as business processes and financial results. The objective is to positively value organizations adopting best practices in these areas to pursue their competitive agendas. The methodology employed by Kleinwort Benson for constructing portfolios of this kind uses a scorecard system, which parallels the principles of models like the EFQM's Business Excellence Model and Investors In People, along with inclusive and corporate governance approaches to business. It provides a clear focus for performance measurement and cross-organization comparison.

Applying the methodology to measuring organizations for potential inclusion in the portfolio, Kleinwort Benson conducts a Fundamental Evaluation Assessment, which analyzes cash flow, sustainability of growth, sensitivities of financial performance, and improvements in individual measurement targets. It also examines other key parameters:

- Price/earnings ratio
- Dividend yield
- Discounted cash flow
- Net asset valuations

When aggregated, all these parameters help determine the most undervalued, and therefore attractive, future organizaiton structure, or inclusive, portfolio.

Prior to launch, the model was tested against a sample of 350 U.K. organizations based on market capitalization: it outperformed them for the previously discussed measures above by 16 percent in the short term and 38 percent in the longer term. Kleinwort Benson calculations predicted that a 1 percent change in sales growth, and in employee and supplier value added for portfolio organizations would give a 24 percent improvement in operating profit, a 5.3 percent lift to return on capital, and a 43 percent improvement in economic value added.

ECONOMIC VALUE ADDED

EVA Applications

The latter figure for the Kleinwort Benson portfolio is one indicator for the increasing adoption of EVA since the early 1990s. However, a second driver was the fact that current financial reporting standards require organizations to prepare balance sheets showing what would be left for creditors if the organization were dissolved. This suits both creditors and bankers, but not shareholders, who are left with little idea of what the business assets are worth.

The proposition is that economic value, and not accounting value, should be the primary approach to financial measurement. A substantial body of empirical research indicates a positive relationship between EVA or economic profit improvements and enhanced share prices and these organizations also tend to outperform others in their sectors. As noted, Coca-Cola is an excellent example of this in practice.

To recap, EVA measures the increase in economic profit, which is operating profit after taxes less charges for the cost of capital, generated from one year to the next. The methodology adds back spending conventionally charged against profits such as R&D, marketing, and good will, which appears on an EVA balance sheet as assets and not deductions, as in traditional accounting. Aggregated over time, the formula provides a total market value added (MVA) figure, which is an organization's market value less the capital tied up in the business. In effect, then, EVA examines and measures a business from a shareholder's point of view and alters the accounting system accordingly.

EVA has four attributes:

- Measures corporate performance
- Prioritizes capital expenditure, including the cost, funding, and payback of acquisitions
- Provides incentive comparisons
- Helps communicate with Stern's so-called "lead steers," dominant, price-setting investors active in any stock market

Marketplace and investment community need are what drive EVA. It has a high correlation with MVA, so managers cannot win unless shareholders do so, too. This is because they have different accountabilities

and because the methodology lengthens corporate and individual decision horizons. In short, high economic value added convinces institu-
tional investors to acquire the organizations stock. Its principles are
applicable to most industries and cultures; for example, half of stock
market–listed organizations in the Pacific Rim territories now apply
EVA. However, two types of organizations are resistant to this new form
of financial measurement: bureaucracies like government agencies or
public utilities and those where risk taking is not encouraged.

That said, exemplar Coca-Cola has been committed to EVA principles
since 1983, driven by its founding mission "to create greater value for
share owners." In an organization as large as Coca-Cola, achievements
are not always easy to measure or comprehend, which is why EVA was
adopted as an easy-to-use tool to measure financial performance. Since
1995, EVA-based financial measurement has been deployed across the
entire organization to guide business unit activities and decision making based on the cost of operating capital employed. Each is accountable
against monthly, quarterly, and annual targets for its economic profit
and EVA at two levels, net income and operating capital, after producing a three-year business plan annually, from which the budget for the
current year is approved.

Formal reporting monitors progress against budget, business goals,
and profit targets, with management being encouraged by Coca-Cola
to influence its own EVA by adopting three strategies related to local
contexts and business conditions:

- Investing in projects related to corporate strategy that generate
  returns in excess of the cost of capital
- Growing net income, improving volumes and revenues, creating
  efficiencies for better operating margins, and ensuring that costs
  and expenses grow more slowly than revenues
- Reducing operating capital costs through efficiencies and eliminating low-return or unnecessary activities

Notably, too, Coca-Cola determines annual and long-term incentives
for eligible employees and executives based on performance against
economic profit targets. This ensures that management teams are
clearly focused on the key business drivers.

EVA, Compensation, and Incentives

This latter point on incentives is a critical success factor for EVA. It
was not until five years or so after designing the EVA methodology that
it recognized the importance of compensation links to the model. If
performance measures were aligned in one direction with incentives

based on other criteria, managers would naturally focus on the direction rewarded by incentives. Accordingly, an EVA-related compensation system was launched in 1990, which is based on improvements to economic profit. Incentives are typically paid with one third immediately awarded in cash in addition to base salary, plus two thirds deferred at risk, should performance fall below targets. The second element comprises both cash and share options and may be deferred for one to several years. This type of plan aligns shareholder and employee interests. As EVA can be measured layer by layer through the business, staff get incentives according to activities they can actually influence, unlike stock prices, on which they have little direct influence.

The phased payment also makes employees and managers view EVA performance over the longer term because it carries financial disincentives for poor performance. In fact, a whole family of EVA-based incentive ideas can be designed that incorporate one year's performance improvements into the following year's base compensation levels.

Broadly, this is how EVA incentives and compensation work at U.S.-based Lucas Varity and VarityPerkins in the United Kingdom, the case study in this chapter. EVA permeates every level, from the boardroom to the shop floor. The bonus of the chief executive and those of senior managers are determined solely by whether they achieve their EVA targets. Every decision and action results from EVA principles, to focus everyone on returns that exceed the firm's cost of capital. At VarityPerkins, bonuses based on EVA targets comprise a minimum 10 percent of salary for all staff, rising to higher percentages for directors and senior executives. The organization's profit-related pay schemes are also linked to EVA performance.

Business targets are reset annually, based on the previous year's actual performance and predetermined annual EVA improvement targets. As the model recommends, some senior management bonuses above a certain level are "banked," meaning withheld or deferred, against the next year's performance. VarityPerkins says this achieves three outcomes: it prevents any manipulating of figures by managers to artificially inflate bonuses, helps instil a longer-term business focus, and tends to level out peaks and troughs in bonus patterns. These targets drive business plans and performance, which gives a structure to budget and reward setting. Managers know what they have to achieve, and nothing gives incentives to management like an EVA incentive scheme.

Critical Success

EVA deployment and leadership are critical factors for the successful application of EVA. The most effective approach is for an organization to establish a steering committee of all senior operating managers, typically twelve, including the chief executive officer, finance director, and heads of planning and HR. However, you must be careful to ensure that all managers participate so that everyone feels they have a stake in ensuring EVA success. You have to educate employees, too. Explain, keep them up-to-date and reinforce your message. The process takes a very strong commitment from an organization's chief executive officer in championing EVA and accepting its consequences. Without this top-level drive, people will simply play the system and return to the familiar performance game.

This latter point is the very key to success. Leadership is critical and has been the most significant factor behind the successful adoption of EVA throughout Varity. Operating management must also buy in, and much effort is required in training and communication. These points apply to all VarityPerkins employees, 30 percent of whom are also shareholders. A sixteen-page EVA booklet is given to all employees, with monthly updates by newsletter, and the importance of EVA is reinforced as one element of total quality training programs.

ACTIVITY-BASED COST MANAGEMENT: CONTEXT

If the question of value is a central tenet of EVA, cost is endemic to financial measurement, overheads, labor, productivity, the cost of quality, and so on. However, whereas traditional cost accounting systems provide data without difficulty, accurately identifying the cause of cost is less certain an activity and, therefore, effective cost control. This point has given rise to activity-based cost management (ABCM), or activity-based costing. In effect, this is a contemporary methodology that can add on to existing cost accounting methods or act as a cross-functional process that identifies non–value-adding activities and cost drivers. Especially for the latter situation, ABCM is a substantial contributor to strategic decision making, process improvement, and performance measurement.

Its strategic framework hinges on two principles, internal capability and external positioning through commercial strategy. The former incorporates structure, processes, skills, methods, and so forth, and features four measures:

- Activity-based budgeting
- Resource management
- Capacity management
- Process measurement

Positioning concerns customer needs, competitors, and shareholders and also has four measures:

- Costing
- Profitability
- Portfolio analysis
- Pricing and estimating

Underpinning ABCM, Develin[2] argues, is a commitment to change management that takes an organization from its current position to a future vision through a variety of means, such as:

- Reengineering
- Rebalancing resources
- Rethinking service provision
- Benchmarking
- Continuous improvement

The critical consideration is better product and customer profitability, as driven by customer needs and behaviors. Adopting activity-based costing makes an organization rethink and measure the cost drivers in process performance. It means asking two questions: What value is added where in a business activity? How can this process be improved?

Better cost management was the rationale for Shell International Exploration and Production (EP) deploying activity-based costing (ABC) in parallel with the principles and best practices of asset management. There are four interacting reasons for this:

- Falling oil prices
- Rising operational costs
- Different reporting structures within the organization
- Lower profitability

The business context for ABC at Shell EP is certainly revealing. The organization is the world's largest operator of its kind, active in eighteen countries with interests in a further twenty-seven, and produces 4 million refined barrels of oil and 450 million cubic meters of gas a day. Reserves of these "product flow" assets total 9 billion barrels and 1,400 billion cubic meters, respectively. However, assets are broadly classified into five groups:

- Product flows
- Knowledge, through best practices and technology

- Knowledge and risk management
- People skills and competencies
- Services

The fundamentals of activity-based costing can be universally applied to all aspects of operations and the petroleum resource life cycle from exploration to abandonment. Also, the method can supply a range of detail, from management summaries to specific analyses with equal merit. As interpreted at Shell EP, these fundamentals are:

- Using common classification structure for all activities in the organization's business model, expenditure costed is defined as the consumption of resources while undertaking an activity upon an asset with each element having appropriate levels of reporting.
- There is clear definition of individual accountabilities, based on a corporate asset register, for two roles, asset holders with single point and total accountability as determined by the chief executive who then delegate work on their assets to other asset holders or activity executors. A key success factor is the quality of internal customer/supplier relationships between these roles.
- The activity-based costing methodology, although primarily dealing with cost elements in corporate management systems, includes other considerations, introducing life cycle thinking in asset reference plans, for example.

In relating activity-based costing to asset management at Shell EP, the organization has to deliver what it promises in terms of the internal return on investments and alos externally, for its reputation as a prudent and cost-effective organization.

Where there have been lapses in asset performance and asset integrity in the past, hindsight often highlights a weak emphasis on making assets work, poor integration of activities and inadequate control. Asset management addresses these shortcomings by determining roles against the five previously mentioned groups. In addition to the asset holders, three other roles act as service providers: process owners, responsible for best practices and technology; risk advisers, for standards and policies; skill managers, for people assets.

A key step in managing assets is to build relationships between the asset holders and their service providers. These should be as close as practicable to external commercial arrangements through service agreements. The asset management model shows how asset holders provide goods or services for each other and are judged on the criteria that are significant for their kind of asset, whether cash flow, compliance, integrity, or a combination of all three.

It is a general view that activity-based costing applies only to calculating product or process costs in manufacturing organizations or, indeed, for organizations like Shell that have complex structures. Nonetheless, the methodology can also be used effectively in service environments, as exemplified by the U.S. Internal Revenue Service (IRS). The adoption of ABC in relation to cost management and continuous business improvement in a federal agency, in line with the previously mentioned point concerning the process and value-added dimensions of ABC, builds on business processes. This is because these processes comprise activities that convert inputs to outputs. The methodology organizes all cost information on an activity basis, behind which is a fundamental belief, that cost is caused and that those causes can be managed. The closer you come to relating costs to causes, the more helpful accounting information will become in guiding management decisions.

Whenever IRS did cost-benefit analyses in the past, difficulty was experienced in apportioning labor, overheads, and general support costs using traditional accounting methods, a not uncommon experience in any bureaucratic organization. But, resource use and management had become a critical priority with significant efficiency pressures in federal departments throughout the 1990s, hence, their adoption of ABC.

IRS defined staff outputs in the collection division as "products" and "product streams" and was able to determine which costs applied to which units and business processes. Applying ABC, one project produced remarkable first findings. It found that a product stream in the Laguna Niguel district of California, which had annual costs of $1.36 million had 74 percent of activity costs supporting non–value-added activities. As a result, further analysis concentrated on four major collection division activities: processing cases, investigations, resolution of cases, and case closures.

The IRS found that two of these items had 94 percent and 98 percent non–value-added activity, respectively, with the other two at 64 percent and 69 percent. These numbers, with their related costs, provided the ammunition recommend several changes to the current method of doing business. The IRS identified sixteen improvement opportunities to eliminate or minimize non–value-added activities and demonstrate hard dollar savings. Both gave immediate muscle to the case when presented to agency executives, and their buy-in was almost undeniable.

As to learning points from initially applying the ABC methodology, three employees were eager for change to occur and were creative in suggesting solutions; cross-functional teamwork enhances improvement opportunities; and the inclusion of administration or support staff in projects helped reduce non–value-adding impacts.

OVERVIEW

Having considered issues such as value, balance, integration, and strategic financial measurement, one point is clear about this aspect of corporate performance: in leading organizations it is being, at minimum, reconsidered or, at best, completely rethought. The impact is affecting finance and accountancy professionals, too; for example, some financial directors now speak of reengineering the function. Here is a recap of the significant issues:

- Traditional financial measures have limitations, being nonpredictive, historically biased, and focused on inputs. Therefore, by their nature, they cannot proactively drive business change, which is a fundamental requirement of any organization facing competitive realities.
- Thus, a newer emphasis is emerging on value creation and measurement, that is, the application of economic value–added principles or discovery through measurement and then elimination of non–value-adding activities.
- Financial measures should relate to all others in the business as an integrated, strategic performance measurement portfolio with linkages apparent to help nonfinancial personnel understand their importance. Balance is a key word here.
- In financial terms, balance also applies to measuring the basics of revenues and costs, with cost management, as an internal control, being more widely interpreted through process focus and methodologies such as activity-based costing.

A significant point needs adding: as pressures insist that traditional financial measurement systems be reviewed, reshaped, and realigned, new, applied ideas are emerging, which have to be evaluated, and will continue to be so. Two examples suffice. First, different models are being devised by specialist consultancies and, sometimes, by leading organizations themselves. For example, Develin & Partners designed the Overhead Value approach, a process-focused, cost reduction mechanism, while Caterpillar Inc. adopted a transfer pricing method to help resolve its competitive problems in the early 1990s. This is a cost-improvement process aligned with market-based profit center transactions. Both are itemized, not as recommendations, but to highlight that over time, many similar developments can be expected that work in practice for proponents. Finance directors and other executives concerned with strategic performance measurement must remain aware of these possibilities.

The second example concerns a burgeoning business issue, the environment. For all organizations, environmental impacts and environmental performance measurement are becoming critical considerations in strategy for heavy manufacturers and service firms alike, partly because of a "green" groundswell but also through growing public pressure for social accountability. Expectations are high and corporate reputations may be at stake. Thus, for example, Nortel Canada operates an Environmental Performance Index, which gives a single rating on twenty-five parameters of production and the environment in relation to annual sales. Financial measurement plus input from this function's professionals helped create the Index. A similar arrangement exists at Danish industrial enzymes giant Novo Nordisk. Its Eco-Productivity Index, which is applied at all worldwide sites, measures resource utilization for raw materials, water, energy, and packaging. Efficiency, waste reduction, and cost elimination, the very meat of traditional financial measurement, are key attributes.

As a final consideration on trends that are driving a rethinking of financial measurement, the social dimensions of corporate governance and public accountability must be taken into account by any astute executive. Can these dimensions be measured internally? Perhaps they cannot be measured, or only with difficulty, but if they are increasingly considered as investment criteria, as with the Kleinwort Benson funds referred previously, for example, the effects might become considerable. After all, they impact on the ultimate financial measure for public organizations, the stock price, and equity value for any other business borrowing money, both of which could be adversely affected if all elements of business activities and measurement are not blended into some view of coherent, strategic performance.

In the United States, major organizations such as Coca-Cola, AT&T, Wal-Mart, and Quaker Oats have become advocates of EVA. A particularly enthusiastic organization is the Varity Corporation, based in Buffalo, New York. EVA permeates every level, from the boardroom to the shop floor. The bonus of the chief executive and all senior managers bonuses, are determined solely by whether they achieve their EVA targets. Every decision and action results from analysis that uses its principles in order to focus us on ensuring that every investment produces a return that exceeds their cost of capital. This approach enables the corporation to directly align management and shareholder interests, which produces a critical outcome. All personnel think and act like shareholders, whether they are senior managers engaged in strategic decision making, total quality teams in their plants making decisions about capital expenditures, or employees taking action to reduce shop floor costs.

For Varity, EVA is not just a financial measure. It is too often regarded as being about investment appraisal alone, but to really work, it has to be a way of running the business. EVA bridges any gap between short-

and long-term business planning because, whether you are purchasing tools or revisiting processes, the same decision criteria used for each.

VARITYPERKINS, UNITED KINGDOM

Context

The quest at VarityPerkins for creating sustainable shareholder value has been a significant issue in contemporary business since the early 1980s, more recently fueled by the trends toward corporate governance in the 1990s. Shareholder value is often perceived as purely increasing operating efficiency, measured historically by conventional practices, budgets, margins, profits, cash flows, earnings, dividends, and so on. However, a growing number of primarily multinational organizations are interpreting shareholder value more widely to incorporate value-adding growth and the positive avoidance of value-destroying business activities. The aim is to maximize investor wealth through value creation, using the concept of economic value added (EVA).

EVA is a measure and driver of added value for corporate activities and the deployment of resources. In some organizations, EVA has become a framework for reengineering financial management systems in order to more effectively manage shareholder interests internally and decentralized value-based planning.

EVA Snapshot

Fundamentally, EVA is based on the market value of assets and, in principle, is similar to net discounted cash flow. It is a means of measuring genuine economic profitability, that is, value created by an organization, by factoring the cost of capital into conventional profit and loss accounts. Therefore, EVA can be defined as posttax operating profit minus the cost of capital: in other words, the difference between the return on capital and the cost of capital.

If this return is greater than cost, EVA is positive and the organization is creating value, but if it is negative, the business is, in effect, destroying value for its shareholders. However, a negative EVA could be perfectly compatible with an organization showing a profit in conventional terms. However, organizations that do not reduce the extent to which their reported profits fail to cover their cost of capital are unlikely to report consistently increased profits in the longer term.

A substantial body of empirical findings and research indicates that improvements in EVA have a strongly positive relationship with increased share prices and that organizations with high EVA returns tend to outperform their market sectors. Applying EVA involves examining a business from a shareholder's point of view and altering the accounting system accordingly. Rather than using liquidation values, EVA measurement focuses on cash and cash-generating assets. Sums conventionally deducted, such as deferred tax, goodwill amortization, and R&D expenditure, are added back to profit.

Cost of capital is also relevant from a shareholder viewpoint as an investor usually has to pay the opportunity cost for having money tied up in an organization. For EVA purposes, this is based on a combination of risks: the yield on safe investments, the risk of shares versus bonds, and the risk of that particular organization are three examples. The resulting percentage is combined with the cost of the organization's debts to provide an overall "cost of capital" figure.

Adopting EVA

The difficulties faced by the group in the mid-1980s meant that cash management and shareholder value were very high on the agenda, with the first being almost as important as profit and loss accounting. There was an emphasis on maximizing the use of assets by squeezing cash out of them, so the concept of an asset charge, which is central to EVA, was aligned with the organization's ideas of making assets work more effectively.

Parallel moves in the mid-1980s saw VarityPerkins reorganized into three engine manufacture and supply organizations, for small, medium and large engines, plus businesses handling distribution, licensees and overseas joint ventures, parts sales and engineering design and development. Early in 1996, a business was also established to focus on developing activities for the Asia-Pacific region. As the business is to manufacture and sell diesel engines, it could have been centrally organized along functional lines, but in this type of organization, it is difficult to find who is accountable for profits. The corporate thrust was to drive responsibility for profit down the organization, so the principle of separate subsidiary businesses was adopted, as was the principle of outsourcing those activities that were not critical to the success of engine design and manufacture.

For example, the parts warehouse facility in Manchester, U.K., is managed by Caterpillar logistics. In this sector, the firm is a leader in warehouse management performance, so it makes sense for it to handle this aspect of the operations. Outsourcing nonessential operations has allowed the firm to develop a low-cost manufacturing base, doing internally only what it believes it can do better than other organizations. As a result, it manufactures less internally than almost any other diesel engine manufacturer in the world. Apart from the basic parts, everything is bought in.

The decision to adopt EVA across Varity was made in 1993 in order to introduce a simpler method of measuring the achievement of corporate objectives, therefore replacing several different, and not necessarily compatible, performance measures. In addition, EVA was perceived as:

- Helping to build a new continuous improvement-based culture
- A means of bridging the gap between short- and long-term business
- An effective way of linking incentives to actual performance

EVA was seen as meeting all these criteria. It is perceived as a business performance measure that VarityPerkins has found is appropriate to such disparate areas as:

- Examining capital investment decisions
- Evaluating acquisitions and divestments
- Measuring business performance
- Rewarding staff performance
- Goal-setting
- Communicating financial results
- Assessing strategy

These areas had previously been measured in terms of return on average assets, cash flow, net income, working capital ratios, and a number of other metrics. The firm wanted a measure that would bring different elements of corporate performance together so decisions would not be made inconsistently and in isolation. EVA is more all-embracing than most other financial measures. It is more user friendly and easier to report. Managers can tell each month the amount of EVA generated by each of the businesses. By applying EVA, they can be certain that buying an organization, investing in machine tools, developing a product, or rewarding performance are all assessed on the same basis. This is the technique's great strength.

EVA underpins the organization's emphasis on total quality and business excellence. EVA is about year-on-year improvement and naturally feeds into total quality. In effect, total quality is the means and EVA is the result. The VarityPerkins view is that an EVA-based management framework:

- Enables business opportunities to be evaluated on a consistent basis
- Allows the assessment of relative returns on different projects and activities
- Encourages an appreciation of the organization from a shareholder-value viewpoint

Fundamentally, it encourages managers to act as "shareholders," who then become motivated and rewarded on that basis. EVA is therefore fully compatible with total quality and its focus on continuous improvement. EVA creates the environment for improvement, acting as both a measure and a driver.

EVA Implementation

The introduction of EVA measures took place across Varity over a twelve-month period. Definitions of the concept were established and a number of changes made to the group's traditional accounting system to make it more cash-based. Adjustments included relating pensions accounts to a cash base and the capitalization of leases.

EVA targets for Varity and its subsidiaries were calculated, and these were then integrated into existing financial systems. Three major streams of training were provided for participants at board level and below within VarityPerkins (including identifying EVA champions) plus across individual businesses. The concept of an EVA champion is akin to having someone responsible for best practice. As an example, individual directors in the group are now responsible for their own strategic action plans designed to deliver planned growth over the next five years. The managing director of Perkins Engines Peterborough, the business for mid-range engines, is responsible for cost-based management techniques, of which EVA is an important part. His informal title of EVA champion is one way of ensuring that in applying techniques such as Kaizen, manufacturing process reengineering, and the management of business costs, there is someone responsible for ensuring that best practice is shared throughout the group.

The drawing up of a practical definition of EVA for use in VarityPerkins was a compromise between theoretical purity and operational simplicity in order to get an understandable measure. A number of decisions were made to establish the EVA accounting structure:

- Cost of capital
  - Single or multiple? Single. Varity uses a target debt equity ratio, which allows for decisions to be made in line with where the organization wants to be.
  - Constant or variable? Constant, based on cost of capital plus cost of debt.
  - Capital structure? Target 40 percent debt-capital ratio.
  - Pre- or posttax? Pretax. For most investment decisions, tax is irrelevant. Where it is an important factor, as in tax leverage it can be factored in, but 99 percent of the firm's calculations are made simple by using pretax figures.

- Definition of net operating profit
  - Good will amortization? No, good will is a component of business assets that shareholders have paid for: as they are seeking a return, good will should stay on the balance sheet.
  - Operating leases? Capitalize.
  - Treatment of gains or write offs? Reverse.
  - Reorganization costs? Reverse or amortize.

- Capital employed
  - Long-term liabilities? To be included.
  - Cash? To be included

Applying the system involves a certain flexibility to allow time for projects to become established. For example, the organization might recognize that an expansion into South East Asia in line with strategic objectives might make a loss in the short term.

If EVA is to work, it forces you to take long-term measures to expand the organization. You can only do so much to maximize the use of existing assets, so to enhance EVA in the long run, the business has to grow. Therefore, on certain selected strategic investments for EVA calculation purposes only, short-term losses will be capitalized, for a period not exceeding three years, and then amortized. The keys to successful implementation of EVA include senior management leadership. This is critical, and the involvement of the chief executive has been the most significant factor behind the successful adoption of EVA throughout Varity. Group operating management must also buy into EVA, and much effort is required in communication and training.

Communicating the benefits of EVA has been extended to all VarityPerkins's employees. It also features in total quality training programs, albeit focusing on the means of delivering business outcomes through total quality–driven, continuous improvement.

A sixteen-page booklet explaining EVA, its importance and links with continuous improvement has been distributed to all staff and monthly changes are communicated via newsletters. Employee involvement is significant because 30 percent are currently Lucas Varity shareholders through stock purchase schemes launched in 1995.

Incentives and EVA

EVA is also strongly linked to performance incentives. Lucas Varity has a financial target of annual incremental increases in EVA and has developed an EVA-based financial management structure. The parent group also estimates its stock market position at a certain point and the gains in EVA required to drive share values to this position. These are then broken down and allocated as annual targets to organizations within the group.

Developing Systems

A key priority in implementing EVA was establishing an EVA-based financial management system. This is based on the long-term objective of maximizing market value added (MVA), with financial targets set in EVA terms, and business planning focused on strategies to maximize EVA.

MVA is defined as the difference between assets calculated in terms of EVA and an organization's capitalization value. To raise the share price by a certain value over a known period of years, the level of annual increases in EVA required to give an incremental MVA is calculated. This annual increment gives the corporate financial targets for Lucas Varity and its subsidiary businesses.

The main elements of developing a financial management system based on EVA at VarityPerkins are:

- Capital budgeting: accepting all projects that produce a positive discounted EVA
- Business valuation: discounted future EVA and capital book value
- Acquisition: limit premium on book value to expected future value of EVA
- Disposal: divest activities where sales value is greater than the book value plus net present value of EVA
- Accounting: adjust traditional accounting to focus on cash investment and cash returns

The EVA Links to Strategy

Forging links between EVA and strategy is essential, along with a reappraisal of the business-planning process. The latter has evolved over the years into three critical elements. One aspect examines the organization's market share and key external influences; a second looks at VarityPerkins through the eyes of customers and involves an external competitive assessment; and in the third, the top four or five strategic objectives are defined and strategic action plans to deliver them are drawn up.

Many organizations have nothing to link their strategic plans with financial objectives, but the finance and planning director must know what the top strategic activities to deliver the projected increases in sales and profits. The organization's strategic action plans include milestone and performance targets and are all evaluated on an EVA basis.

By using EVA as a strategic tool, business growth can be planned and the actions required to deliver it are identified. Inexorably, EVA leads to better evaluation of the strategies proposed to deliver the growth plans in the organization. The particular advantages are the interlinkage between all elements of business planning and the strategic intent. Many organizations may have similar aspirations and financial projections, but they do not take them further to develop consistent action plans. With EVA, nothing is inconsistent.

The technique also influences the VarityPerkins strategy on mergers and acquisitions. Estimates of the potential EVA to be generated by a target organization make it clear whether a premium on the book value being demanded by the vendor is excessive. Similarly, if the price offered for a Varity organization exceeds its EVA targets, then it may make sense to sell. In fact, using EVA to develop strategy encourages a consideration of mergers where no acquisition premium is paid, as in the 1996 Lucas-Varity merger.

EVA in Practice

Day-to-day decisions by employees at all levels affect VarityPerkins' EVA in two areas, profit growth drivers and capital stewardship drivers. The profit growth drivers include:

- Total quality initiatives
- Sales and marketing activities
- Margin enhancement
- Productivity gains
- Customer service
- Tax planning

The capital stewardship drivers include:

- Receivables management
- Preventative maintenance
- Payables management
- Supply chain management
- New investments
- Asset sales

Applied in this way, everyone in the organization can see how these factors affect EVA. One example is the more effective management of payables and receivables. In fact, the receivables cycles are down from 78 days in 1992 to 53 days and, in the largest VarityPerkins business, 48 days. VarityPerkins states that since introducing EVA it has seen rising sales revenue and profits and business units have recorded significant benefits:

- Reduction in cycle times and changeover times
- Increased inventory turnover
- Elimination of waste
- Reorganized and upgraded machining facilities
- Enhanced margins

EVA was also used to make the decision to proceed with a joint venture with ISM, the acquisition of Dorman Diesels, the sale of Gardner, and the outsourcing of parts warehousing. At a Varity Corporation level, EVA has also had an impact on portfolio management, such as the sale of Hayes Wheels, in which Varity had a 46 percent stake, and it also subsequently affected the decision to initiate a share buyback scheme. Seeing a relatively higher cost of equity versus debt, the organization repurchased 7 million shares, or 17.5 percent of outstanding common stock, in two stages up to 1995. In the United Kingdom, share repurchase schemes are not as common as in the United States, but this was seen as a very responsible move. In effect, the organization was saying to shareholders: "We do not need this at present, it is your cash." Buybacks are very supportive of the EVA concept of organizations being managed on shareholders' behalf.

Although, like other organizations, VarityPerkins uses a number of operating measures to monitor different aspects of operational performance, first-time pass rates for delivered quality, operator productivity, and so on, it is somewhat unique in the United Kingdom for the way in which it has developed a business planning and reporting system that is truly EVA-based. EVA is therefore an all-embracing structure for measuring and driving progress in Varity. It is more than just a measure. It acts as a driver of change and continuous improvement from a shareholder's point of view. The requirement to deliver year-on-year increases in shareholder value continually challenges the firm to seek better ways of doing business. Figures are available on how it might do so. In 1992, the Varity Corporation had a negative EVA of $150 million. The corporation set a five-year target to reach a positive EVA and, by 1995, had reached 80 percent of this target. In 1994 Varity Corporation had a positive MVA of $573 million but an EVA of negative $22 million.

NOTES

1. A. B. Fisher, Corporate Reputations: Comebacks and Comeuppances, *Fortune*, vol. 133(4), 1996, pp. 90–97.

2. Develin and Partners, a U.K. consulting firm that specializes in this area.

10

Knowledge Management and Measurement

CRITICAL TRENDS AND PRACTICES: THE CONTEXT FOR VALUING KNOWLEDGE

By the year 2000, U.S. multinational, Dow Chemical Company, was making over US$125 million a year from licensing fees for its intellectual property rights. By cutting the number of active patents to 16,000, around $40 million in tax obligations will be saved over a ten-year period. American insurance giant USAA has an IT-driven customer feedback and knowledge system that boosts sales, cuts costs, and contributes to the bottom line. Ford's digitalized technical and customer information system, called Fordstar, is a virtual learning network linking six thousand global dealerships which extends training but helps to cut costs. For several years, Swedish financial services group, Skandia, has published an *Intellectual Capital* supplement to its annual report, primarily for investor and client readership. These corporate snapshots indicate four dimensions of knowledge management, which is exploding throughout the business world as a multifaceted armory for enhancing competitiveness, direct bottom-line results, more customer knowledge to increase loyalty, virtual learning, and public reporting.

Leading consultancies are also active. Consider that the Price Waterhouse Cooper's internal knowledge network has over two thousand databases, which its employees worldwide can access for best practices, studies, and expert opinions. Similarly, Arthur Andersen's Global Best

Practices initiative has a knowledge repository with 18,000 pages of world-class business practices for people in seventy-six countries.

To share perspectives and extend the knowledge dialogue, leading organizations are themselves proactive. Virtual knowledge collaborations are increasingly common through the Internet and videoconferencing and the building of organizational intranets is becoming a corporate priority. Dow's, for instance, has 28,000 electronic workstations.

What is organizational knowledge? Is knowledge management anything more than a fancy phrase or intellectual exercise for most of the business world? Does it represent a sustainable commercial proposition? Can all the dimensions of knowledge be effectively identified, captured, classified, understood, applied, measured, and valued? What is driving the wider knowledge movement other than pockets of individual best practice among pioneers?

KNOWLEDGE MANAGEMENT

The term *knowledge management* is now widely used in the literature. Where employed the tendency is to define it narrowly to focus on a specific aspect relating to either knowledge, innovation, or learning. For example, Hedlund and Nonaka[1] and Hedlund[2] use the term to describe the relationship between tacit and articulated knowledge in relation to different levels of carriers (individual, group, organization, and interorganizational). Although an appropriate usage of the term, it is argued here that knowledge management consists of more than just this one very specific aspect. One possible cause for lack of usage is confusion and ambiguity over the meaning of the term *knowledge*. As detailed in earlier sections, few authors clearly define what they mean by *knowledge* or differentiate it from related concepts such as learning, information, data, and expertise. To use Hedlund and Nonaka[3] as an example again, despite making significant academic contributions to the field, they rely on the *Oxford English Dictionary* for their definition of *knowledge*[4] and state that they "have not been able to extract clear or commonly shared definitions."[5]

Approaching the topic of knowledge management from the perspective of information science (librarians), there is a tendency for authors to concentrate on component activities. An example is Choo's definition of:

> information management as a cycle of processes that support the organisation's learning activities: identifying information needs, acquiring information, organising and storing information, developing information products and services, distributing information, and using information.[6]

It is when placing *information management* (*knowledge activities*[7]) in its organizational context that the authors realize the necessity of establishing a link with changed behavior.

What is required is a definition of knowledge management that is founded on firm philosophical grounds, adopts a holistic organizational view, and is capable of supporting empirical research into the phenomenon. The theme emerging from the literature is that knowledge management is a process.[8] It has also been argued that there is a link between conducting activities, acquiring knowledge, learning, changing behavior, and as a result of changed behavior, conducting revised activities. Consequently, for the purpose of this book, knowledge management is defined as the process of managing the cycle of capturing knowledge from organizational activities and learning from that knowledge about scope for improved organizational effectiveness through changes to behavior and organizational activity.

This approach is similar to that found in some of the more recent learning organization literature, which implies a more holistic organizational view and attempts to relate learning to observable outcomes. Likewise, the application of autopoiesis and chaos theory shifts the focus from cognitivistic and connectionist approaches of organizational knowledge to one of organizations as autopietic systems.[9] von Krogh and Roos view organizations as living, self-producing systems.[10] Organizations have their own history and identity, which affects their ability to acquire new knowledge, learn, and subsequently change. The authors suggest that change has occurred when a new paradigm is reflected in everyday organizational language. This view is complementary with the proposed definition of knowledge management.

The knowledge management process is continuous, concurrent, and multidimensional. Knowledge management is continuous in two respects. First, organizations may continuously cycle through the process. Changed behavior results in revised activities, which renews the cycle. Second, activities do not stop so that knowledge can be acquired, nor does learning stop to allow behavior to change. The various components of knowledge management progress concurrently. Activities are conducted concurrently with knowledge acquisition, and learning, while behavior continues to evolve. It is also argued that knowledge is managed at multiple levels of the organization and that these interact. For example, the activity of managing an alliance itself will result in learning and changed alliance management behavior. This activity may be concurrent with operational activities to share knowledge between alliance partners to develop a product, for example. Lessons learned from collaborative product development are likely to result in changed alliance management activities, and vice versa.

This interrelationship can be diagrammatically illustrated by the components of knowledge management continuing concurrently, with the results of each component are fed into subsequent components. Figure 10.1 shows activities, knowledge acquisition, learning, and behavior evolving over time (on the horizontal scale); the results are depicted as sinusoidal. *Knowledge management* involves managing this cycle.

The approach taken here differs from that of Boisot and Child,[11] Nonaka,[12] Hedlund,[13] and Nonaka and Takeuchi.[14] These authors have struggled with the complexity of managing knowledge within the two parameters of codification and diffusion. In essence, they have studied how to get tacit knowledge out of individuals and to diffuse it among groups and organizations. Although this is an important aspect, from the perspective of strategic alliances, codifiability and diffusibility are but small components of the problem domain.

Choo, on the other hand, adopts a holistic approach but constructs a model (*information management cycle*) comprised of knowledge activities[15] leading to adaptive behavior.[16] Although it is useful in supporting his focus on the activities themselves, the model is not based in either philosophy or learning theory. The major disadvantage of the model is that there is no clear link established that is empirically researchable.

The knowledge management framework (see Figure 10.2) details what has been achieved from reviewing the literature to this point. A relationship has been established between alliance activities, knowl-

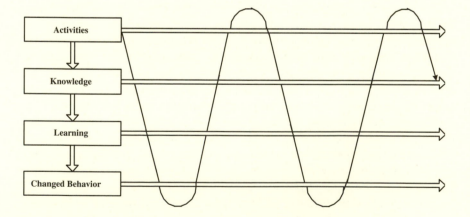

Figure 10.1 Knowledge Management as a Continuous Process

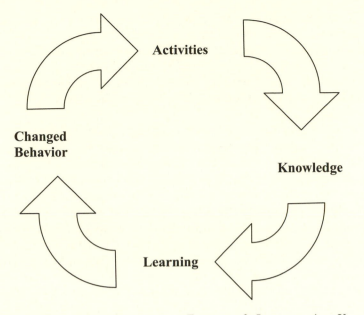

Figure 10.2 Knowledge Management Framework Incorporating Knowledge and Organizational Learning

edge, learning, and changed behavior. Reviewing the literature on knowledge has enabled the term to be defined, major characteristics to be analyzed and key knowledge activities to be related to this model. Reviewing the organizational learning literature has enabled learning to be defined, highlighted the major organizational learning issues to be relevant to the research topic, and related key organizational learning activities to the model. Two areas of research remain outstanding to complete the model. First, there remains a need to review the strategic alliance literature to reveal the alliance-specific issues likely to be of relevance. Second, the information technology literature must be reviewed to identify the role that information technology could play in alliance knowledge management.

Reviewing the organizational learning literature reveals an absence of empirical research investigating in detail how knowledge is managed within organizations. Many of the case studies presented or alluded to in the research literature are restricted to broad examples of how exemplary organizations claimed to have learned. There is generally no attempt to verify these claims or to deal in a more granular form exactly what happened. Questions left unanswered include:

- What knowledge was acquired?
- Where was it acquired, and by whom?
- How did the organization learn from this knowledge?
- How was learning manifested in changed behavior?
- What evidence is there that these changes are attributable to learning and not some other, possibly random, influence?

In summary, there has been much academic debate about theoretical issues such as organizational cognition, taxonomies of learning, and learning activities. There is also much prescriptive advice on how organizations should learn, based on superficial examples of claimed successes. There is, however, an absence of empirical research giving clear evidence of organizational learning that reveals the pragmatic difficulties encountered by organizations. Representative of calls for research into knowledge management is that of Garvin, who explained, "We need clearer guidelines for practice, filled with operational advice rather than high aspirations."[17]

A 1996 APQC knowledge management benchmarking study of eleven organizations found a "vast treasure house" of knowledge, know-how, and best practices.[18] If tapped, this information could add millions to the bottom line and yield huge gains in speed, customer satisfaction, and organizational competence, the report suggested. In effect, the study noted, several other drivers appear to be converging under the broad theme of competitiveness:

- Downsizing and restructuring have led to the loss of expert knowledge and practices.
- Information technology investments have created great enabling potential for knowledge management practices.
- Global organizational structures are requiring a coordination of dispersed knowledge.
- There is a capacity to innovate, either for new products or services, and to avoid reinventing the wheel.
- Business pressures occur, such as reduced costs and cycle times and increased speed of response.

To recap on the drivers or contributory factors for knowledge management initiatives, the key words are *competitiveness, customer value, core competencies, information technology as the enabler, innovation, organizational learning,* and *better financial performance.*

In terms of how these drivers help define what an organization means by knowledge, rather than pure information, the following interpretations are distilled from case reports and research studies described in this chapter:

- Intellectual capital: patents, copyrights, trademarks, licences, technologies, and so on
- Best practices: practical solutions developed in the course of business activities that require transfer
- Knowledge assets: brands, names, commercial rights, and other intangible forms of value
- Know-how: skills and expertise related to an organization's processes or activities, including external influences such as market trends and regulation
- Organizational memory and intelligence: "hidden" knowledge resources and the intellectual capabilities of stakeholders, employees, shareholders, customers, and suppliers
- Learning: formal capabilities, wisdom, scanning capacities in relation to the external environment

Clearly, these dimensions represent a kaleidoscope of knowledge. Without question, any organization could cite specific examples for each, representing an immense source list of potential, if not already exploited, information. This is the context for valuing knowledge, which is one aspect of its measurement and can be done if this potential is recognized. Key here, if opportunities are not to be wasted, is to shape knowledge into a coherent and dedicated strategy or framework for action that aligns with business imperatives. In fact, avoiding waste in its widest sense is a central issue in knowledge management.

PUTTING A VALUE ON KNOWLEDGE

Consider, for instance, this apocryphal story from the U.K. Patent Office. One process at a British chemical organization was producing unwanted sludge, a problem that its R&D unit could not resolve and that was costing the business in terms of remediation. An inquiry to the Office's Search and Advisory Service as to whether a solution for the process problem had been patented revealed that one had been devised and filed some years earlier by one of their own experts. The story illustrates, not just lost opportunity and wasted resources, but also hidden value, a central principle of knowledge management.

Dow Chemical is valued at over US$21 billion on the U.S. stock market but, according to traditional accounting practices, it has a book value of approximately US$8.3 billion. The difference reflects its intellectual capital, or corporate knowledge, which led to the creation of an intellectual asset management (IAM) function in the early 1990s to ensure that this resource produced maximum value.

However, in reviewing Dow's 29,000 patents at the time, function experts discovered that 15 percent of them were worthless, yet still retained a tax liability of $250,000 each over a ten-year period. As noted, by abandoning or licensing out over 13,000 patents, significant savings were made. Dow spends more than $1 billion annually on R&D and, on average, files 1,200 patents a year. The IAM review has focused on the degree to which each patent could provide future value or become a core competence of the organization. For instance, 200 items in the current patent portfolio are regarded as fundamental building blocks for the chemical giant's different businesses.

A key point is the need to review. For all Dow's patents and know-how, the fifteen-member IAM function assesses what the organization holds, identifies the "owner," and attaches a value expressed as a percentage of the net present value of the business. This allows intellectual assets to be measured, managed, and increased, in effect, cutting the costs of maintaining them, increasing licensing incomes, and therefore providing a critical link between intellectual asset issues and business strategy.

European-based pharmaceutical manufacturer Hoffman-La Roche addressed one aspect of the knowledge management process in order to speed up internal documentation, sometimes amounting to 200,000 pages, for the eventual approval of new drugs by the U.S. Food and Drug Administration (FDA). Drug development is a critical success factor given that those sold worldwide can earn more than US$1 million in one day. Time, efficiency, cost, and quality are the business issues. Reducing development time meant staff at Hoffman-La Roche had to clearly understand the context, regulatory requirements, and information content of what they assembled for the FDA approval submission.

If knowledge is not shared, major inefficiencies may occur in clinical trials and effort or knowledge is duplicated. Information or expertise is widely dispersed throughout the 60,000-plus employee group. Systematic knowledge trees were designed, detailing types, sources, and databases of expertise and tracing knowledge links; in effect, these define who communicates what to whom and when. These systems are now decentralized and accessible to any drug development project team in Hoffman-La Roche.

Two significant outcomes resulted. The structure helps employees understand the importance of the knowledge they create and the process revealed much hidden value. Using the new process, one team expected a three-year time scale for obtaining FDA approval but, by working with the knowledge trees and specialists, halved the volume of data needed for internal documentation. Approval time could now be as low as nine months.

Texas Instruments' strength in knowledge management has two dimensions: transferring knowledge and best practices through its Office of Best Practices (OBP), established in 1994 (detailed in Chapter 4), and innovation, or knowledge creation. Both were exemplified when an internal solution was devised to increase capacity in wafer fabrication which, when disseminated worldwide, saved $500 million. It occurred because the organization leveraged its operational knowledge. Knowledge management is interpreted by the global semiconductor manufacturer at three levels:

- Operational efficiency, which has been effectively achieved
- Product development and leadership, the current priority
- Customer intimacy, including knowledge programs for business intelligence and market trends, which will assume greater importance in the future

The critical issue is that the firm is competing in a knowledge race to business and organizational excellence of three phases, understanding, deployment, and execution. In this, OBP is the engine to keep the momentum going by maintaining the highest quality of sources and information. To TI and its OBP, knowledge management is a strict discipline and not just a valuable idea.

As far as outcomes in these vignettes, bottom-line benefits are evident in all through cost savings or greater revenues. Significantly, however, putting a value on exploiting knowledge resources involved creating an intellectual asset structure at Dow, rethinking a knowledge process at Hoffman-La Roche, and at Texas Instruments building a transfer network that acts as a knowledge brokerage. So far, three issues have been revealed, the business case for knowledge management, the link between this and value creation, and how value is leveraged in practice. Advisers must explore these and other issues.

Recalling that Dow Chemical Company expected to earn $125 million a year in licensing fees from patents, as described in this chapter's case study, the figures should be achieved because business management understands its intellectual property position and develops plans to leverage these assets. This has not always been the case, for three reasons:

- It can be difficult to identify and measure intellectual assets.
- Resources, time, and budgets can be stretched in a lean organization, which inhibits potential value creation.
- An organization may not initially be clear over the impacts or value that licensing might have on business units.

Dow lacked even a basic language for R&D and business managers to use when talking about intellectual assets in terms of how they were brought together and valued.

Taking a lead from the structure that Dow now has in place, managers seek alternative sources of revenue as their understanding of intellectual capital increases. Their job has been to make the process user-friendly to which business managers can relate. It accelerates ideas by cutting through bureaucracy, inefficiencies, and disconnected processes. A critical point is to generate new ideas, knowledge creation, rather than just managing existing knowledge. Organizations are having to reconsider the sources of innovation and growth as a result of downsizing and reengineering. Distinguishing between two types of knowledge is important: explicit, through manuals, courses, and practices, and tacit, which is acquired by experience. Although the former is straightforward to quantify and measure, the latter is difficult to articulate, being ambiguous by nature. It is the process of transforming tacit into explicit knowledge that builds a knowledge-creating organization.

The preoccupation with knowledge in many organizations can be likened to picking the early fruits instead of focusing on the roots. Knowledge management can be sustained only by the latter, also, with restructuring, that organizations are suffering from "corporate anorexia." Downsizing means there is a danger of losing corporate memory, so new opportunities have to be created through innovation. Certainly it is vital to maximize existing knowledge but, at the same time, you must also nurture your intellectual capital. To do so effectively means shifting inhibiting mindsets. One of these is a too strong emphasis on definitions, meanings, and indicators. It is far better to be roughly right than precisely wrong. Knowledge management can be overcomplicated.

Whereas knowledge management can be built on common sense and practical wisdom, this is not yet common practice. Too many knowledge management managers do not stand back and reflect for a while, or indeed, demonstrate the patience to wait up to three years for the results to emerge. Similarly, that rushing into tactical solutions is a common practice and a mistake. This tends to be a buckshot approach to get quick results, which sometimes demonstrates an element of keeping up with the Joneses. Putting tactics before strategy diverts an organization.

The key is to understand business strategy, which, is often a short-coming as executives can be too keen to ask, "Where do we start?" in a kind of knee-jerk reaction to the knowledge management trend. Not enough consideration is given to strategic issues, including:

- Managing organizational capability
- Recognizing the competitive attributes of intellectual capital
- Evaluating what the term means, as tailored to the organization
- Appreciating the need for the technology as a facilitator

- Deciding what information or knowledge is critical for business success

Knowledge is not fully understood as an asset to be strategically managed as its management is sometimes regarded as a convenient overlay. This means the topic must be put squarely on the chief executive officer's agenda. It is at that level that the process has to start if the management of intellectual assets is to become a core capability. There are two critical questions: Where is the most significant value creation lever in relation to achieving or sustaining competitive advantage, and how, then, will the use of knowledge become a differentiator?

Other emerging trends are:

- A greater inclusion of intangible assets in knowledge management thinking at corporate levels
- New knowledge management roles emerging to facilitate the relationship between people and technology
- Alignment with strategic performance frameworks such as balanced scorecards
- The use of technology as a driver and enabler, as in virtual networks

A disconcerting trend is the tactical rush to install a database. Everyone has an urge to put everything on a database without considering strategic or business issues. Do they have an understanding of what knowledge management means? Is there a common language? And if people are not involved in any dialogue, will they become contributors? Who contributes to knowledge and repositories is the big issue.

CORPORATE BEST PRACTICE IN KNOWLEDGE MANAGEMENT: SEQUENT COMPUTER SYSTEMS

Evolution of Knowledge and Value

Knowledge management at Oregon-based Sequent Computer Systems has been strategic since it began drafting enabling technology in 1993, prior to significant developments over the next two years. The goal of knowledge is not to find truth, but to achieve effective performance. From very early on, the firm has believed that knowledge should be internally self-consistent and structurally complete. Sequent needed to view knowledge as, not what is right, but what works, or even what works better. Partial, or even empirically incorrect or philosophically muddled, bodies of knowledge, have been, and are, effective.

The job is to produce the infrastructure and processes that take this kind of effective commercial knowledge to those who can use it, the customers. The main reason organizations are learning to manage their knowledge is because it leads to smarter, well-equipped sales teams designing better systems in the customer's place of business. In turn, this makes the customer successful.

Sequent also sees it as a "moral issue" to make customers successful, so its selling process is an intraorganization commitment. The customers buy from Sequent on the expectation that they will not only get a project that is successful but also learn what the firm knows. Part of the business is to give away intellectual property through the engagement with customers.

Sequent Computer Systems is a twenty-year-old information technologies organization founded by eighteen people, seventeen of whom came from Intel with backgrounds in sales. The organization now has over two thousand employees, almost half of whom operate from fifty-three field locations in the Americas, Europe, and Asia. Its business is information intensive, skill intensive, and knowledge intensive in having to provide complex, highly customized IT systems for large commercial firms operating in high-risk, high-reward environments. One reason the firm decided to make knowledge management a priority is for survival. If it tried to compete in the commodity or volume game, it probably would not win. Instead, management does a lot of soul searching because it has to. It deals with customers who did not succeed with IBM or Packard Bell, so it really needs to understand the business.

In the definition, design, and deployment of its systems, Sequent makes extensive use of its collective skills, knowledge, and experience so that current or new customers can benefit appropriately from the key learning of Sequent's dealing with previous customers. This is seen as a replication of tested knowledge, which minimizes the risk associated with complex projects. As such, it is essential for Sequent to capture, systemize, and reuse as much of the knowledge generated in projects with customers as we possibly can. By managing its knowledge, and at the same time, keeping the cost structure stable, the organization has reached $1 billion in revenues, up from just $450 million in 1994. It absolutely lives or dies by the knowledge of its people. The business model is, in fact, constrained by the skills of its employees. When it wins deals, it is because of the employees.

In 1993, the first draft of knowledge management technology was written in Sequent's corporate development department. Message-based repositories were put on the Web and announced within a closed circle. At that point the firm was immediately faced with different technological problems:

- The issue of publication
- Meta-data, information on when a certain message is old and should be refined or deleted
- Logical design of the warehouse
- Physical implementation
- Operations and management procedures

After addressing these issues, the knowledge channel began to renovate itself. Throughout 1994, a prototype of the technology Sequent was using to capture, transfer, and reuse knowledge had been up and running. This system, the Sequent Corporate Electronic Library (SCEL), was formally introduced in 1995. It works on a publisher and consumer relationship, with publishers putting knowledge into the system and consumers using it. Librarians organize the knowledge while executives manage it and track SCEL's use.

Also in 1995, knowledge management appeared as a formal objective in both the corporate strategic plan and the strategic marketing plan, which also identify explicit knowledge management initiatives. Its model for these revolves around four key innovation principles: construction, embodiment, dissemination, and use. Construction is the making of knowledge through complex processes involving creation, synthesis, theft, libel, and reinterpretation. Constructors always need to embody their innovation, the second element. This is the transformation of knowledge that is tacit (held in the heads of knowledge workers, for instance) into processes, practices, equipment, materials, and culture. Next, embodiments are disseminated, with the distribution of embodied knowledge throughout an organization. Ultimately, through dissemination, they get used. This is the place where they find out whether the knowledge works.

Managing and Measuring Knowledge: The Dimensions of Implementation

As the context for managing and measuring knowledge, it is worth emphasizing two points raised in earlier sections. First, Sequent Computer Systems took nearly three years before knowledge management was deployed to the satisfaction of management and the customers. Second, a "tactical rush" is evident as organizations move into this arena. Also, from the kaleidoscope of interpretations cited earlier, implementation might be considered an especially complex task. There are eight significant knowledge processes:

- Generating new knowledge
- Accessing knowledge of value from external sources

- Representing knowledge acquired in documents, databases, software, and so on
- Embedding knowledge in processes, products, and services
- Transferring existing knowledge
- Using accessible knowledge in decision making
- Facilitating knowledge growth through culture and incentives
- Measuring the value of knowledge assets and the impact of knowledge management

APQC identified six key interpretations of knowledge common to the eleven participants of its study:

- Knowledge management as a business strategy
- Transfer of knowledge and best practices
- Customer-focused knowledge
- Personal responsibility for knowledge
- Intellectual asset management
- Innovation and knowledge creation[19]

The Center for Business Innovation makes two points on knowledge management as guiding principles behind its research agenda and corporate programs: what an organization knows and its speed of learning are the bedrock of sustainable advantage and the tasks of generation, codification, and transfer are critical concerns for management.[20]

The importance of behavior, organizational design, cultures, and learning should be highlighted. They spell out a particular executive challenge on knowledge management. The challenge is to discover how knowledge can best be handled, utilized, and measured, so the message therefore is to make it visible, build the infrastructure, and raise managers' awareness of the value of knowledge and its culture.

Measuring Intellectual Assets

No other knowledge management area is as underimplemented as measurement. In terms of importance, the benchmark group tends to rate measurement lower than any other category. Although some organizations are beginning to develop indicators to manage knowledge, their attempt to link these to financial results is often weak. This could ultimately destroy knowledge management initiatives. Organizations that are able to create and use a set of financially justified measures to guide their knowledge management activities seem certain to come out ahead in the long run.

Some of the measurement indicators are difficult to measure in practice, whereas others are, arguably, easier to measure, for example, employee attrition rates, submissions to knowledge bases, and expenditures on training and R&D. With a proven intellectual asset management process, this form of measurement at Dow Chemical Company (the end-of-chapter case study) is advanced, but is still evolving. As the case study details, measures ensure process effectiveness and enable more accurate predictions of future intellectual asset valuations to be made.

The biggest dilemma is identifying the best measures of value contribution and process execution to ensure these leverage human, customer and organizational capital. Measurement is an iterative process, driven by four principles:

- Measures are a tool for alignment between vision, strategy, organizational outputs, and individual activities.
- Indicators and trends are as important as value targets becuase the latter reflect success after the fact by evaluating outcomes.
- A small set of meaningful measures to direct organizational action is especially important when measuring the value contributions of intellectual assets.
- The act of creating measures for intellectual assets, in and of itself, can lead to value creation.

Dow emphasizes that there is a more overarching principle, which concerns the organization as a whole. First and foremost, all intellectual asset measures align with the current hierarchy of business measures including those for corporate, global business, functional, and employee purposes. The Swedish Skandia Assurance and Financial Services group attributes its remarkable growth from three hundredth in world-league tables to third position, plus a 1000 percent rise in annual premiums over five years, to its multifaceted interpretations of intellectual capital.

Intellectual capital is something you cannot touch, but it still makes you wealthy. However, the implication of wealth does not necessarily mean money. Skandia's market value is created by financial and intellectual capital, the latter represented by the hidden value that sustains performance. This comprises two other building blocks of capital which are elements of the so-called Skandia Value Scheme:

- Human: core competencies, skills, key people, trademarks, concessions, and innovation
- Structural: IT systems, customer databases, and distribution systems

Perceived as a dynamic concept, there are six other forms of capital. Flowing from structural capital, they are customer and organizational capital. The latter then creates process and innovation capital, and finally, from this, intellectual property and intangible assets. Intellectual capital is, therefore, the sum of human and structural capital plus all the other forms of capital.

By perceiving capital in this way, the firm can codify, recycle, and use the idle capital (which most organizations have). However, it is not fixed; the firm reviews and refines intellectual capital every six months. Skandia strives to quantify all its hidden value through the Navigator management and reporting model, which has four focuses:

- Financial focus: value added per employee, personal expenses, total organization expenses, and education investments against gross written premiums
- Customer focus: accounts per employee, numbers of people with sales-related tasks, and education investments in relation to numbers of accounts
- Process focus: number of years an employee has been at Skandia, numbers of people in leadership positions, IT-experienced staff, and an empowerment index
- Renewal and development focus: education investments per employee, numbers with degrees, recruitment ratios, and percentage of employees below the age of forty

Through each focus, indicators and measures or groups of baseline ratios have been devised to plot trends and determine which intellectual capital factors should be strengthened to improve business performance. Applied to human capital, Navigator model focuses each include several measures. The Navigator model provides balanced reporting by adding ratios for intellectual capital to traditional financial measures. This process leads Skandia to a whole, systematic management of hidden value which also helps them cultivate investor and customer relationships. That is why Skandia publishes the *Intellectual Capital* supplement to our annual report.

New metrics are required for hidden assets so that organizations can measure the costs of intellectual capital and its potential for growth. However, often they do not understand what knowledge management is in the first place. Although we can suggest that the key indicators are in four cost performance areas: quality, attracting new customers, losing customers, and innovation, it is not easy to link these with knowledge management. Few organizations have achieved this. A second issue is what data will be used for if it does become available. If we assume that measuring intellectual capital relates back to different aspects of customer performance, it should have a predictive value in revealing trends. However, demonstrating links to specific financial outcomes is very difficult. Indeed, the issue is cause and effect.

Taking a strategic view, which must therefore drive a rethinking of how knowledge assets are measured the unmeasurable has to be measured. However, traditional financial accounting mechanisms fail to calculate or calibrate the most important resources of the organization, its intellectual capacity. Instead, current mechanisms treat people as liabilities or expenses instead of assets. The business case must be defined in order to justify investment strategies in the human and social capital of the firm. Measuring intellectual capital is far more than a metrics, or even internal, issue. If we recognize that articulating an organization's hidden value through intellectual capital is the only means of sustaining growth and wealth creation, there are substantial implications for corporate accounting and reporting. These arise because of the need to balance three aspects of business performance. Being based on past performance, traditional accounting systems are not helpful which means wider perspectives have to be adopted by the profession. It requires a fundamental rethink of strategic performance measurement, where the beauty will always come from balance.

Taking a broad overview of managing and measuring knowledge, knowledge has to align with core business processes. How knowledge is introduced into work processes is as important as the design of the processes themselves. Knowledge, best practices, behaviors, and individual skills are the least exploited assets of the contemporary organization, which, if they can be exploited, will rapidly improve performance. However, these assets are not widely emulated or transferred, partly because people are not aware that the knowledge exists or cannot access it if they do.

There are few incentives to seek out knowledge. To be able to leverage knowledge for competitive success has several crucial factors:

- Building a knowledge architecture
- Creating ownership of subject matter to draw in new knowledge
- Providing information in accessible forms, including databases
- Identifying areas of knowledge collection and creation
- Designing processes around knowledge
- Encouraging a culture of collaboration and sharing

In effect, these factors lead to the creation of a virtual network for transferring knowledge and best practices. Few organizations are anywhere near making effective use of their best practices, but through virtual networks, the rate of collaboration and knowledge sharing has accelerated.

OVERVIEW

Clearly, the widely varying communities of dialogue and practice in knowledge management represent an amorphous threshold of different interpretations, standards, and levels, from the relatively cerebral principles at Skandia to Dow's focus on patents or the transfer of easily defined and deployed best practices at Texas Instruments. In between, there are many other corporate experiences. However, for any knowledge management situation or attempt, two points are vitally important. First, intellectual assets, if not exploited, are a sheer waste of resources and competitive advantage. Second, any organization with knowledge resources of some value absolutely has to address this imperative. Management and measurement are crucial considerations, as already indicated. Moreover, as a starting point, a knowledge review rather than the "tactical rush" into technology and databases is key to reveal the strategic issues throughout this chapter.

The business environment, with its changing conditions and performance shortcomings, will certainly drive this review, along with a realistic appraisal of organizational and competitor capability. The first agenda item should address some aspect of better customer performance. Organizationwide dialogue to communicate direction and the need for change is also essential.

As to broader trends and how agendas may be shaped by external influences in this area, little of significance has occurred in knowledge management. In 1995, knowledge management was new but, six years on, it is still new and little has changed. The same organizations appear on conference platforms, and the core group of applied thinkers is also the same. One would think that, in this era of hard-nosed chief executive officers and less than effective internal performance measures, significant penetration should have been evident. However, even though executives and organizations appear to be overwhelmed with issues, I expect the next two to five years will change the face of knowledge management and measurement.

It may well take at least two decades to see through the implications of intellectual asset management, since the world is moving from an industrial to a knowledge era. The new source of wealth is *knowledging*, which should be jointly explored by organizations and their customers, from strategic dialogue to strategic planning and back to dialogue. (*Knowledging* is the creation and management of knowledge within an organization. Sharing and retrieving data from a database is not knowledge or knowledge management. Organizations need to identify, store, manage, and learn from the knowledge that they have and continue to obtain.) This raises the virtual enterprise concept based on trust to share each other's knowledge. Since few organizations would score even 20 out of 100 for good practice, this point implies significant cultural change.

The key is to create a culture of valuing that makes knowledging possible. As it is more beneficial to share rather than protecting or withholding knowledge, this culture will demonstrate the progressive empowerment of people.

CASE STUDY: DOW CHEMICAL COMPANY, USA

Context

Intellectual assets (IAs) are usually defined as incorporating patents, copyrights, technology, trade secrets, brands, trademarks, computer software, engineering drawings, corporate names, licenses, and commercial rights. They are intangible assets without physical dimensions which derive from the people, processes, systems, and culture of any organization, irrespective of sector or core capability.

In recent years, the concept of know-how is being added to these intangibles in the form of individual skill and capabilities which make up organizational knowledge. Some leading organizations in this area refer to the dimensions of know-how as human capital, corporate IQ, and organizational memory. But are these trends any more than an intellectual exercise? To what extent is an intangible asset a commercial proposition? Can intangibles be classified, audited, and valued? Can organizations make or save money from them? Some organizations obviously believe they can, for example Coca-Cola, which has a trade name estimated to be worth over US$11 billion. This can sometimes create an enormous gap between book value, based on hard assets, and market value, which takes account of the intangibles.

Dow's Intellectual Assets

In 1995, Dow's book value was estimated at around US$8 billion, versus US$21 billion in market value which, when simplified, estimates the technology-driven enterprise's intellectual assets at US$13 billion. In the same year, sales reached US$20 billion, US$25 million of which was from the licensing of intellectual property. Of greater significance, however, is that these licensing fees were conservatively targeted to reach US$125 million by 2000, a fivefold increase in the same number of years. The figures should be achieved because business management understands its intellectual property position and develops plans to leverage these assets. However, this principle has not always been actively pursued in the past for a number of reasons.

First, in a knowledge-based, matrix organization of fifteen major business units, 12 percent of its 40,000 workforce are R&D specialists, who are issued around 1,200 patents a year. It can be difficult to identify and measure intellectual assets. Secondly, in any lean organization like Dow's R&D function, resources and operating budgets can be perpetually stretched, which tends to inhibit potential value creation. There are usually too many good things to work on within R&D. Finally, the organization has not always been clear, or confident enough, in knowing what impact or value licensing might have on its business units.

In the past, the only things Dow licensed were those technologies that the organization was clearly not going to pursue, inferring that the best assets with market potential were used by themselves or were not exploited for reasons mentioned previously, while trying to out-license those with dubious commercial appeal for Dow proved less than successful. Like most organizations, Dow had a firm grasp on the indicators that monitor how well hard assets produce value, but it lacked even a basic language for talking about intellectual assets in terms of how they were brought together and valued. It was crucial for R&D groups to speak a language that business managers understood if resources were to be leveraged to their full potential.

This view is confirmed by Dow Chemical's patents portfolio, which can be both a revenue stream in terms of licensing but also a substantial cost. In the early 1990s, 29,000 patents were held, derived from 11,000 inventions, some of which can cost as much as US$250,000 each through tax maintenance fees and acquiring costs in their typical lifetime of ten years. This amounted to a total tax obligation for the organization of about US$200 million over a given decade.

In addition, annual patent department expenditure runs at $30 million a year on maintaining the portfolio, litigation, writing agreements, and so on. Significantly, 15 percent of its patents, some now recognized as vanity patents, had little worth yet still retained an annual tax liability. At present just over 200 patents are considered to be the fundamental building blocks for Dow's businesses. That is less than 1 percent of the portfolio.

Apart from costs of intellectual assets, we must add another consideration. In keeping with many organizations with silo functions, or discrete business streams, Dow recognized that cross-functional connections or transfers were often not being made. A useful idea or patent might exist in another business without it being evident elsewhere, which represents lost opportunities. Appreciably, then, at Dow, critical questions were faced in the Intellectual Asset Management (IAM) function when they first convened in 1991 in order to articulate how value is created from its work. What are Dow's intellectual assets? Where are they? How are they identified and classified? Can they be measured, valued, and managed? What are the sources of leverage? What can be the financial contributions to the bottom line? Can the organization effectively exploit all its technical know-how?

Valuing and Managing Intellectual Assets: First Steps

From once producing a handful of chemicals at the turn of the twentieth century, Dow Chemical now has over two thousand related products, fifteen business units, and almost fifty joint ventures. Around half its revenues come from markets in Europe, Latin America, and the Pacific Rim. Its cultural attributes are technology driven, globally focused, and conservative in the American Midwest tradition.

The first steps toward intellectual capital valuation and management can be likened to a journey, although hardly one ending in the light of experience. It is a journey that has been guided by six significant influences or imperatives:

- The thinking of gurus like futurist Joel Barker at Infinity Limited and Yale University's John Robin: the former reasoned that intellectual properties would be more valuable than physical assets in the twenty-first century, which is actually happening now (Robin's work concerned service value, the difference between book and market value)
- Financial realities in directly contributing to the bottom line, paybacks, profits, cash flows, and so on, and enhancing corporate return on investment and shareholder interests
- Competitive realities, driven by shorter product life cycles and time to market, rapid technological change, global sourcing capability to meet customer demand, and intense competition, together insisting that the organization has to continually reposition itself and seek, not just one, but several competitive advantages
- Faced with these realities, an insistence in the IAM function that any intended discoveries and applications have to serve strategic business goals
- The need to forge an environment that creates new intellectual assets and fundamentally involves cultural change
- Collaborative work with like-minded individuals and organizations, for example, Skandia AFS, Canadian Imperial Bank of Commerce, and the concept of intellectual capital management

The latter firm helped Dow shape the Intellectual Capital Model, shown in Figure 10.3, which comprises human, organizational, and customer capital. Each is interdependent and, through knowledge

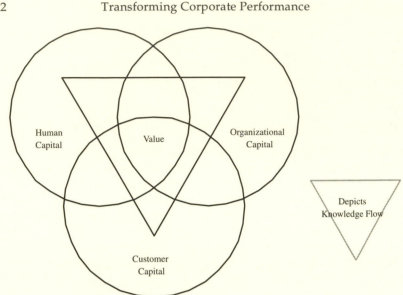

Figure 10.3 The Intellectual Capital Model

flows between them, able to create value. The model conceptualizes their relationships that together capture and create intellectual capital, which, if managed effectively, bring value and ultimately lead to financial outcomes. It is simple and exciting in practice. In one example, manufacturing technology centers and global technology leadership teams at Dow leverage corporate knowledge, brainpower, intellectual property repositories, customers, suppliers, and competitors to identify best practices. This is a first source of leverage. A second source occurs when best practices are applied to improve product quality or process efficiency, thus demonstrating the point of achieving strategic goals previously noted.

IAM Process Model

Underpinning this practical example and developing from the Intellectual Capital Model is the process itself, shown in Figure 10.4 and implemented in 1993. It is a focusing framework for all IA dialogues within and outside the organization and has six phases:

- Phase 1: Strategy integrates intellectual assets into strategic business thinking by leveraging existing assets, identifying those required to fill strategic gaps and addressing threats to freedom of practice and competitive advantage

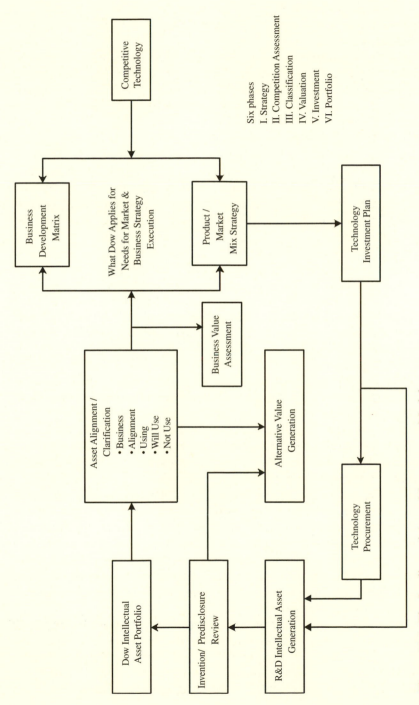

Figure 10.4 The Intellectual Asset Management Model

- Phase 2: Competitive Assessment entails understanding the competitive environment in which an asset resides, such as assessing a competitor's IA and its anticipated response to Dow's strategy and actions
- Phase 3: Classification organizes intellectual assets in terms of their value or potential value to the organization, with three umbrella classifications: (a) using, (b) will use, and (c), will not use. In the event of classification, (c) an asset will be sold, licensed, donated or abandoned
- Phase 4: Valuation focuses on aligning IAM with strategy, ranging from standard approaches for best guesses to a disciplined methodology, called the Dow Technology Factor™ Method. This is a combination of methodologies developed with consultant AD Little, which gives snapshot estimates of financial contributions from intangible assets, expressed as a percentage of net present value.
- Phase 5: Investment fills strategic gaps by assessing outside intellectual assets and/or capabilities, and then determining whether to acquire them or develop new assets internally. If the business is successful in the latter, they are added to the portfolio.
- Phase 6: Portfolio legally defines, articulates, and organizes intellectual assets, using common reporting templates and an extensive computer database.

An example of how the process is applied to business units that are responsible for their own intangible asset costs and revenues is the Dow Latex Business. After reviewing the Intellectual Asset Portfolio, it was decided that a significant number of patents provided no value. By allowing these to expire or by abandoning them, the business was able to save over US$200,000 in annual tax maintenance fees, which directly contributed to bottom-line business performance.

Reinforcing this example, the process is continuing and iterative for all business units, another of which has created anew revenue stream out of its application. The process is a new platform for business opportunities because in the past, some business managers might not know that they have, for example, three patents underpinning their competitive advantage. Taking on the intellectual asset process, they now look for alternative sources of revenue as their understanding of intellectual capital increases.

The IA function's job has been to make the process user friendly and one to which business managers can relate. It accelerates ideas by cutting through bureaucracy, inefficiencies, and disconnected processes. The result is a new climate of rediscovery in Dow, which, in principle, builds on organizational IQ and memory. However, to be successful, the process alone was not enough. Anew structure with IA champions had to be created.

IA Structure

Dow Chemical's supporting structure for the intellectual asset process was put in place after the model was introduced into business units in 1993. It comprises intellectual asset management teams (IAMTs), dedicated intellectual asset managers (IAMs) or champions in the businesses as in-house experts, and a central IAM Technology Center. Dow Chemicals have not built a functional empire; the entire intellectual asset organization is integrated into business units as a support group, which helps add value at the business end. This way, the staff has credibility and is in touch with the opportunities and challenges facing the business units. They are more likely to be listened to this way.

The first structural element is the one hundred or so IAMTs, which are closely aligned with the businesses in order to manage the process and IA portfolio. Team members are multifunctional front-line managers, who meet two to three times a year to review the portfolio and make recommendations on its disposition. In this capacity, they provide the critical linkage between intellectual asset issues and business strategy, thus optimizing cost gains and maximizing leverage.

Since 1992, the teams have been led by intellectual asset managers, the second structural element. Apart from helping the function reengineer processes to make the IAM model work, they also identify best practices and create new tools. They act as champions, advocates, and, in some senses, visionaries to encourage business ownership of the process. Significantly, they are perceived as change agents, the focal point for cultural change, as the IAM process continues to evolve. Through their IAMTs, managers are responsible for minimum standards:

- Developing and maintaining an intellectual asset plan aligned with the business strategy
- Reviewing the intellectual asset portfolio at least once a year
- Identifying key intellectual assets, meaning those defined as giving Dow a competitive advantage
- Classifying intellectual assets by utilization
- Managing portfolio costs
- Where appropriate, doing a competitive technology and portfolio assessment
- Creating and staffing Intellectual Asset Management Teams and facilitating their meetings
- Leadership and advocacy for the IAM vision and process implementation

- Making recommendations for licensing, abandonment, donation, and utilization of intellectual assets.

The IA managers' work is supported by Dow's Intellectual Asset Management Center, a small work group located within the IA function. This has ten primary responsibilities:

- Maintaining a communications network
- Sharing best practices
- Continuous process improvement
- Database support
- Administrative support
- Leadership
- Career development of IAMs
- Training and manuals
- Measurements
- IAMT support

Through adopting this structure and the IA process, in all, over sixty processes, methods, and tools have been developed or reengineered. However, the critical success factor is having capable, dedicated, and focused people. If the intellectual asset managers had been unfamiliar with the subject and only able to work on IAM goals for 10 or 15 percent of their time, this entire effort would have died a slow death. The window of opportunity to focus IA resources and thinking was there for Dow, but only for a limited time. Fortunately, the staff knew it and planned projects accordingly. They also completed projects as quickly as possible to give themselves new tools, and also to make an immediate and positive impact on the businesses.

Measurement and Valuation

Despite a proven model with successful examples to date, combined with effective leadership and advocacy sustained over a ten-year period, the measures taken at Dow have been critical to successful implementation. Strategically, they have ensured process effectiveness at each stage, and enabled more accurate predictions of Dow's future value development and contribution to be made. Measurement is a Dow corporate norm, and IAM is no exception. The need is for simple, meaningful measures that align employee goals with those for functional plans and business strategy. The biggest dilemma is identifying the best measures of value contribution and process execution to ensure they leverage human, customer, and organizational capital.

Clearly, intellectual asset measures are still under development, but the iterative process is driven by four principles:

- Principle 1: Measurements are a tool for alignment, giving critical feedback to ensure that alignment exists between vision, strategy, organizational outputs, and individual activities. They set boundaries, focus the organization, help translate vision into improved performance, and result in sustainable competitive advantage. The intellectual asset issue is for organizations to consider whether all their assets are captured and aligned within these systems.
- Principle 2: Measurement indicators and trends are as important as value targets; the latter reflect success, but whether targets have been achieved can only be known after the fact as they evaluate an outcome. Indicators, on the other hand, are measures of focus and momentum for predicting performance and making rapid decisions to impact outcomes. Most of what organizations measure in the area of intellectual assets falls into the indicator category, for example, strength of customer relationships; capabilities and loyalty of employees, suppliers, and customers; robustness and utility of the organizational knowledge base; market recognition of brand names; and development of intellectual property.
- Principle 3: Measure the minimum and make it easy to act on. A small set of meaningful measures to direct organizational action is a fundamental design principle, which is especially important when measuring the value contributions of intellectual assets. The organization will tend to ignore soft or abstract areas unless people buy into the measures, can gather the data with a minimum of additional effort, and know what to do with the information once they get it.
- Principle 4: Focus inside first and outside last. The act of creating measures for intellectual assets, in and of itself, can lead to value creation for organizations.

Selecting a model and specific measures heightens awareness of the interdependencies between the soft side of the organization and its ability to deliver hard value. This forces the organization to critically examine how well it manages intellectual assets, builds consensus, and sharpens the focus on managing a complete set of value drivers. Focusing on the management needs of internal stakeholders first ensures that the measurement of intellectual assets is more than just a public relations maneuver. This point may be extended by saying that it is tempting to impose a model and a set of measures which broadcast well externally. However, if this is the organization's starting point, the businesses may report measurements but will probably not use them to make decisions.

The points concerning public relations or an inability of measures, or their users, to aid the decision-making process are fundamental issues that Dow has painstakingly avoided. Returning to the earlier comment that measurement is an organizational norm, first and foremost, all intellectual asset measures must align with the business' current hierarchy of measures. These are:

- Corporate: stock price, earnings per share, dividends, and growth targets
- Global business: economic profit, net present value, and fit with corporate strategy
- Function: value creation, people management, and maintenance of competencies
- Employees: competencies and personal goals

Targets and Indicators

As an example of how intellectual asset measures are aligned with this hierarchy, and therefore business strategy, several business units are piloting the use of the previously mentioned indicators and value targets. This also illustrates the continuing process of developing measures.

One value target is percentage of current sales protected by intellectual assets. Thus, if say 50 percent of sales in a business provide a distinct competitive advantage by commanding a higher price or gaining greater market share, the strategy has to focus on the maintenance and renewal of those assets. In practice, this will be achieved by having IAMs and their teams collaborate with business unit managers.

A second example of a value target, and the most important of six in the Dow intellectual asset measures portfolio, is the amount of net present value in any business that can be attributed to intellectual assets. As this metric may be affected by competitive breakthroughs or litigation, the Dow Technology Factor methodology is used to compute and reflect current business assumptions about intellectual asset strengths, risks, and opportunities. Intellectual asset–related net present value is therefore tied to business conditions.

Finally, one important indicator measure is a snapshot ratio, which helps the business visualize R&D as a capitalized investment rather than an expense. This is important for three reasons. First, as highlighted in the introduction, is the difference between Dow's market value and its book value, the former being a major influence on stock price and thus an important business contribution from the organization's intellectual assets. Second, the organization spends over US$1 billion a year in research and, from atypical industry time scale for product innovation to market in 10 to 12 years, Dow aims to halve this. In some cases, it has achieved two years. Also, it aims to significantly improve the standard product success rate of about ten to one. These points raise an important implication, premium price, enhanced market share, and competitive advantage are directly impacted by effective intellectual asset management. Third, significant moves in the last three years have been achieved in valuing and managing patents, an unimpressive area of business performance until the IA process was implemented.

Achievements

Since its implementation in 1993, the IA process has fundamentally reinvented how Dow Chemical regards, classifies, values, and makes money from its original portfolio of twenty-nine throusand patents. Patents were a natural first priority for the IA process partly because rationalization was so evident, but also the IA function would have a high probability of success, virtually a prerequisite nowadays for any major change program to make business managers sit up and take note.

Since applying the process to patents, their existence has become transparent through all fifteen business units and, therefore, the organization as a whole. The portfolio has been rationalized, given the business costs involved in maintaining them and that others were dormant or of poor quality, such as vanity patents.

Of 16,000 patents now, 43 percent are being used and exploited, including the 200 or so that are Dow's core capability building blocks; 42 percent have optimistic prospects and 15 percent are being dispensed with. For the latter, as noted in the IA process classification third phase above, options include sale, licensing, donation, or abandonment. Also, patent abstracts have been produced for ease of access, cross-transfer, and reference.

The business has itself benefited substantially. Over US$40 million in tax obligations has been saved over a ten-year period which has translated into bottom-line performance in most business units. Naturally, too, with a more focused portfolio, the speed at which licensing revenues increase will be enhanced. Third, and perhaps most significantly, an accurate, or desirable, valuation now exists for all patents.

Through applying the Technology Factor™ methodology, Dow has conducted hundreds of internal valuations and now understands the parameters of value growth and preservation for patents. Dow has set the business context for patent sales or licensing which is useful if, say, five organizations are interested in one and have different value connotations. They now know what their value is, which aids both sales and negotiations.

The patent scenario also has strategic implications. By further developing a measurement tool that Dow has used for fifteen years, called the patent tree, business managers can assemble, visualize, analyze, and explain patents in terms of their own portfolio along with any or all of competitor patents.

By examining variables such as market dominance, breadth of coverage, blocking, and opportunities, data can now reveal competitor intentions, which is crucial to Dow's future competitive advantage. Incorporating standard hardware and software, common networking, and database management, the system has rapidly facilitated easier access and data integration. It allows Dow to do all the things it could not do before. It puts the right information in front of the right people at the right time and, as they can now sell integrated solutions instead of separate products, significant commercial advantages will ensue for Dow and its customers.

Valuing Know-How

Extending from patents and IA systems, substantial resources have been put into articulating the concept of know-how which fully extends the IA function's original vision between 1991 and 1993. Intellectual Asset Management Teams have been addressing three questions:

- What is the key technical know-how in a business segment?
- Where does it reside?
- How is it articulated?

In dialogue with business units and as a result of expected consensus by late 1997, know-how will have two effects and a substantial impact. First, technical people will be able to focus resources on technology or processes that win competitive advantage, and second, business managers can embrace developments within their own business context or conditions.

Just as standard workstations put the right data in front of the right people at the right time, the cumulative impact of articulating know-how does so same for knowledge. Hence, the crucial link is forged to knowledge creation and the ultimate objective for all IA function efforts, contributing the creation of more value for the organization than ever before. It is then a straightforward step in the journey toward intellectual capital valuation.

For this phase, Dow reviewed its third intellectual capital prototype, which was targeted for presentation to the board in 1997. Top management support for the IA function's work has always been given and is a critical factor in success. Three outcomes emerged from the prototyping, when related to the IA process. First, Dow Chemical will have, for the first time, an intellectual capital vision for the entire organization, with strategic, functional, business, and employee dimensions. This will reveal how each creates value. Second, bearing in mind the US$13 billion difference between book and market value, intellectual capital valuations will improve and will appear in the annual report and accounts, initially as a supplement. The final outcome, and undoubtedly of longer-term impact on Dow's competitive advantage for the millennium, is managing knowledge and organizational learning more effectively, which again relates back to value creation.

Then Dow begins to examine itself as a learning organization, which, through the IA process, can impact on business performance and results. All along, this has been the strategic intent, to take what the firm is already doing well, stand back and understand it, reengineer processes and measures, and then manage the whole enterprise even more effectively.

Dow is thus prepared for the era of knowledge, or knowledge management, with all its potential opportunities and gains. Organizations that succeed in this area will leapfrog their competitors and flourish. When Dow Chemical achieves that capability after a long, five-year period of evolution, the business impacts will be of breakthrough proportions rather than just increments along the way.

NOTES

1. G. Hedlund and I. Nonaka, Models of Knowledge Management in the West and Japan, in P. Lorange, C. Chakravarthy J. Roos, and A. Van de Ven (eds.), *Implementing Strategic Processes: Change, Learning and Co-operation* (Oxford: Blackwell Publishing, 1993), pp. 117–144.

2. G. Hedlund, A Model of Knowledge Management and the N-form Corporation, *Strategic Management Journal*, 15 (Special Issue) (1994), pp. 73–90.

3. Hedlund and Nonaka, Models of Knowledge Management.

4. *Oxford English Dictionary* (1992): "The fact of recognizing as something known, or known about, before; recognition" is the more comprehensive definition, whereas (Models of Knowledge Management, p. 121), rely on *know,*which among the OED's fourteen other listed meanings, also encompasses"to understand the way, to be able."

5. Hedlund and Nonaka, Models of Knowledge Management, p. 121.

6. C. W. Choo, Information Management and the Intelligent Organization: Roles and Implications for the Information Professions, *Proceedings of the 1995 Digital Libraries Conference: Moving Forward into the Information Era,* 27-28 March, Singapore (1995), p. 83.

7. R. Daft and G. Huber, How Organizations Learn: A Communications Framework, *Research in the Sociology of Organizations,* 5 (1987): 1–36.

8. I. Nonaka, The Knowledge-Creating Company, *Harvard Business Review,* 69(6), (1991): 96–104; I. Nonaka, A Dynamic Theory of Organizational Knowledge Creation, *Organizational Science,* 5(1) (1994): 14–36; Hedlund and Nonaka, Models of Knowledge Management; C. W. Choo, Towards an Information Model of Organizations, *The Canadian Journal of Information Science,* 16(3) (1991): 32–62;

C. W. Choo, Information Management and the Intelligent Organization; C. W. Choo, *Information for an Intelligent Organization* (Bedford: Learned Information, 1995); T. H. Davenport, *Process Innovation: Reengineering Work through Information Technology* (Boston: Harvard Business School Press, 1993); J. McGee and L. Prusak, *Managing Information Strategically* (Chichester, U.K.: John Wiley, 1993); I. Nonaka and H. Takeuchi, *The Knowledge-Creating Company: How Japanese Companies Create the Dynamics of Innovation* (New York: Oxford University Press, 1995).

9. G. von Krogh and J. Roos, *Organisational Epistemology* (Basingstoke, U.K.: Macmillan, 1995).

10. Ibid.

11. M. Boisot and J. Child, The Iron Law of Fiefs: Bureaucratic Failure and the Problem of Governance on the Chinese Economic Reforms, *Administrative Science Quarterly, 33* (1988): 507–522.

12. I. Nonaka, The Knowledge-Creating Company; Nonaka, A Dynamic Theory of Organizational Knowledge Creation.

13. Hedlund (1994), A Model of Knowledge Management.

14. Nonaka and Takeuchi, *The Knowledge-Creating Company.*

15. Daft and Huber, How Organizations Learn.

16. Choo, Information Management and the Intelligent Organization.

17. D. A. Garvin, Building a Learning Organization, *Harvard Business Review, 74*(4) (1993): 78–91, p. 79.

18. APQC, *Knowledge Management Benchmarking* (1996).

19. Ibid.

20. Center for Business Innovation, *Managing the Knowledge of the Organization* (Boston: Ernst & Young, 1995).

11

Strategic Performance Measurement Overview

MEASUREMENT REVIEWS AND AUDITS

As a brief overview of the preceding chapters, three observations stand out. First, business change is forcing organizations to rethink how they interpret, or what they do concerning four broad aspects of corporate performance: strategy, processes, people, and systems. Together all four encompass the main chapter themes discussed in this book.

Second, it is clear that performance measurement is a driver of change and improvement, provided it is interpreted strategically and other elements realigned accordingly. This affirms the point in Chapter 1, that it is a competitive issue in its own right.

Third, and unquestionably, measurement has to deliver against heightening expectations from diverse constituencies of stakeholders, hence the importance of avoiding the tag of sector laggard or, in some cases, a more primary need of simply staying in business. Effective delivery from measurement makes commercial and strategic sense.

Certainly, raising performance measurement to a strategic level is of critical importance. Each chapter indicates how this might be achieved through key questions, case reports, and guidelines. Employee measurement, one of the most difficult areas according to studies, acts as a snapshot to illustrate this point. Widely applied, it is generally perceived as merely a *feel-good* or public relations exercise, which, in practice, can have little real worth.

However, raised to the strategic level, it insists that issues like satisfaction and retention should be measured, as two examples. The first may indicate misgivings about the organization, whereas results from the second certainly demonstrate what employees will actually do about it if the organization or its climate do not improve. The strategic implications are inescapable.

Each chapter has many similar examples to help shift focus from the tactical to strategic, which raises a further two considerations. The first concerns specific areas of measurement. If, say, customer measurement is being reviewed, reviews are a useful starting point. If it is a continuation of strategic performance measurement, who participates? Best-practice organizations recognize that "themed" reviews of this kind do not only involve an area's specialists, they have to be cross-functionally representative, too. As a result, quality professionals must contribute to reviewing customer measurement, an HR expert will aid a process measurement focus group, and finance people have perspectives to help grapple with measuring intellectual capital.

The second consideration is pure strategy. Pulling together all aspects of performance measurement covered in these chapters requires the highest level of review, which must be related to critical success factors and key performance indicators. Focused on business conditions, capability, and the organization's destiny, strategic reviews tend to be cross-functional for greater effectiveness, rather than being simply the collective wisdom of a selective few executives. Thus, departmental managers, functional heads, or process owners will contribute, ensuring greater rigor and more balanced perspectives.

The outcome of this type of measurement review in best-practice organizations is often one sheet of bullet points under key sections (typically, *strategy, processes, people* and *systems*). This is the classic "one-page," "vital few," or top-tier approach to priorities favored by many successful executives. That said, however, strategic watchwords have to be considered at a review stage:

- Avoid nonpredictive indicators
- Measure value-creating factors
- Consider measuring innovation, learning, and change
- Devise both short- and long-term goals
- Ensure that measures and targets align with strategic objectives
- Avoid the "for interest only" syndrome

However, prior to this type of strategic review, or sometimes succeeding it, an organizationwide measurement audit of lower-level tactical activity supports the higher level and achieves three things.

It establishes current status, and can then identify improvement opportunities. In addition, an audit will also reveal the degree to which corporate measurement is focused, balanced, and integrated (the three key words of this book), and also identify any shortcomings in the process itself.

What happens to data, how it is analyzed, the contribution it makes to better decision making, and the actions that result are four important issues to have in mind during an audit. Given that many organizations are still functionally structured, measurement audits can be useful in stand-alone departmental settings, though line of sight to business objectives has to be an underpinning intention. For example, evaluation audits of HR performance and programs is an increasing practice as a forerunner to rethinking and transforming what this function does and achieves. Also, recalling the point that measurement has to deliver, reviews and audits establish whether this can be, or is being, achieved, along with attendant issues and shortcomings. Arguably at this point, the real work on performance measurement begins implementation.

Implementation Guidelines

When addressing customer measurement in Chapter 6, remember that after sharpening the strategic focus, all the rest is implementation and the big issue here is not collecting data, but deciding how it is used to best effect. Companies never seem to think this through; yet transforming data into organizational action is the most critical step of all.

The most frequently encountered performance measurement issues by far is implementation. Often, performance measurement projects are introduced to get quick returns, like improving productivity, without thinking through the longer-term implications or the fundamentals of corporate change. Other critical issues include:

- Linking hard measures with soft, for example productivity metrics with employee satisfaction or performance management
- Identifying leading indicators, that is, those that have a direct link to the outcome of improved capability
- Measuring innovation
- Competing with finance, how budgetary measures complement other sets, and the extent to which collaboration exists between financial and other executives

Considering these issues, the most frequently encountered implications include changing the budgeting and planning processes, rethinking compensation plans and reviewing IT systems.

The process of determining *strategic* performance measures is almost as important as the measures themselves. When senior officials discuss their strategic direction and the measures to track this on an ongoing basis, they benefit from the process. As the process gets driven down into the company and discussed with subsequent layers of management and employees, best-practice organizations that have been studied say this depth process has a unifying effect. They report that it improves communication and a sense of shared mission far more than, in the words of one executive, "posting a bunch of mission statements around the plant." Most managers agree on other key factors for implementing strategic performance measures: The process must be initiated from the chief executive officer down as well as from the bottom of the organization up; managers warn that otherwise, individual units will not have the authority or buy-in to accomplish a companywide effort.

Companies already have between 50 and 80 percent of the information they need to construct a strategic performance measurement system. A number have built from the familiar, revised accordingly, and then devised only those new measures that are vital to their organization. However, companies should be careful to build on the familiar yet not be chained to it. Managers stress that a company should only measure what it wants to manage strategically, many report having too many measures. Finally, a performance measurement framework is essential as different managers need different types and numbers of measures. For instance, senior executives may only want a broad overview of corporate status, whereas plant managers may need far more measures to track progress, but in either case, they have to relate through an integrating framework.

There are key steps in shaping this type of framework: First, define the business purpose and success model and be clear on where success comes from. Second, identify the relationships that are key to success, which can be financial and nonfinancial. These tasks should be balanced if the business is to deliver against intentions and strategy. Constructing such a framework is an iterative process in three phases: define success, map out the processes, and revisit the results against original definitions. It is also looped to incorporate feedback so, in effect, you go round the circuit and continually improve it.

Avoiding Common Problems

Examining this notion of measurement process improvement touches on common problems encountered in organizations. Feedback is important because measures wear out; the measurement process is never absolute and it does affect behavior. You must be aware, however, that even good measures eventually influence people more to affect the measure itself rather than achieving the goal. Avoid putting any special measures on a pedestal because this is a dangerous practice. Elevating measures to an absolute status is to risk imposing your definition of reality on the business instead of perceiving the actual situation.

Ultimate success in strategic performance measurement occurs through strong employee relationships and reinforces the idea that the Investors In People process must constitute a crucial element of any measurement system. Consideration should be given to how recognized approaches such as balanced scorecards and business excellence methodologies fit with the organization's measurement framework. (This issue is examined in Chapters 2 and 3.)

Avoid the "sameness" or the danger of becoming a "me-too" organization, which often accompanies the adopting of established methodologies. Never forget that the unique elements of your own business must be central to strategic performance measurement. U.S. companies have a long history of collecting data and information, but they have rarely asked themselves what should be done with it to improve capability and performance. Executives are more concerned with how their organizations stack up against others, which raises two problems. First, there appears to be a limited corporate capacity to understand and apply appropriate methodologies, followed by shortcomings in evaluating what is meant by business capability. Either way, there is a big learning curve to experience.

There are three implementation issues:

- Define hard, measurable goals rather than using general descriptions of purpose.
- Identify desired outcomes.
- Insist that analysis leads to some form of improvement action.

Of note, too, the process must link with employee and executive measurement through performance management systems, and onto compensation plans and business objectives. To return to the point that introduced this chapter, the business issue is about differentiating between efficiency and effectiveness in regard to the outcomes of measurement.

Do not get lost in micro measurement or the minutiae of metrics that choke an organization and lead to missing the "big business" pictures. Measure right and you will get the right measures. Rethinking strategic performance measurement starts with putting a laser-beam focus on outcomes or results, with the ultimate objective being to deliver improved sets of result, and not sets of measurements.

Consider two questions: What will drive the results? Which tools or measures will get the organization where it needs to be? Then implement, making sure you cover all the important points at the right time.

In overview, there are two connections between performance measures and strategy delivery to consider. One is for executives to assess whether strategy is actually being implemented, and the second is to influence behavior. If an organization gets the right measures in place, it will encourage people to behave in certain ways with those behaviors helping them achieve business objectives and make recommendations.

To start with, you must define business objectives by getting all senior managers together. The design or redesign of measures follows, tied to objectives, in two ways and through a feedback loop. Top-level measures flow to local or line measures, which then relate back to the former and support business objectives. Then, you must implement and manage. However, and fundamentally, you must give people a clear picture of the business, their contribution to it, and the practical links between the two. In this way, corporate behavior will eventually change.

Glossary of Terms

Book value: The value of assets recorded in financial accounts. With few exceptions, these are all tangible assets, such as buildings, plant, and machinery.

Breakthrough, breakthrough goals: Dramatic performance improvements, often realized in short periods, as distinct from continuous incremental improvement. *Kaizen* is the Japanese word meaning *incremental improvement* and the title of Masaaki Imai's 1986 book, *Kaizen: The Key to Japan's Competitive Success.*

EFQM Model for Business Excellence: The European Foundation for Quality Management (EFQM) model features nine elements or criteria, which are grouped, for convenience, into Enablers and Results. The Enabler criteria are concerned with how results are being achieved, whereas the Results are concerned with what the organization has achieved and is achieving.

EVA: Economic Value Added, a method that gives a measure of value added generated by the business after various accounting adjustments. *Value* in the context of business markets is the worth in monetary terms of the technical, economic, service, and social benefits a customer receives for the price paid for a market offer. *Value added* is where the level of value is increased or initially attached to a business activity.

Intangible assets: Assets that are not physical or tangible in nature, and therefore more difficult to identify and count as discrete entities.

Intellectual capital: The intangible assets of an organization not normally valued on the balance sheet, including knowledge, information, and experience that can be put to use to create wealth. It includes not just know-how, but also customer loyalty, processes, databases, and intellectual property such as brands, trademarks, and patents.

Market value: The total market capitalization of an organization, that is, the share price on the stock market multiplied by the number of shares outstanding.

Index

About the Author

MICHAEL A. MILGATE is CEO and managing director of a group of IT companies in Australia. He has worked with a number of national and international organizations as a marketing manager, business development manager or consultant in a variety of service, engineering, and technology-based industries. He has held a number of academic positions in management and marketing areas and currently holds master's degrees in commerce, in education, and in law, and a Ph.D. in marketing and international business. He is a fellow and Certified Practicing Marketer of the Australian Marketing Institute and a fellow and Chartered Marketer with the Chartered Institute of Marketing in the United Kingdom. This is his fourth book.